Hanna Sheehy-Skeffington

IRISH STUDIES

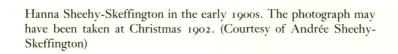

Hanna Sheehy-Skeffington in the early 1900s. The photograph may have been taken at Christmas 1902. (Courtesy of Andrée Sheehy-Skeffington)

Hanna
Sheehy-Skeffington
Irish Feminist

Leah Levenson
and Jerry H. Natterstad

SYRACUSE UNIVERSITY PRESS   1986

LEAH LEVENSON is a freelance writer whose biography of Francis Sheehy-Skeffington, *With Wooden Sword*, was published in 1983. She worked with her late husband, Samuel Levenson, on his biographies of James Connolly and Maud Gonne.

JERRY NATTERSTAD received his Ph.D. from Southern Illinois University at Carbondale and is currently professor of English at Framingham State College. He is the author of *Francis Stuart*, and his articles have appeared in the *Dictionary of Irish Literature*, as well as in such periodicals as the *Journal of Irish Literature* and *Eire-Ireland*.

Library of Congress Cataloging-in-Publication Data

Levenson, Leah.
  Hanna Sheehy-Skeffington, Irish feminist.

  (Irish studies)
  Bibliography: p
  Includes index.
    1. Sheehy-Skeffington, Hanna. 2. Feminists—Ireland—
  Biography. 3. Ireland—Social conditions. I. Natterstad,
  Jerry H., 1938–   . II. Title. III. Series: Irish
  studies (Syracuse University Press)
  HQ1600.3.L48 1986   305.4'2'0924 [B]   85-26223
  ISBN 0-8156-0199-9 (alk. paper)

Manufactured in the United States of America

Contents

IRISH STUDIES

Irish Studies presents a wide range of books interpreting important aspects of Irish life and culture to scholarly and general audiences. The richness and complexity of the Irish experience, past and present, deserves broad understanding and careful analysis. For this reason an important purpose of the series is to offer a forum to scholars interested in Ireland, its history, and culture. Irish literature is a special concern in the series, but works from the perspectives of the fine arts, history, and the social sciences are also welcome, as are studies which take multidisciplinary approaches.

Irish Studies is a continuing project of Syracuse University Press and is under the general editorship of Richard Fallis, associate professor of English at Syracuse University.

IRISH STUDIES, edited by Richard Fallis

Acknowledgments

I N THE PREPARATION of this biography, we have relied heavily upon primary sources—Hanna Sheehy-Skeffington's correspondence, diaries, and writings (published and unpublished), as well as miscellaneous papers. The bulk of this material is housed in the National Library of Ireland and we are indebted to the library's staff, in particular Fergus Gillespie and Donall O'Luanaigh, who did so much to lighten our task. Ken Hannigan of the Public Records Office in Dublin was also helpful, and valuable material was made available to us by The Hoover Institution on War, Revolution, and Peace at Stanford University.

We are grateful to the relatives of Hanna Sheehy-Skeffington—Pan Collins, Judge David Sheehy, Garry Culhane, and Conor Cruise O'Brien —who not only graciously consented to talk with us but, in the case of Pan Collins, also furnished photographs. To one member of the family we are especially indebted: Andrée Sheehy-Skeffington, Hanna's daughter-in-law. She not only consented to our use of material donated to the National Library of Ireland before it was catalogued but sacrificed documents that were needed for her projected biography of her husband, Owen Sheehy-Skeffington. For all she has done and for her friendship, we thank her.

So many people offered material and consented to be interviewed that it would be difficult to list them all, but a few must be mentioned: Sighle O'Donoghue, Monk Gibbon, R. Dudley Edwards, Roger McHugh, Eilis Ryan, Seamus Scully, Seamas O'Buachalla, Maire Comerford, and Dr. Samuel Davis. We thank them as well.

Summer 1985   L.L.
                                                                   J.H.N.

Foreword

 OMETIMES the neglect of significant figures after their deaths tells us more about a society than it is prepared to admit to itself. It is not simply an inability to perceive the contribution made to the society by such people: their neglect may conceal a deep-rooted resistance to seeing the nature of their significance on the part of the community.

Hanna and Francis Sheehy-Skeffington have had to wait a long time for a biographer. In life they were inextricably bound together by ties deeper even than those of devoted conjugal love. They shared a vision of Irish society which had in it elements of pacifism, antimilitarism, a dislike of churchly authoritarianism and the excesses of nationalism, and each taught the other the meaning of feminism.

Francis was mindlessly gunned down on Easter Wednesday 1916 by a crazed military officer. Hanna was to live until 1946 a life of passionate involvement in the formation of the new Ireland that emerged in the south after the founding of the Free State. She addressed herself to all the pertinent questions that were set aside as being too embarrassing or too challenging to that society humiliated by civil war, and dependent on financial and institutional resources of a limited nature.

It was not her left-wing politics (after all Hanna Sheehy-Skeffington had been identified with the "votes for women" campaign and was the editor and main journalist of the *Irish Citizen* for many years); it was rather what constituted "left-wing" politics in the new Free State. In Hanna's own words, when she stood for election as an independent candidate in 1943, her campaign was about "equal pay for equal work, equal opportunities for women, the removal of the marriage ban on teachers, doctors, and other skilled women, the restoration of jury rights, the abolition of the Means Test, proper pensions for the aged, widows and the blind . . .

proper meals and free books for school children." But her ideas on the reform of local government and on state censorship were brushed aside to await a more liberal climate.

Perhaps that age is approaching. It is no accident that the first complete study of Hanna Sheehy-Skeffington has been done at this time. Leah Levenson, author of *With Wooden Sword: A Portrait of Francis Sheehy-Skeffington*, and Jerry Natterstad, author of *Francis Stuart*, have detached Hanna from the charismatic aura that surrounded Francis and thus given us in an absorbing totality an Irish woman whose prodigality of talents was matched by a generosity of spirit. The authors have rendered honour and vindicated the pursuit of history by the story they unfold in the following pages.

History Department   Margaret MacCurtain
University College, Dublin

Hanna Sheehy-Skeffington

The Fashioning of a Militant

N FRIDAY, 28 April 1916, one day before the Easter Rising ended in bitter surrender for the Republicans, Hanna Sheehy-Skeffington learned that her husband, Francis, had been executed by the British military two days earlier. They had had tea together on Tuesday in Dublin and she had left him shortly before seven P.M. to return home; from then until Friday morning she had heard nothing but rumors of his whereabouts. The truth, when it came, was shattering. On the morning of Wednesday, 26 April, without trial or hearing, her husband had been taken into the courtyard of Portobello Barracks and shot. She was, at thirty-eight, a widow with a seven-year-old son.

The Sheehy-Skeffingtons' marriage had not been an ordinary one. They had depended upon each other for intellectual stimulation, for companionship, for love, and for laughter as well. Together, from the time they had first met during their university years, they had been tireless advocates of pacifism, feminism, socialism, and nationalism. Together, they had fought for a free Ireland for both women and men.

It was difficult for Hanna to believe that she would never see her young husband again—he was only thirty-seven when he died—but when the terrible truth could no longer be resisted, her grief was mixed with fierce anger. Speaking before audience after audience in both Ireland and the United States, she swore to carry on his work. This woman, an ardent feminist who for more than a decade had served as a symbol of enlightened independence for the women of Ireland, apparently saw no irony in vowing to carry on her husband's work. Given the period and her own tendency toward self-deprecation, the emphasis is not surprising.

At the time of Francis's summary execution, Hanna Sheehy-Skeffington could already look back upon substantial accomplishments. She had played a prominent role in the formation of the Irish Association of Women Graduates and Candidate-Graduates, a powerful organization in the furthering of educational opportunities for women. She had been largely instrumental in forming the Irish Women's Franchise League, the strongest force in Ireland for obtaining votes for women. She had written numerous articles on the need for changes in the status of women in every field and was much in demand as a spokeswoman for votes for women and freedom for all of Ireland. Furthermore, her contributions as a writer and editor to her husband's paper, the *Irish Citizen*—perhaps the most important voice for the feminist cause during the period—had been indispensable.

Her values had a complex genesis, but many of them, especially the most important, can be traced to her family background. From her father's side, the Sheehys, she inherited a strain of pacifism and an intense nationalism; from her mother's side, the McCoys, she acquired an unshakable independence of spirit as well as a keen sense of self-worth as a woman.

Her grandfather—her father's father—died in 1899 at the age of eighty-seven, and she could recall his aversion to bloodshed and his fervent commitment to an independent Ireland. He had been a native Irish speaker, he told her, but in his day pupils at the National School he attended received at the end of the day a stroke of the cane for every word of Irish they spoke. He had felt the bite of the cane on a number of occasions.[1]

A more radical strain of nationalism came from David, Hanna's father, who unlike his father was actively involved in the cause of Irish freedom. He was a member of the Irish Republican Brotherhood, was active in the Land League, and over the years spent many periods in jail for his beliefs—in Tullamore, Mountjoy, and Kilmainham jails, to mention the more prominent. One episode in particular reveals the strength of his commitment to a cause he believed just. In 1887, while serving as an M.P. from South Galway, he was held in a Sligo jail for some two weeks pending trial before a Crimes Act Court. At that time his wife was dangerously ill and prison officials agreed to release him, with bail, if he would promise not to speak publicly or commit any unlawful act before the trial. This he refused to do, with the result that he was quickly tried.[2]

According to one account, he was charged with "inciting certain persons in his speech delivered at Clonmel" and sentenced amid cheers for him from those in attendance, including some of the police. During his four-month jail term, he refused to wear the prison garb of the common criminal, insisting instead on parading around his small, sparsely furnished cell in his undershorts even in the coldest weather. Many times the warders dressed him by force, but as soon as they left his cell he would remove his clothes again. He was a political prisoner, he argued—after all it was his Land League agitation that had subjected him to this—and was not to be treated as an "ordinary criminal." "What I did," he wrote his father, "I did under a strong conviction, and solemn sense of duty and honour."[3]

David's older brother, Eugene, was also an outspoken and militant nationalist. They had both begun their education at the Jesuit College of St. Munchin's in Limerick, but both had been withdrawn from that institution by their father because its pupils were obliged to take an oath of allegiance to the Crown. The boys then entered the College des Irlandis in Paris to complete their studies for the priesthood. When a cholera epidemic broke out in that city, David was sent back to Dublin but Eugene remained.[4] After ordination he served as curate of Kilmallock, County Limerick, and then as parish priest of Bruree in that same county. A liberal and an agitator, Eugene was active in the Irish Republican Brotherhood, and so deeply involved in the Land League that he became known as the Land League priest.

Early in the 1900s, Father Eugene had a serious brush with the church. It was discovered that, during an ecclesiastical mission to the United States, he had collected funds for the league. For this he was suspended from his priestly functions by his anti-Land League bishop. Not willing to accept his bishop's action, Eugene made two trips to Rome where he fought "the battle of my life," as he wrote John Devoy, leader of the Republican Brotherhood forces in the United States.[5] His victory was complete, however, and his functions restored by the pope. This experience seemed not to have intimidated Father Eugene for he was on the first committee of the Gaelic League and was one of only two clerics who attended the Rotunda meeting when the Irish Volunteers were formed in 1913.[6] It was he who administered spiritual consolation to the 1916 rebels in the General Post Office—a building he left only after it was ablaze.

The exploits of Father Eugene and the jail experiences of their father when he was a member of the Fenian Brotherhood never failed to fascinate the Sheehy children. Hanna, especially, developed a great affection and admiration for her uncle and of all the children she was his favorite. She must have noted, as her brother Eugene had, that neither her father nor her uncle, for all they had endured, bore any enmity toward the English people. They were fully aware, as Eugene pointed out, that a sizable majority of the British had twice voted in support of Home Rule for Ireland. The real problem was a Tory clique that ignored the wishes of the people and "Ireland's just demands." When in 1914 Eugene applied for a commission in the British Army, Irish Regiment, his father could condone his decision since David saw the war as being fought for the rights of small nations.[7]

So active had David Sheehy been in the Fenian movement when he returned from Paris that, after a time, he was forced to flee to the United States to avoid prosecution. Back in Ireland after his exile, he met and married Elizabeth (Bessie) McCoy, whose parents, like his own, were County Limerick natives. Bessie, as she was always called, was some five years younger than David and, as family legend has it, left the convent school she was attending to marry him. (Since records indicate that she was twenty-five when she married, this is unlikely.) Born in Curraghmore, in County Limerick, she was a bright, witty, ambitious, strongwilled woman who wielded considerable influence over both her husband and her children. Her grandson, Conor Cruise O'Brien, writes that she "intended quite consciously, I believe, to preside over the birth of a new ruling class: those who would run the country when Home Rule was won."[8]

If that was so, she got off to a fine start by having six children in eleven years: two boys and four girls. Hanna was the first; Margaret was born two years later; two years after that, Richard; a year later, Eugene; two years later, Mary; and then, two years after that, Kathleen. For those times it was not an exceptionally large family, nor was the rapidity with which Bessie bore the children remarkable. What was unusual, indeed quite unusual given the attitudes prevailing in most families of the day, was the attention Bessie gave to the development of her daughters. They were never made to feel that females were inferior and this had its effect upon all of them but especially upon Hanna, who was most like her mother. Bessie was quite conscious of the resemblance and perhaps somewhat threatened by a daughter whose forcefulness, intellect, and moral earnestness were equal to her own. Hanna, Conor Cruise O'Brien wrote, "would have made a great reforming Mother Superior in a medieval order. When she took up a cause she did not let it go."[9]

Johanna Mary (Hanna) Sheehy was born in County Cork on 24 May 1877. All of the other Sheehy children were born in County Tipperary where David Sheehy owned a mill in Loughmore, near Templemore. Consequently Hanna's earliest memories were "the sound of the mill-wheel and of the waters of the Suir, the smell of fresh bread from the adjoining bakery."[10] She also remembered vividly her first visit to Dublin, before the family moved there permanently. She had stood on O'Connell bridge and been thrilled with the view—one she was always to admire "at all hours and seasons." She had asked her aunt, whose hand she was holding as she stood there, if this were really Ireland, for she had the country girl's distrust of the town and was afraid she had wandered outside Ireland's borders. Reassured, she could relax and enjoy the scenery.[11]

Her fondest recollections, however, were reserved for 2 Belvedere Place in Dublin, where the family took up residence toward the end of the century. Home for her was always the large, comfortable, Georgian house with its high granite steps, pillared doorway, and balcony, situated in a quiet residential street just off fashionable Mountjoy Square. Here, amid the constant bustle of a large and energetic family and the comings and goings of the many visitors, she spent the greater part of her youth.

The Dublin she grew to love as a girl was a small city with mudwall cabins along the banks of the Tolka and no buildings beyond. Rathfarnham, Santry, and Dollymount were merely villages, a day's journey away. Two-horse trams clattered over the cobbles at a leisurely pace, taking an hour or more to get from Nelson's pillar to Phoenix Park; at the bottom of Parnell Square a third horse waited to help pull them up. It was rare in those days to see anyone riding a bicycle, and once Hanna observed "a woman mobbed at Aston's Quay" for having the temerity to be seen on one. Theater at the time featured Sarah Bernhardt, Barry Sullivan, Lillie Langtry, and Mary Anderson. Operas were performed in the old Leinster Hall. There were the old Metropolitan Hall and the Hardwicke Theatre with portly Edward Martyn in attendance. There was the opening night of Yeats's *Cathleen ni Houlihan* and there was the row over his *Countess Cathleen*—a slur against the Irish, some felt, if not the faith. On the political front, there were the battles in the House of Commons over Gladstone's Home Rule Bill, and there was the tragedy of Parnell's adultery and fall from public grace.[12]

Since both the Sheehy and McCoy families were devout Roman Catholics, all the children attended Catholic schools in Dublin and, of course, the Catholic university. Almost without exception their friends were Catholics. But, as Conor Cruise O'Brien notes, the "aspiring middle class of Belvedere Place" did not subscribe to the Ulster Protestant slogan,

Home Rule Means Rome Rule. Ireland, they felt, should be ruled by their class—not by the Catholic church nor by the Protestant ascendancy— and this would necessitate training the best. The Jesuits were already "helping to train such an *elite*," O'Brien said, and so was his grandmother Bessie.[13]

The Dominican Convent on Eccles Street, founded in 1882, was rightfully considered the best day school available for girls, and this was Bessie's choice for her daughters. Hanna was from the first an outstanding student and, for a time, devout enough to want to become a nun. All four of the daughters were in fact bright and each won exhibitions—money prizes granted at three levels of secondary education—with Hanna winning them at each level. Bessie encouraged the girls to compete for these prizes just as she did her sons, although it gradually became clear to the females that, ultimately, equal intelligence and ability did not produce equal opportunities or rewards. This unsettling lesson, plus Bessie's independence and drive, prepared the way for the Sheehy girls' gravitation toward the feminist movement and women's suffrage.

At the end of the nineteenth century, the education of females was based on the assumption that only through wifehood and motherhood could they find true fulfillment. On the second level, for instance, though girls were competing in increasing numbers and with increasing success in intermediate board examinations, only two types of establishments were available to them: day schools where fees had to be paid, and the more exclusive boarding schools with correspondingly higher fees. Of more than one hundred and fifty second-level schools, approximately three were free. The result was that the vast majority of females—the poor—received only four years of schooling. Even at the university—for the very few who got there—the situation was far from ideal. Though no distinction was made between men and women insofar as taking the Royal University examinations was concerned, women were not permitted to attend lectures and, because of this barrier, were unable to prepare adequately for the examinations.[14]

Those women who, like the Sheehy girls, began to campaign for a better education usually came from the day schools—that is, from the middle class. But there was not complete harmony within this group. Some members wanted a "longer, broader and a more intellectually stimulating education for women, which, however, would be definably different from men's." Others, like Hanna, felt that women were the intellectual equals of men, that the difference in sex did not mean any difference in ability, and that their education should, like that available to men, fit them to enjoy participation in "the inherent rights of mankind." This, they felt, they could obtain only through social and political equality.[15]

The ability of the young Sheehy children to win scholarships was fortunate, for there was never much money in the Sheehy household. David had given up the mill for a career in politics. From 1885 to 1900, he was a Nationalist member of Parliament representing South Galway and from 1903 to 1918, an M.P. representing South Meath. Though an M.P.'s stipend was not large and though it was the Sheehys' only source of income, the children always felt themselves members of a prosperous and privileged family. By Dublin standards, indeed they were. Domestic help was easy to obtain with wages mostly paid as room and board, so there were always servants to do the chores. The Sheehys were possessors of that patina of gentility which went with professionalism and enabled Bessie to look down upon those who were "in trade"—a condescension that she extended to the uneducated as well.

When Hanna was eighteen, her studies were interrupted by incipient tuberculosis. Travel in Germany and France and time away from school seemed to restore her health, and soon she was back in Dublin and enrolled in St. Mary's University College, where in 1896 she was received into the Association of the Children of Mary—an indication of a continuing religious interest.[16] Always an excellent and serious student, Hanna's record at the university is best summed up in a letter of recommendation from one of her professors, written in 1903:

> As a pupil of mine for some eight years, Miss Hannah [sic] Sheehy M.A. has read a very wide course in English Literature. Her acquirements in this subject are much above the level attainable by a brilliant student who does not unite to superior mental equipment, a rare capacity for steady persistent application. In the Intermediate examinations and in those of the Royal University, Miss Sheehy uniformly won high distinctions; but these only inadequately indicate the full measure of her ability and scholarship. She has considerable powers of critical appreciation.[17]

As her professor suggests, Hanna's university career was distinguished: she received a scholarship in 1897; a B.A. from the Royal University with second class honors in modern languages in 1899; and an M.A. with first class honors and a special prize of twenty-five pounds in 1902.

Among Hanna's papers are three essays, written in 1901 and 1902, entitled "Early English Literature," "The English Novel," and "Satirical Literature in English." Considering her years, the essays show insight and thorough preparation. They also show a considerable amount of prejudice, as witness this passage in her paper on English satire. In discussing the development of the genre in that country, she notes that "when the satirist appears behind his figures to point their real meaning for himself, the subtle pleasure is completely dispelled and instead of being served up a piquant bouquet, we are forced to partake of a sour ill-timed moral discourse." This fault she attributes "to the over-didactic tendency of the English race," which, she feels, all too often dominates its satirical literature. The best English satires, she maintains, "are due in great measure to foreign influence, working either from outside through French, Spanish and Italian literature models, or from within, owing to the contributions of Irish and Scot[tish] writers in English."[18]

In the main, research for her essays, as well as studying in general, was done at the National Library in Kildare Street. It was an ideal place to work and also to meet and talk with fellow students, both male and female. Here she would sit at one of the small desks in a large, circular room lined with tall bookcases. The talk was usually confined to the dimly lit hallway beyond the main desk or to the steps of the curved portico looking out on a fine courtyard formed by the library itself, the imposing Georgian facade of Leinster House, and, just opposite, the National Museum. Out on the steps of the library Hanna could see a young James Joyce and a young, bearded Francis Skeffington in animated conversation.

Much of Hanna's social life during these years centered around home. Since David Sheehy was heavily involved in the politics of the day and since both David and Bessie were genuinely hospitable people, nationalist M.P.'s in from the provinces would visit and often spend the night at No. 2 Belvedere Place. All the children had lasting memories of conversations about controversies in the House of Commons, the glories of Home Rule, and about Gladstone and Parnell. With the Sheehys, the custom of "evenings" or "afternoons" took the form of "Sunday evenings." Both parents placed a high premium on intelligence and the most intellectual—and often the wittiest—students were among their regular guests during the years the children were in school; the young people looked forward eagerly to those occasions of good conversation, charades, dancing, and singing.

The list of university students who frequented the Sheehy Sunday evenings is most impressive. In the light of literary history, the most important proved to be James Joyce. Actually, his friendship with the Sheehy boys predated university days. Stanislaus Joyce calls James's visits to their home "the only experience of what might be called social life that my brother had in Dublin." Though Stanislaus liked David Sheehy, he claims that James thought him "pompous and inclined to lay down the law" and preferred Bessie. As Stanislaus saw the family, there were "two clever brothers and four clever sisters, one of them a really handsome girl."[19] This may have been Margaret, for she was considered the handsomest, but possibly it was Mary, who was thought of as the prettiest and with whom James Joyce was said to have been secretly in love for many years. By 1926, however, his infatuation must have been well over, for a letter from Margaret Sheehy to Hanna that year indicated that he could not remember which of the sisters had attracted him.[20]

There with Joyce on those Sunday visits were John Francis Byrne (his closest friend at the university and the model for Cranly in *A Portrait of the Artist as a Young Man*), Tom Kettle, Cruise O'Brien, and Francis Skeffington. Stanislaus Joyce attended occasionally as well, and he recalls that when he first went there as a young boy he met a girl—one of Hanna's university friends—who took him aside and, to his delight, spent most of the evening talking to him about sports. Completely captivated, he was very disappointed that he never saw her there again.[21] Most accounts of these evenings mention simply the boys who attended, but apparently the daughters and their friends were a decided asset.

All of the Sheehy girls, according to Patricia Hutchins, were lively and attractive, displaying "that pleasant-sounding, half-humorous intonation, the accent of the Ireland-educated gentlemen and gentlewomen of another generation."[22] Hanna in fact was only modestly attractive, with dark hair, oval face, deep-set blue eyes under heavy brows, prominent nose, and firm, resolute chin. Though not as physically appealing as her sisters, she was considered the most intellectual and the wittiest, her wit often quick and biting. Margaret, two years younger, with a strong and lasting passion for theater, was the one who was in charge of drama for the Sunday evenings. She achieved a minor success when one of her plays, *Cupid's Confidante*, was actually performed by the Dramatic and Literary Society in the X.L. Cafe in Grafton Street. Both she and Joyce performed in this one—he in the role of the villain, Geoffrey Fortescue. It was not surprising that, many years later when she was living in Canada, she formed a little theater group which performed Irish plays. Mary, some

seven years younger than Hanna, was beautiful, vibrant, and educated—
she studied at the Dominican and Loreto Colleges and was a graduate of
the Royal University. Passionately opposed to the government because
she considered it male chauvinistic, she was equally opposed to the church
for the same reason. She was a likely source for the "dark full-figured"[23]
Emma Clery in James Joyce's *Stephen Hero*—a girl who, young Stephen
senses, had not "reserved herself for him."[24] Mary said later she had no
idea that Joyce even found her attractive. It was the nationalistic Thomas
Kettle, tall and handsome with the look of a dreamer and poet, who
caught her eye. Kathleen, the youngest, was considered the most tractable
of the girls, but she was to show the Bessie Sheehy persistence when she
refused to be dissuaded from marrying Cruise O'Brien—a stand for
which her son, Conor Cruise O'Brien, is, of course, grateful.

Hanna's intelligence, her quick wit, and, it is very possible, her dep-
recation of her own charms, appealed to Francis Skeffington immediately.
The gaiety and the whole atmosphere of the Sheehy menage did as well.
Different from anything he had known previously, the evenings brought a
warmth into his life that, though he may not have realized it, he needed.
The only child of Joseph Bartholomew and Rose Skeffington, he had been
taught at home by his father, a supervisor of education in the National
Schools system and a strict disciplinarian. His mother, forty years old
when she married twenty-two-year-old J. B. (as Francis's father was always called), must have been something of a maverick to make such a
match, but there is no indication that she played anything other than a
secondary role in the Skeffington household. One or two letters to her son
over the years indicate that she resented her husband's dictatorial temperament and what she considered his lack of generosity with money, but this
resentment took no overt form. J. B.'s education, and her lack of it, may
have been the cause of her passivity. He held a doctorate from the Royal
University and had a strong, inquiring mind. By all indications, he gave
his son a splendid education. But he was a stubborn, dogmatic, hot-tempered, extremely religious man, and the atmosphere in which Francis
Skeffington grew up was oppressive. Partly in reaction to it, however, he
emerged a staunch feminist, a pacifist, an internationalist, and a young
man with strong doubts about the Catholic church and the value of a religious upbringing. Having acquired his father's stubborn streak, he never
varied from his beliefs—he only added to his causes. In Hanna, he saw a
nonconformist like himself.

Skeffington became a university character in short order. His dress would have guaranteed that, if his ideas hadn't. He wore, always, rough tweed suits, knickerbockers, and boots that seemed too large. He was only about five feet five inches tall and appeared frail; with a soft, reddish-brown beard, he resembled George Bernard Shaw. The student body soon came to know his ideas on pacifism and feminism as well as his attitude toward drinking and smoking, vivisection, and the eating of meat. As relatives noted later, Hanna and he bore a rather striking, almost familial, resemblance to each other—high forehead, straight nose, rather deep-set eyes and high cheekbones; at five feet three inches, she was only slightly shorter than Francis. Hanna, however, was inclined to look somewhat sombre, while Francis's eyes sparkled with wit and good humor.

At the Sheehys, Skeffington's northern accent stood out. Born in County Cavan, he was very young when the family moved to Downpatrick so that his father might take up his duties as district inspector for the Downpatrick School District. Roger McHugh, in a profile of Skeffington, draws a vivid picture of him: "Skeffington had something of Ulster earnestness in his direct manner of confronting you, of briskly shaking hands, of replying to some absurd case which you had invented 'just for the cod of it' with an invitation to develop your point of view in public in the Phoenix Park the following Saturday at 3 P.M. sharp; and he would walk briskly away, leaving you with a totally unwanted sense of responsibility."[25] His "Ulster earnestness" Hanna found most attractive. There is an item in her 1907 diary, however, that reads: "F. has a new awful habit of walking around 'thinking'—hope he'll drop it."[26]

By 1901 matters were becoming quite serious between Hanna and Francis. In January of that year they had what seems to have been an innocent rendezvous in Paris. In subsequent months they saw a great deal of each other in the National Library, took long walks together, and wrote to each other almost daily. By the following year, they were attending meetings of the Contemporary Club together. "Most interesting evg.," she jotted in her diary, "though woman's question was shunted by Chairman."[27] Both she and Francis spoke that night and it was then also that she met Anna M. Haslam, secretary of the Irish Women's Suffrage and Local Government Association, and Miss Oldham, two prominent figures in the feminist movement who were soon to become very important to Hanna.

Marriage was entering into their thoughts by February 1902. Hanna noted in her diary that month: "Frank's loneliness—his ideal was that one should not always stand alone, that Love made up for all. And so it does!"[28] But her strong conviction about the importance of independence and personal accomplishment for women made it difficult for her to accept without hesitation the implications of Frank's position; marriage, with all that she felt it entailed, was a matter about which she had serious doubts.

An otherwise unmemorable story Hanna wrote in 1901 called "Life's Choosing" reveals just how intense her misgivings were at the time. As the piece opens, Madge Stevenson, a student at a convent school, is participating in a summer retreat on woman's vocation in life. A priest, speaking to the group, is telling the girls that woman's first duty is "her domestic duty" and adds, unimaginatively, "The sphere of man is the outer world, the sphere of woman is the home." Madge flatly rejects the clerical view, which was also essentially society's view. On the other hand, Lucy Molloy, her friend and fellow student, agrees with the priest and argues that if a woman mixes in politics and business "she is sure to get coarse and slangy," to be too much "like a man." Lucy plans to marry and not "waste any time bothering my head over such nonsense."[29]

Her friend does marry early and writes Madge that she is having a fine time attending plays and balls. While Lucy is blissfully wasting her time, Madge devotes herself to journalism and literary criticism, rejecting a proposal of marriage from Lucy's brother Terence, who has just finished medical school. Lucy's bliss, however, is predictably short-lived as her marriage collapses in financial ruin and she goes home to her mother.[30]

Like Madge, Hanna rejected the conventional attitudes, perpetuated by the church, toward the woman's role; also like Madge, she rejected the conventional attitudes toward marriage. It was indeed the fear she would lose her independence if she were to accept Francis's proposal that lay behind the story. Despite her uneasiness, however, by June 1902 she and Francis had decided to marry in 1903 come what may.

It was always Hanna's spoken contention that it was Francis Skeffington who sparked her interest in feminism. Given her family background, her education and intelligence, and the general restlessness of educated women in Ireland during that period, it is impossible to accept this premise. On the votes-for-women front, for instance, much work was being done internationally and, in Ireland, the Dublin Women's Suffrage Society was formed in 1874, followed by the Irish Women's Suffrage and Local Government Association, which was founded in 1876 by Anna and Thomas Haslam. Thanks to the Haslams, a group of Irish women and men were developing a keen interest in women's suffrage and better conditions for women generally. In 1899, also, the nationalistic women's organization, Inghinidhe na hEireann (Daughters of Erin), was formed. A Hanna Sheehy, growing up in a politically and socially aware household, would have been very conscious of all of these advances.

Certainly a number of her feminist principles were firmly in place as early as 1901. That year the Royal Commission on University Education, considering changes in higher education, named Hanna to a subcommittee that prepared a questionnaire for all women graduates of the Royal University. Her own responses to the various questions indicate that she believed any changes in the system, to be effective, had to apply to both men and women equally. Without "absolute equality," she said, the present structure might as well be kept. Consistently enough, she rejected the idea of women students attending their own colleges and competing only among themselves, calling such a scheme "utterly ruinous to women's education" and arguing that they should go to the same general colleges as men, share the same curriculum and lectures and compete with them on examinations and for degree honors. "There are many advantages," she wrote, "for both sexes in a complete system of co-education."[31]

One issue raised by the questionnaire involved the possibility of establishing an association composed of degree candidates and graduates for the purpose of looking after the interests of women. Given the "crisis" in university education and the absence of women on the Royal Commission that would be deciding the future of education for them, Hanna was wholeheartedly in favor of the proposal. "A permanent organization is greatly needed," she maintained, "and should be open not only to men and women graduates and Candidate B.A.s but to any persons interested in the question of women's education."[32] Of 282 replies to the proposal, 277 approved of such an association. On 14 March 1902, a general meeting was held in Dublin to discuss the matter and early in April a recruiting letter was sent out over the names of A. W. Haslett, M.A., and M. O. Kennedy, B.A., asking those wishing to join to so indicate. Hanna gladly signed.[33]

Thus the Irish Association of Women Graduates and Candidate-Graduates was established. The need for it was obvious. Almost at once two hundred members were enrolled, with voting rights restricted to those who already had earned their degrees, and very soon branches were established in Belfast, Cork, Derry, and Galway. The association, nonsectarian and nonpolitical, had as its stated objectives providing means of communication and mutual action in matters concerning the interests of the university women of Ireland; equalizing educational opportunities for

men and women; and supplying the membership with a placement service—a clearing-house for applicants and employers. Judging by Hanna's
initial response to the proposal, she may not have been completely satisfied with an organization open *only* to women.

One involvement, either personal or organizational, led to another
for Hanna. In September she received a letter from Anna Haslam, enclosing a report of the Irish Women's Suffrage and Local Government Association and asking her to join. "It is exceedingly important that we should
have as many educated women as possible amongst our published list of
supporters," she wrote. "Your name has been forwarded to me by Miss
Roper, B.A., Manchester, as one of those who signed the Women Graduates Petition in March."[34] Naturally, Hanna joined and a friendship was
established with Mrs. Haslam that, although Hanna would grow impatient with her lack of militancy and what she came to consider the stodgi-
ness of the association, lasted as long as Haslam lived.

A Union of Ideals

O N 27 JUNE 1903, Hanna Sheehy and Francis Skeffington were married in the Roman Catholic chapel of the university at St. Stephen's Green. It was a beautiful wedding and they were a handsome couple, but there was, apparently, one discordant note. Disregarding the intense disapproval of J. B. Skeffington, Hanna and Francis, as proof of their thoroughgoing feminism, took each other's names; henceforth they would be known as the Sheehy-Skeffingtons. Though the step was not entirely without precedent, it was for 1903 still quite revolutionary. Francis's father, not noted for his liberal spirit or his forgiving nature, was never able to accept their decision graciously and, many years later, told his son that, if he needed help, he could turn to the Sheehys since he no longer bore the Skeffington name exclusively.[1]

The next weeks were busy and exciting. For their honeymoon, the couple decided on a cycling trip. They visited Cork, had a week in Killarney, cycled all around South Kerry and around the coast, doubled back to Killarney for a few days rest before climbing Carrantual, Ireland's highest mountain, and returned to Dublin late in July. By early August they had settled into their first home at 8 Airfield Road, Rathgar, at that time an area mostly inhabited by upper-middle-class professionals. The street, a cul-de-sac, contained well-kept, single-family dwellings, each with its box hedge. Soon they were busy pursuing their careers. Hanna was teaching modern literature part-time at St. Mary's University College, Donnybrook, and at the Dominican Convent, Cabra. Francis was serving as the first lay registrar of University College, Dublin. He was also working on a novel and beginning to receive a little recognition as a journalist, with pieces appearing in publications such as *New Ireland* (a "Weekly Journal Devoted to the Industries, Language, Literature, and Politics in Ireland"), and the liberal *Freeman's Journal*.

The first years of the Sheehy-Skeffington marriage were beset with more than the usual adjustment problems, as their diaries make clear. Their love for each other was deep, but, as in many marriages, the two were quite different in temperament. Hanna, particularly in those years, was given to serious bouts of melancholia; Francis was possessed of a buoyant, sanguine temperament. Hanna was quicker to pass judgment and to criticize; Francis, though adamant in his beliefs, was extremely accepting of others and willing to listen to their ideas. In addition to temperamental differences, there were financial problems that made adjustment difficult. And, finally, both had received a rigid, Catholic upbringing in a puritanical era, which resulted in ignorance, misconceptions, and fears with regard to sex. Inevitably, both suffered. On the New Year's Day before they were married, Hanna had visited Mother Patrick at the Dominican Convent. The nun had talked of the importance of "moral courage" in a marriage, but this was not the kind of advice Hanna needed, or wanted to hear. As she observed in her diary, no one had ever presented "worthy" thoughts on the subject, "least of all . . . those who taught me!"[2] It was a tribute to the patience and understanding of both—and perhaps to two marriage manuals they ordered late in 1904—that the next year they could report a happy second anniversary.

Less than a year after they were married, Francis decided that he could no longer continue as registrar at the university. His reason for resigning was completely in character. Working with Hanna and members of the Women Graduates Association, he had written and helped to circulate a document requesting that women be admitted to the university on an equal basis with men. Father William Delany, learning of his involvement, pointed out that, as an officer of the institution, Francis had no right to advocate policy in opposition to that of the university. Unrepentant, Francis replied that he thought he had in no way violated official policy. Furthermore, he felt that the admission earlier of women to Trinity College had made it imperative for University College, Dublin, to follow suit. In order to be free to express his opinions in the future, however, he wished to resign his position with six months' notice.[3]

Hanna applauded his action. It did not surprise her that her husband, who always placed a high premium on an individual's freedom to speak, would allow nothing to interfere with his right to champion women. Though she felt that no male was wholly free of chauvinism, Francis seemed as close to being a complete feminist as could be expected. Some months before they were married she commented on "the curious

prejudice of even the best intentioned men," noting that while Francis became irate at the thought of her sister Mary smoking, he accepted rather
calmly the fact that his closest male friends smoked. "Yet this prejudice,"
she wrote, "is unconscious—And it is to be found in the man who of all I
have met is freest from prejudice with regard to women, who would not,
for any wordly consideration, pen a line that might be construed into the
slightest reflection on the progress of women."[4]

Francis's decision to resign had not been made hastily. The attitude
of the university was simply the culminating factor. Shortly before, he
had sent an open letter to *New Ireland* in which he had attacked the bishops
at Maynooth for the warm reception given to Edward VII and had expressed the opinion that their fawning attitude reflected their desire to obtain for Maynooth a share in a grant expected to be given to a Catholic university. Because of his position at University College, he had not dared to
sign his name to the open letter. It was impossible to go on living that
way. Defying convention and establishing a pattern that would never vary
during the brief years of their marriage, Hanna encouraged his decision to
pursue a career as a free-lance journalist. Neither desired wealth; she was
employed, and they were optimistic about the possibilities open to him in
journalism. His salary had been one hundred pounds yearly, a good sum
for those times, but neither ever regretted giving it up.

One of Francis Sheehy-Skeffington's pleasures, and one that led also
to the furtherance of his career, was the young couple's At Homes, held
on Wednesday evenings. With his love of discussion and controversy,
Francis found these evenings both stimulating and amusing. Joyce and
Byrne were often present during the early years, and later there were figures such as Lindsay Crawford, a Protestant and a nationalist; Frederick
Ryan, a young socialist and an aspiring journalist; and Maud Joynt, a
staunch feminist, who seemed able to spark a great deal of controversy.
Much time one night, for instance, was spent on Joynt's disapproval of
pensions and Hanna's support of her stand. People, they both felt, should
be able to save enough money not to need pensions—any other policy
would encourage thriftlessness. Francis disagreed vehemently. People, he
said, should only be expected to live, not to save. The old and weary
worker should be supported by the government. In this instance, as in
many others, Hanna subscribed to a somewhat more bourgeois code than
did her husband.

While Francis seemed quite satisfied with the way the At Homes
were working out, Hanna's attitude toward them was at best ambivalent.

After remarking in her diaries that the gatherings were "getting generally established," she was quick to observe that she found "most of them rather a bore & a bother," though perhaps a quarter had been enjoyable. She did want to try "to work them up better," however.[5]

Tom Kettle was one of those who regularly attended the Wednesday evenings at the Sheehy-Skeffingtons'. He and Francis enjoyed arguing and, in addition, the occasions provided a good opportunity for meeting Mary Sheehy away from the watchful eyes of her mother. In 1905 Kettle was beginning to think of a career in politics. A feminist like Sheehy-Skeffington, he was also becoming increasingly aware that a change in attitude was developing with regard to women's rights. It seemed to him that a new magazine might make his name better known and, at the same time, provide a forum for the ideas he wished to publicize. As a result, in September 1905 the *Nationist* appeared under Kettle's editorship and with Francis Sheehy-Skeffington as assistant editor. The tabloid-sized, sixteen-page paper did not claim to be entirely original or indispensable, but wanted to "devote itself to criticism of contemporary life, construed from the national point of view."[6] Its profeminist leanings could be seen in an editorial in the second issue attacking John Sweetman—Sinn Fein's second president, a country gentleman and an ex-member of Parliament—for offering a scholarship purely for boys. Other donors, the editorial warned, should "understand that his example cannot be generally followed without seriously impeding the modernization of Ireland."[7]

Financial support for the paper was difficult to obtain and this became increasingly so when, as a result of one of its articles, backers began to complain. The offending article had called for "complete independence" from priests in all matters except religion, where they were entitled to "complete deference."[8] It was not very many months before Kettle turned the editorship over to Skeffington completely and not many more months before the *Nationist* was forced to discontinue publication.

Organizations fighting women's battles needed the help of voices like that of the *Nationist* and, happily, it was followed by another publication, the *National Democrat*, brought out by Francis Sheehy-Skeffington and his friend Fred Ryan, who had contributed articles to the earlier magazine. The *National Democrat* continued to carry items of special interest to women and soon was able to report "a substantial feminist advance" when a new regulation passed at the National Teachers' Congress gave women teachers representation on the teachers' executive. Another item pointed out that Catholic women were now being admitted to Trinity College and urged them not to let Catholic men in positions of authority forget it.[9]

In England, the Women's Social and Political Union was making women's suffrage one of the major issues of the day. To the delight of the Sheehy-Skeffingtons, Christabel Pankhurst and a colleague, Annie Kenney, leading figures in the W.S.P.U., had disrupted a meeting in Manchester with cries of "Will the Liberal Party give votes to women?" They had been arrested and sentenced to short jail terms. "A solid wall of prejudice, convention, and conservatism" existed, Francis Sheehy-Skeffington wrote in the *National Democrat*, against which logic was powerless. "I hope the devoted members of the Women's Social and Political Union, undaunted by the abuse which is hurled at them, will proceed from violence to violence until their end is attained. And I have no doubt they will. These women are of the stuff of which martyrs are made."[10] As Hanna wrote much later, "the stone and the shillelagh need no apologia: they have an honoured place in the armoury of argument."[11]

In Ireland, the late nineteenth century had found more and more women becoming actively interested in politics and in the 1860s the Irish Women's Suffrage Association had been formed. Though from 1897 onward there were many members of the House of Commons in favor of granting women the right to vote, these supporters did not include Irish members. For them the first priority was to gain Home Rule, and only when the women's movement became militant did they begin to take notice. George Dangerfield, in *The Strange Death of Liberal England*, dates the rise of militancy from the 1910–14 period. Referring to "The Women's Rebellion" as "above all things a movement from darkness into light, and from death into life," he points out that, "like the Tory Rebellion, its unconscious motive was the rejection of a moribund, a respectable, a smothering security." In his opinion, militancy did not seem to become a force until then and, even then, became only a minor force.[12]

So far as the Irish Association of Women Graduates was concerned, its efforts and those of the *Nationist* and the *National Democrat* were not going unrewarded. In 1907 the Jesuit Fathers issued a report noting that the president of University College, Dublin, had informed the Mother-General of the Loreto Institute at Rathfarnham Abbey that in the future the students of Loreto College could be entered as members of University College if they so desired. "There is an old saying 'Better late than never!'" the report commented.[13]

In addition to the other demands on her time, Hanna's teaching schedule during 1905 was heavier than it had ever been and, secretly, she hoped that it was as heavy as it would ever be. She found teaching demanding, tiring, and often discouraging. To a great extent this was because she was an excellent and a dedicated teacher. She enjoyed her students, was interested in their welfare, and eagerly followed their careers. The nuns, according to her notes, did not approve of her socializing with her pupils, but there is evidence that she did it nonetheless. Still there were days when she found teaching drudgery and a thankless profession; in fact, at one point that year she seriously considered giving it up.[14]

She had started the year with many fine resolutions: to walk more, to keep her diary faithfully, to outline a course of reading for herself, and to try to do some writing every day—"critiques, impressions, pensees," or even just teaching notes and letters. She vowed as well to nag Francis less and to try to help him in his work, at least indirectly, by being in better spirits. On a nationalistic note, she resolved to buy Irish-made goods to aid Irish industry. Ruefully, at the end of the year she noted that she had kept only one of her resolutions: which one she did not say, though it may well have been the one involving her husband because physically she was feeling better that year and "less melancholy of late."[15]

Not always successfully, Hanna tried to fight against melancholy, but she worried also about what she thought was her indolence. Anyone less demanding of herself would surely have thought that she had won this battle. During the winter of 1906–1907 she was studying German, teaching school, writing, speaking, and serving on various committees. She was in demand as a speaker and, for her, this was a great achievement for early on her shyness made public speaking very difficult. Both she and Francis were delighted at her progress. She took particular pride in the fact that while chairing the National Examination Subcommittee for the first time she become involved in a disagreement with the lord mayor over women being relegated to the gallery. "I came off well & showed him up," she noted, and added that she had spoken at three meetings on the suffrage issue.[16] She was much amused at one of these meetings to have a woman ask her, very anxiously, if her husband took an interest in these matters.[17]

All signs were beginning to point to a growing militancy on Hanna's part, to an impatience with empty rhetoric. She was finding the suffragette movement, as it was being practiced in Britain, increasingly attractive. The Haslams' organization was, for her, "too propagandist—needlessly"—and soon she resigned on what she termed "political grounds."

She wanted more direct involvement in public affairs. That she was feeling guilty about what she perceived as her lack of such participation is evident in her lamenting the fact that her "only real Public Work" had been in connection with the row at the Royal University.[18] That activity, however, had certainly not gone unnoticed. James Joyce, in Rome, wrote to his brother, Stanislaus: "I suppose you read about Skeff and his papa-in-law? They harangued student Dublin from a car outside the University Buildings and U. Coll., because God Save the King was played on the organ. 'There was a lady in the vehicle,' the paper says."[19] Of course it was Hanna. In fact, she seems to have been worrying without reason, for there were few controversies in which one or the other of the Sheehy-Skeffingtons did not figure prominently.

On the whole, at the end of 1906, Hanna was pleased with life. Her health, except for the "usual lapses," was good, though her eyes bothered her, and, to her considerable relief, her husband's "journalistic circle" was "widening." Neither marriage nor career had altered the close relationship she had with her sisters, all of whom were very fond of Frank, as they called him, as he was of them. There were lengthy lunches and teas and, that year, much talk of Mary's engagement to Tom Kettle and Margaret's forthcoming marriage to John F. Culhane, a likable young solicitor. Letters and notes were written to each other frequently. When, late in 1905, Mary won a story competition, Hanna, working in the National Library on one of her articles, took time to write her. After offering her congratulations, she cautioned her in a playfully mocking tone to avoid spending her prize money on dresses, ties, or gloves—those "temptations of the flesh"—and to use it, first, to join the Women Graduates Association and then to buy books "that will be a prop to your old age," concluding: "Having put your hand to the ploughshare (purse in this case) do not draw back. There is no compromising with fate. . . . The wages of Sin is Death."[20] This was a battle that Hanna, incidentally, often lost, for she was extremely fond of clothes. Hats in particular she found hard to resist.

Though she felt well, Hanna was never robust and both she and Francis worried about her health. In fact, he took the step of corresponding with her doctor, Elizabeth A. Tennant, presumably concerning a gynecological ailment. Two letters from Dr. Tennant assure him that neither had any cause for great anxiety, that Hanna merely required "a little local treatment," that her condition had nothing to do with "her being a married woman as were she single it wd be just as necessary," and that there was "nothing to prevent her in due course having a family."[21] It was cheering news for Hanna for she had long desired a child. There is substantial basis for the belief that she, like so many of her contemporaries, felt that procreation was really the only excuse for intercourse.

By mid-1908 her health became of secondary importance, for Francis contracted a severe case of diphtheria and nearly died. That winter he had brought out a biography of Michael Davitt and, though the *National Democrat* was extinct, there had been much tiring prepublication work in addition to all his other activities. His illness terrified Hanna. Recalling the "days of anguish" and "fright" at its onset, she wrote him during his convalescence: "I won't forget how near I felt to losing you."[22]

In June Francis went to Youghal, County Cork, to convalesce and Hanna was left to move them from Airfield Road to their new two-story brick home at 11 Grosvenor Place, Rathmines. The move went smoothly with the assistance of Minnie, their maid, and a handyman named Johnny; within a short time Hanna was settled and beginning to get used to the new house and neighborhood, although she felt uprooted. Revealing a sentimental strain that always lay just beneath her rational, practical, sometimes grim exterior, she told Francis of her farewell visit to the Airfield house: "I enclose an elder blossom (now beautifully out there) in form of adieu," she wrote. "I felt lonely for the first time lately over the little house. It seemed to have a mute appeal somehow in its desertion & looked nice, tho' dreary. There was a full moon—well, altogether I had a *serrement de coeur* as I handed away my keys. I do hate pulling up my roots even for a beneficial transplanting somehow. I fear I'll be ever sorry to die!"[23]

During the weeks of Francis's absence, Hanna was left to contend with the usual household difficulties. Servants were, now as before, among the problems. There was petty friction with Minnie, which Hanna tried to control, as she had with other servants. Johnny, a drinker, she thought insolent and "mean & dishonest in small things." She considered it "a social need" to have tea with her parents from time to time and remarked that "consorting with servants . . . is demoralizing to one's social mood" and not conducive to "democratic views." This condescension toward her help was characteristic and hardly becoming to a person who embraced a socialist political philosophy.[24]

Servants were by no means the only problem: there were also her in-laws, always a source of tension for her. "Sorry your mother isn't well," she wrote to Francis, adding, "though it's more than the same old lady would be in my case!"[25] A little later, when Francis's mother was visiting relatives in Downpatrick and J. B. was home alone, Hanna worried that he would expect her to have him to Grosvenor Place for teas or dinners. So upset was she at the prospect that she lashed out angrily: "In fact, I don't pine to see him at all—I see quite well now (if I didn't before!) that neither he nor your mother cares a fluke for me except as a kind of working machine, half-drudge, half-general-worker, & being a vindictive little piece you bet I'm not likely to forget it!" She ended: "You are the only Skeffington that cares an iota for me & after all you're half Sheehy!"[26] Actually Hanna's attitude toward them seems without very solid foundation. There is ample evidence, for instance, in letters from Rose Skeffington to her son that she was always solicitous of Hanna's health and afraid she was overworking. Hanna was probably closer to the truth with J. B., whose rigidity, aloofness, and certainty must have made him something less than the ideal dinner companion or the ideal father-in-law.

Compounding these problems, real or imagined, were Hanna's own physical and emotional health, always delicate, and the family's desperate financial situation. Not everything was bleak, however. Francis's *Davitt* was being praised in nationalist circles and was receiving quite good notices, even if it was not selling very well. In the Sheehy household things were becoming positively intriguing. Eugene, Hanna's brother, seemed to be more than casually interested in a young woman named Aggie Sheehan, whom Hanna had met at Belvedere Place.[27] Sister Kathleen was, she said, studying French with Cruise O'Brien but Hanna wondered where they were studying since it clearly wasn't in the family house. Something seemed to be developing there. "No one suspects anything yet," she told Francis, "& won't of course till it's too late."[28]

By fall, with Francis once more hard at work, Hanna was feeling much better. Resuming attendance at Philosophical Society meetings, they met a couple with whom they formed a close and lasting friendship—James and Gretta Cousins. The Cousinses were both dedicated feminists and even, to the Skeffingtons' delight, vegetarians. Gretta and Hanna had a great deal in common. They were little more than a year apart in age, were well educated, worked closely with their husbands, and spoke and wrote for women's rights without fear. They saw no conflict between being a nationalist and fighting for votes for women. Anything that improved the lot of women would also improve the chances of winning self-government for Ireland, they were convinced. Gretta was an accomplished pianist, holding a Bachelor of Music degree from the Royal Irish Academy of Music in Dublin and, at one time, had accompanied that aspiring tenor, James Joyce, thus establishing her niche in history. But one of her major interests—spiritualism—Hanna did not share with her. Gretta was a practicing medium.

In 1906 Gretta Cousins had attended a meeting of the National Council of Women in London and was inspired by its aggressiveness. She was now searching for like-minded people in Dublin. The Irish Women's Suffrage and Local Government Association—the Haslams' organization—was far too bland for her, though she joined it and tried to breathe some fire into it. Like Hanna, she was convinced that when dealing with the Parliamentary Party militancy was the only possible road. Together they decided that a new, activist women's organization had to be formed. On 4 November 1908, therefore, six women met at the Sheehy-Skeffington's, and the Irish Women's Franchise League came into being. Hanna served as its first secretary, Gretta Cousins as its first treasurer. Just as in the British W.S.P.U., membership was limited to women, though men were allowed to join as associates. Sheehy-Skeffington, Cousins, Thomas MacDonagh (a young poet and friend of the Sheehy-Skeffingtons), and Cruise O'Brien joined immediately.

The Irish Women's Franchise League was destined to play a central role in the votes-for-women struggle in Ireland. As for the make-up of its membership, Gretta Cousins maintained that it was a cross-section of all classes, political parties, and religious groups. The cause for which they were all fighting, she asserted, broke down social barriers. However, Rosemary Owens, in her study of suffrage societies in Ireland, could find little evidence of the involvement of working-class women in such organizations. The Irish Women's Franchise League may have attracted more of them than most of the other suffrage groups (especially during the 1913 Dublin labor disputes) but its membership from all accounts remained primarily middle-class.[29]

From its inception, many women prominent in the nationalist movement were antagonistic to its formation, among them Constance Markievicz, one of the leaders of the 1916 Easter Rising. Writing in Arthur Griffith's paper, *Sinn Fein*, she attacked what she considered to be a tie-in between the I.W.F.L. and the English women's movement. "We hear a great deal just at present of a League that is being started in Dublin called the Irish Women's Franchise League," she commented in a graciously condescending manner. "This League appears to be a very vague organisation, but we see no reason why, when its members have gained a little experience, it should not become something definite and something useful to Irishwomen, and—bar consequence—useful to Ireland." The propaganda of the I.W.F.L., she maintained, should be presented purely from the point of view of the Irish. It might be sufficient for the English woman to fight only for the vote: when she obtained it, she would have a parliament in which she would be represented. The Irishwoman, however, should be attempting not only to win the vote on the same terms as men but first and foremost to fight for a free Ireland in which to use it. To agitate for the privilege of being represented in an "alien Parliament" seemed to her insufficient. So strong was the Markievicz attack that Arthur Griffith felt called upon to add a disclaimer to the article. Of the I.W.F.L., he said: "We shall not condemn it or any body which tends to awaken civic and national consciousness in Irishwomen."[30]

One of the first actions taken by the newly formed organization was to call upon the Young Ireland Branch to put a resolution calling for women's suffrage on the agenda of the national convention which was to be held in February 1909. The Young Ireland Branch had been founded late in 1904 by young idealists who hoped to be able to form a strong enough group to become an effective force in the United Irish League and hasten the attainment of freedom for Ireland. Both Skeffington and Kettle were instrumental in its formation. At its second meeting, Kettle was elected president and both Francis and Hanna were on the executive committee.[31] It seemed to the women in the I.W.F.L. that this was the right group to appeal to. As requested, the resolution was brought to the floor and, though it did not pass, it did bring the question of women's votes before such a body for the first time. It was a victory of sorts. Hanna had never really believed that it would pass. When it came to their attitude toward women, she had never completely trusted either the Y.I.B. or the U.I.L.

About the time the Irish Women's Franchise League was formed, Hanna became pregnant. Apparently this did not hamper her activities. That winter she acted as secretary of the Irish Association of Women Graduates while Maud Joynt, the elected secretary, was in Liverpool, and her name was on the ballot for vice-president. She was, after much study, confident enough of her German to apply to have her name placed on the list from which the 1909 examiners in German were to be selected, and was accepted.

By now an experienced, forceful, and witty speaker, if still inwardly a nervous one, Hanna read a paper before the Young Ireland Branch which was so impressive that the *Irish Nation* picked it up and ran it for three successive Saturdays as a feature story with the title, "Women and the National Movement."³² Without reservation, she stated that the Parliamentary Party's position with regard to women had until that time been extremely backward. Thanks to its black record—the dissolution of the Ladies' Land League, for one thing—she was not at all sure that the women of Ireland would "ever again throw in their lot with Parliamentarianism, or devote themselves exclusively to the Language Movement and Sinn Fein." In the long run, she felt this might be for the best because, in order to build a strong base from which to make their participation in any area solid, they would need to establish it firmly "not on the shifty quicksands of men's sufferance, but on the basic rock of citizenship."³³

On 19 May 1909, Hanna gave birth to a son whom she and Francis named Owen. It was a very difficult birth and, for a time, there was a distinct possibility that Hanna would not survive it. A letter from Gretta Cousins to Francis expressed shock at "how near we all were to losing our dear 'Mrs. Skeffy'" and sympathy for the "dreadful time of suspense" he had just been through. Typical of the Grettas and Hannas of the world, after offering her congratulations on the arrival of their son, she spent the rest of the letter talking about a meeting at which she would like Francis to speak.³⁴

By the time of Owen's birth, his parents had determined to bring him up without any religious training, for both had come to reject organized religion. Hanna's disillusionment with the church and with, in her view, the narrow-minded Catholic clergy was not a new development. On New Year's Day, 1903, she had seen a lay sister distributing food to the poor at the back door of the Gardiner Street convent and had been repelled by the "harsh tones & brutal manners" of the sister, who "hustled about the miserable wretches like so many starving dogs." A few days later she recorded a conversation between Mother Patrick and Mother de Ricci. The former had said that one of the girls was studying medicine and the latter had replied, "Horrid girl!" Hanna's thought was: "You have a male doctor, oh delicate creature."³⁵ The next year she had written: "Hardly went to Mass at all! Not much of this [religion] left now."³⁶ It seems that by then the Sheehy-Skeffingtons had come to the conclusion that the Catholic church no longer filled a need in their lives, and they had become what they called "believing" rationalists and humanists.

Though Francis was always referred to as an atheist, Hanna, for reasons that remain uncertain, was usually labeled an agnostic. It was almost impossible to keep a secret in the Catholic community in Dublin and the Sheehys must have been aware that Hanna and Francis had lapsed, but

Bessie chose not to notice. The archivist R. Dudley Edwards told the story of Hanna's lady friends, good God-fearing Catholics for the most part, taking it upon themselves to see that Owen was baptized, unknown not only to the parents but to one another. As a result, he said, the boy was often said to be "the most baptized baby in Ireland."[37] In Owen's lifelong opinion, his parents had made no mistake. Many years later he wrote that he was always grateful to them for their "determination that their son should be brought up with a free mind and without formal religious instruction."[38]

In the personal life of the Sheehy-Skeffingtons, two other major events took place in 1909. Early that year Rose Skeffington died at the age of 80. She had lived a long life, but this did not soften the pain that Francis felt at her death. He had patiently assumed the burdens connected with her illness while J. B. was away, but now he and Hanna had the additional burden of coping with J. B.'s surprising inability to meet his new situation. Unable to handle even such minor details as the disposal of furniture and papers, he turned to Francis for advice constantly on matters both minor and major.

The Sheehy-Skeffingtons were relieved to put these burdens aside, at least temporarily, when on 9 September Mary Sheehy and Tom Kettle were married. The Kettles were a most attractive couple. Mary, dressed in white satin, was a beautiful bride, with her flashing eyes, high color, fine bone structure, and aristocratic air. Tom, tall, handsome, black-haired, sartorially perfect as always, stood waiting for her as she came down the aisle on David Sheehy's arm. The wedding was held in St. Kevin's chapel of the Pro-Cathedral and Mary's uncle, Father Eugene, assisted the two priests who officiated.

It was almost as happy a day for Bessie Sheehy as it was for Mary. Tom Kettle had always been her idea of the perfect son-in-law (though he did drink too much). David may have had mixed feelings. Dudley Edwards remembered hearing that David Sheehy did not like Kettle because "he kept books on the floor."[39]

Wedding gifts arrived from leading members of Parliament, from friends and relatives, and even from the Parliamentary Party. The Sheehy-Skeffingtons sent not only a writing desk but a set of George Meredith's novels, and James Joyce, always without funds, sent a bound copy of *Chamber Music*. No one would have believed it then, but the latter may have been one of their most valuable wedding gifts.

Three of the Sheehy girls were now married. In 1907 Margaret had married John F. (generally known as Frank) Culhane, whose family were in trade—feather merchants, to be exact. It did not surprise Bessie that Margaret married money. Tall, full-bosomed, and handsome, Margaret had always received a great deal of masculine attention. It was assumed that she was far less interested in education than her sisters, and this may have been so. But all the Sheehy children had a strong sense of responsibility for each other; even though Hanna was two years older, Margaret may have felt that, as a scholar, she deserved every educational opportunity. A third possibility, of course, is that Hanna's brilliance daunted her. At any rate, many years later Eugene Sheehy told Margaret's son, Garry Culhane, that it was Margaret who had "kept us all alive and educated all of us."[40]

Bessie would have preferred that the Culhanes not be in trade. Young Culhane, however, was a solicitor and did rise to the position of Taxing Master to the King's Bench in Dublin City. While she approved of the family's rigorous Catholicism, Bessie was irritated by the way they flaunted their piety. A private chapel was really too much. All this uneasiness was mutual, for they had misgivings about the Sheehys, too. The Culhanes were staunch nationalists but, as their grandson explained it, they felt the Sheehys were striving to "change the status quo with intellect—not guns," which made them uncomfortable.[41]

Mary's marriage left the youngest daughter, Kathleen, the only unmarried girl in the family. A fine scholar, she was interested in the revival of Gaelic and, like the Sheehy-Skeffingtons, in votes for women and in Home Rule for Ireland. Furthermore, by the time of Mary's wedding, she was very much in love with Cruise O'Brien, as Hanna had suspected. Family opposition, however, kept them from marrying until 1912. To Bessie, the practically penniless O'Brien, with his English accent, his agnosticism, and his tendency, she thought, to talk down to her husband, hardly seemed the best choice for her daughter. David, too, had reservations, objecting to O'Brien's criticism of the Parliamentary Party to which he himself was extremely loyal. Nonetheless, Hanna and Francis did their best to smooth the way for Kathleen. The freedom of the individual was being violated, they felt. After all, it was Kathleen's decision to make.

For Hanna, though, family matters had to take second place to the feminist movement, which was gaining momentum in Ireland. The Irish Women's Franchise League, to which she was devoting much of her time and energy, was now firmly established in Dublin. It held monthly meetings, which were well attended. The Daughters of Erin, one of the few

women's organizations she did not join, was also flourishing. Unlike the
I.W.F.L., it was attempting to fashion the women's movement around the
issue of Irish independence. "Freedom for our Nation," it proclaimed in
1909, "and the complete removal of all disabilities to our sex will be our
battlecry!" Its monthly magazine, *Bean na hEireann* (Women of Ireland),
was the first and only journal devoted to Irishwomen's nationalist activities.[42]

It was impossible for those women who proceeded on narrowly nationalistic lines to see that the English suffragettes' experiences could serve
as a guide for the Irish. The Sheehy-Skeffingtons, however, were well
aware of this, and open-minded. In one of his many letters to his father,
Francis urged him, late in 1909, to hear Emmeline Pankhurst, England's
foremost suffragette, at Albert Hall, "if you can get in. It is her last London speech before her Canadian tour."[43] But the Sheehy-Skeffingtons
were also vigilant. Writing to a fellow Y.I.B. member a bit later, Francis
informed him that the I.W.F.L. was extending its operations to the provinces. The reason: the Women's Freedom League in England was sending
emissaries and attempting "to run the Suffrage movement in Ireland on
purely English lines; and they must be forestalled."[44] As Hanna pointed
out in one of her articles in the *Irish Nation*, English opinion should not act
as a guide for Irishwomen, although, she thought, "there is a certain
amount of false courage displayed in protesting this overmuch."[45]

Articles by Hanna were beginning to appear quite regularly in the
Irish Nation. The April and May issues of 1910 carried her summary of the
life of Mary Wollstonecraft, who had done pioneering work for women's
rights. In successive issues she discussed the goals of the I.W.F.L. and
replied to attacks that critics were making on what they considered to be
the narrowness of the league's aspirations. One point that she made was
quite fresh. These critics, she maintained, were seeing the situation
through men's eyes. "To fight men's battles for them and to neglect those
of women has always been regarded as true womanly, though when men
fight for their rights on the broad basis of humanity they are not accused
of selfishness. The cause of an oppressed group is fully as great as that of
an oppressed nation and deserves no taunt of narrowness."[46]

Considering the small number of committed workers involved, the
accomplishments of the I.W.F.L. were impressive, and not limited to
purely feminist matters. For example, Maud Gonne, deeply involved in
the cause of feeding school children, had talked with Hanna Sheehy-
Skeffington at the Women's Franchise League offices about how troubled

she was over the situation in the schools. Hanna, she said, had immediately asked Mrs. Conroy, the secretary of the league, to ask the Dublin Corporation to meet with a delegation to take up the problem of providing dinners for the children. As spokeswomen, Hanna named herself in her capacity as president of the league and Maud Gonne as president of the Daughters of Erin. When the Dublin Corporation told her that it was unable to do anything without a special act of the British Parliament, Hanna drafted such an act and Maud took it to London, where it was presented in the House of Commons without change. Unwilling to wait for parliamentary action, the I.W.F.L., the Irish Trade Unions, and the Daughters of Erin formed a school feeding committee and proceeded to supply meals to needy children.[47]

Militant and nonmilitant methods alike were employed to gain attention for the issue of women's right to vote, and the battle was carried to the doors of Parliament. Members of Parliament were heckled by I.W.F.L. members and, on occasion, Irishwomen wound up in English jails. In Ireland, they took their story all over the country, with varying degrees of success. When in 1911 the Conciliation Bill, proposing votes for women, was coming up for its second reading, the I.W.F.L. sent members and friends a persuasive letter instructing them to write their representative, ask that he cast his vote for the bill or, barring that, absent himself from the House or abstain from voting. Plans were made to send "a strong Irish Contingent" to Westminster should the bill be reported unfavorably.[48] On this same matter, Hanna arranged for the preparation of a petition to be submitted to the House of Commons. A splendid, lengthy document, it clearly and forcefully stated the case for passage, but like earlier petitions it fell on deaf ears.[49] The setback merely reinforced Hanna's belief that militancy was the only way. Another proof of the effectiveness of direct action could be seen that same day—the day of the census boycott.

With Charlotte Despard as the leading spirit, the Women's Freedom League decided to organize a boycott of the 1911 census. The I.W.F.L. took up the idea immediately and greeted with glee Madame Despard's ringing statement: "I am not going to tell whether I am a wife or a widow, whether I have had children or not, or the ages of those in my household, until I am a citizen."[50] Plans were kept secret but apparently word went out from the I.W.F.L. headquarters that women were to stay away from home on census day. Gretta Cousins and her maid spent the night in a vacant house near their home, thus making it possible for James to write on his form that he had been "unable to give a true enumeration" of his household since the women were "absent in protest against being officially classed with children, criminals, lunatics and such like."[51]

According to an *Irish Times* report, "a number of supporters of the case absented themselves on Sunday night from their residences, and were accommodated by leaders of the plot, who were willing to refuse any information regarding them on the Census form and to take the consequences of such a refusal." The *Times* estimated the number who participated in the boycott in Dublin as "exceedingly small." Although this may have been true, the publicity was invaluable and the suffrage groups did unite behind it—militant and nonmilitant alike. A few days after the boycott, Mrs. Pankhurst came to Dublin to speak and, when interviewed by Sheehy-Skeffington, said that hundreds of thousands in Ireland and Britain had managed to avoid being counted.[52] It seems likely that both Mrs. Pankhurst and the *Times* were showing bias, yet the issue of "votes for women" was being widely discussed for a few days and the militants were not too wide of the mark when they called the boycott's results a clear victory.

The growing militancy of the women continued to come under attack by the press. When militants disrupted a meeting in Belfast at which Winston Churchill spoke, the *Leader* responded with one of its usual diatribes. This "annoyance," it was sure, would damage the Home Rule effort. "We confess that politically we do not like the imitation Suffragette gang in Ireland," the paper acidly remarked, "and since they did their little worst in Belfast . . . we like them less." The piece went on to express satisfaction that the votes-for-women bill had been defeated and confidence that "all Irishwomen outside the coterie were delighted also."[53]

Near the end of her life, Hanna wrote her version of the Belfast meeting. "He [Churchill] was then a Liberal—and a Home Ruler of sorts, and the Orange blood was up." As a consequence, he was not allowed to speak in the Ulster Hall but spoke instead at the Gaelic sports grounds "in the heart of the Green Quarter." The suffragettes, however, "gave no quarter to British visiting Ministers." Hanna and another I.W.F.L. stalwart attended the meeting—"how we secured tickets I know not, but we usually had a friend or two in various camps"—where they were joined by five Belfast women. Following their "usual plan," the seven drew numbers, took their stations in various parts of the audience, and then, in turn, shouted "Votes for Irishwomen," allowing a pause after each shout. The tent in which the meeting was held was overflowing, and there were police in abundance stationed outside. Hanna's number was three.

The first heckler was like a bombshell; she got her word in and van-
ished, so did the second from another part, and after due interval my
turn came—again from another quarter. By that time tempers were
breaking—how many more would there be? I brought my Dublin accent along, an extra offense of course. After my interjection, the
crowd did the rest; I was seized and hustled to the top of a rough
flight of steps leading to the soggy field. Two rough and angry stewards held me. One said, 'Let's throw her down the steps,' and made a
grabbing gesture. I turned and caught the lapels of his coat with each
hand firmly, saying, 'All right, but you'll come along too!' I wasn't
thrown down.[54]

Hanna's fighting spirit did not go unnoticed by her father-in-law.
Over the years the hot-tempered J.B. had blamed her—though he tried
not to cause an actual rift—for his son's militancy in the women's movement, as well as for his attitude toward money, and for the path he followed to earn his livelihood. His acrimony had increased with the years
and, finally, Francis was forced to come to Hanna's defense. "I cannot allow you to insult or attack my wife," he wrote his father. "No amount of
pecuniary or other indebtedness would induce me to condone this."[55]
There is no indication that his stand changed J. B.'s opinion.

Stones and Glass

HE LAST DAY of March, 1912, was declared Home Rule Day and celebrated with a nationalist rally in Dublin for which between 100,000 and 250,000 people turned out.[1] A third Home Rule Bill was soon to be introduced but no provisions were to be made in it for enfranchising women. The members of the Irish Women's Franchise League placed the blame for this squarely upon the shoulders of the United Irish League and blamed the Young Ireland Branch for not putting pressure on the league.

The weather that day was perfect and the huge crowd orderly. The night before the rally a group of women had chalked "votes for women" on walls and fences and in the morning twenty-three women paraded quietly through the streets carrying signs calling for votes for women. The crowd's reaction to them was courteous but, when they reached Dawson Street, they were rushed by an organized group of Parliamentary Party stewards. Posters were snatched from their hands, and they were shoved about without mercy. In the scuffle, Hanna's glasses were broken: they wanted to blind her to the defects of the party, she said later.[2]

A few days after the rally, Hanna spoke at an Irish Women's Franchise League meeting. She pointed out that not a single member of the Parliamentary Party had voted for the Conciliation Bill, which if incorporated in the Home Rule Bill would have given a limited vote to women. This, added to the treatment by the stewards, convinced her that it was time to resign from the Young Ireland Branch and she called upon the other members of the I.W.F.L. to follow her lead, urging them also to resign from any league-connected organization. Her call for such action did not meet with unanimous approval but, after much discussion, they decided that a deputation should be sent to the national convention of the

United Irish League to be held in the Mansion House on 23 April, at which time the Home Rule Bill was to be considered once more.[3]

Hanna's brother-in-law, Tom Kettle, took issue with the decision in an *Evening Telegraph* item headed: "The Irish Suffragettes determined to send a deputation, notwithstanding intimation that it will not be received." He also complained that the I.W.F.L. was becoming too closely allied with the British Women's Social and Political Union. As soon as Hanna read this, she sent off a reply to the paper. "Professor Kettle is hard to satisfy," she began, but, as he very well knew, the I.W.F.L. was nonpolitical and entirely independent of any other group. As for the deputation, she could not see how the convention organizers could "face the shame" of refusing to receive as prestigious a group as theirs would be: a daughter of Sir Charles Gavan Duffy, a great-granddaughter of Daniel O'Connell, women graduates, doctors, artists, Poor Law guardians, women from all parts of Ireland.[4] However, the convention organizers, as Hanna soon found out, could.

The convention opened to an overflowing crowd of approximately five thousand delegates. Outside the Mansion House, Hanna and some thirty women were busy handing out votes-for-women leaflets to the delegates. Other groups of women who attempted to join them were stopped by the police.[5]

Hanna and Gretta Cousins, as the convention got underway, tried to gain admittance and, later, tried to speak to Redmond, leader of the Parliamentary Party, as he was leaving the Mansion House; both attempts were unsuccessful. During the day Hanna got a chair from the hall and tried to use it as a platform, but she was bodily removed by the police, and when her husband attempted to hold on to the chair it was taken from him by force. Students throwing bags of flour at the women and protesters distributing anti-suffrage leaflets added to the general confusion. One such leaflet read: "Irish women condemn the masculine conduct of Sheehy-Skeffington [presumably Hanna, not Francis] and Cousins. Beware of the English Pankhurst and their Irish Cousins."[6] The confrontation became serious indeed for, according to a letter from a friend and fellow member of the I.W.F.L., Hanna fainted but "returned again to the fray" when she recovered. Though the writer admired Hanna's courage, she nevertheless felt that the militants were injuring the women's cause in Ireland,[7] a view shared by others both in and out of the I.W.F.L., Mary Hayden, the ardent feminist, among them.

The Irish Women's Franchise League, being a nonpolitical organization, could take no official position against the Parliamentary Party, but the Sheehy-Skeffingtons could. Hanna's resignation from the Young Ireland Branch was followed by her husband's, and their action was commended by Patricia Hooey, a journalist in London who was president of the Irish Women's Suffrage League. She had resigned her secretaryship of the Irish Parliament Branch, since she could no longer in good conscience work with the current leaders. In her opinion, her action and that of people like her did not indicate that they were any less nationalistic than before.[8]

Immediate and strong support for the stand of the Irish militants came from the Women's Social and Political Union in London. In mid-April an article appeared in *Votes for Women*, its organ, accusing the Parliamentary Party of setting out to sabotage the cause of women's enfranchisement, and declaring that it was now "a fight to a finish between Suffragists and the Nationalist Party!"[9] In order to carry on that fight, the leadership of the union was beginning to feel that the time had come for the Irish Women's Franchise League to have a permanent representative in London. Annie Kenney, on behalf of the W.S.P.U., wrote Hanna: "You are so far away, and it seems a pity that there should not be someone to whom you can send letters at once to get them into the Lobby." If the I.W.F.L. could afford it, Kenney felt it should send one of its "best workers and Lobbyers" so there would always be someone "on the spot to get questions put, to Lobby Members of Parliament, and to give her whole time to watching the Irish situation."[10] It was a splendid but impractical idea. Not only was it impossible from an economic standpoint but already many Irishwomen felt that the organization was working too closely with its British counterparts. Yet Hanna agreed completely with Kenney's concluding admonition. "Do as we do in England," Kenney wrote, "simply pester the lives out of Cabinet Ministers, leaders of the Irish Party, the Labour Party." Letters should go out to all of these men, she said, indicating that the Irishwomen meant business.[11]

As the militancy of the women increased, it was met with a silent boycott of their activities by the press. Clearly the suffrage movement needed a paper of its own—one that would represent both militant and nonmilitant wings and one whose columns would be open to contributions reflecting the points of view of all suffragists. Once more, as they had in founding the Irish Women's Franchise League, the Sheehy-Skeffingtons and Gretta and James Cousins decided to meet the problem together. As a result, on 25 May 1912, the first issue of an impressive, eight-page weekly called the *Irish Citizen* appeared. It had not been easy to raise the necessary capital but help had come from the Pethick-Lawrences, a husband and wife team prominent in the British suffrage movement, as well as from many others. The result was a publication that would prove to be a bible for the Irish suffrage movement.

One of the paper's first major stories, written by Hanna, covered a mass meeting sponsored by the Irish Women's Franchise League and held the first day of June in the Antient Concert Rooms in Dublin. The purpose of the meeting was to demand that the Home Rule Bill in committee at this time be amended to include votes for women. All of the suffrage societies were represented and, in addition, such organizations as the Women Workers' Trade Union, the Ladies' Committee of the Irish Drapers' Assistants' Association, and the Daughters of Erin. Hanna was on the platform with other luminaries of the women's rights movement and was much impressed to find that "for the day at least" there was such unanimity among the various women's groups. Showing strong signs of female chauvinism, Hanna wrote that "women possess the genius for organization, for skilled manipulation of effect" which, combined with their "unfailing attention to details," produced meetings much more picturesque than those organized by men. For her the decorations—vividly colored banners and pennants which emphasized the "exclusively feminine platform"—proved her point.[12]

The conclusion of Hanna's article reflected the confidence that the meeting inspired:

> Home Rule or no Home Rule, Westminster or College Green, there is a new spirit abroad among women: whether the vote is reluctantly granted by a Liberal Government or wrested from an Irish Parliament, to women in the end it matters but little. Politicians and parties (Irish and English alike) if they do push on their Home Rule ship, regardless of warnings, 'full steam ahead,' will be iceberged and their male monster will founder—that is all. But the women who are behind this world-movement will most surely achieve their purpose. I am almost sorry for the politicians at their party play, those little legislators blindly making little laws for those who make the legislators.[13]

With great enthusiasm, a resolution was passed calling upon the government to amend the Home Rule Bill by adopting the local government register, which included women, as the basis for the election of the new parliament. Copies of the resolution were circulated to the cabinet and to all the Irish M.P.'s, with a request that they insist this amendment be added to the bill. When no replies were received, the Irish Women's Franchise League members took action. On 13 June 1912, windows were broken in the General Post Office, the Customs House, the Land Commission Office, and the Ship Street Barracks by Kathleen Houston, Marjorie Hasler, Maud Lloyd, Jane Murphy, Margaret Murphy, Marguerite Palmer, Hilda Webb, and Hanna. All were arrested. Hanna and Margaret Murphy were charged with breaking nineteen windows and remanded for a week on five pounds bail, which Francis Sheehy-Skeffington paid for both of them.

An *Irish Times* editorial expressed horror, deploring "this childish campaign of window smashing" and hoping that it had been done without the knowledge of the "responsible leaders of the Irish Suffrage Movement."[14] It was answered within a week in the pages of the *Irish Citizen* with a full page headed, "Why We Throw Stones at Government Glass-Houses," giving statements by the eight women involved; Hanna's remarks cited the lack of success achieved by peaceful means. "Constitutionalism has failed to evoke response," she wrote. The Conciliation Bill was dead and the Parliamentary Party was responsible. "If reason does not penetrate Government departments, flints will. I have always realized the potency of the dock. Thoreau says somewhere that the time may arise when the prison may be the only place of honour left to an honest man. Many a brave Irishman has proved the truth of that axiom in the past; it is now for Irishwomen to realise citizenship by becoming 'criminals.'"[15]

If the editors of the *Irish Times* needed proof of the effectiveness of militancy, they had only to note an Irish Women's Franchise League meeting held in Phoenix Park the day after their editorial appeared. More than a thousand attended. During the question period, Mrs. Palmer took one side of the platform, Hanna the other, and both explained very effectively why they were willing to go to jail. According to the *Irish Citizen*, the meeting was "the best propagandist gathering that has been held in Dublin since the first meeting addressed by Christabel Pankhurst in 1910."[16]

The remand week having ended, Hanna and her co-conspirators appeared in court. The scene was impressive, with over two hundred women present and with the prisoners being handed bouquets of flowers as they were brought into the courtroom. Hanna conducted her own defense, by all accounts ably. She and Marguerite Palmer saw this as an excellent opportunity to make political speeches. Disregarding constant interruptions from the police counsel and the magistrate, Hanna listed the constitutional methods that had been used unsuccessfully in Ireland from 1876 to the very last mass meeting which had just been held. Her remarks were greeted with such applause and cheers that, finally, the courtroom had to be cleared. As the women were ushered out, they could hear Mrs. Palmer shouting, "Keep the flag flying" and Hanna urging them to "remember Mr. Asquith is coming in July."[17] He would be the first prime minister to visit Ireland in an official capacity.

In his closing remarks, the counsel for the prosecution, Gerald Moran, stressed the defiance of the prisoners and pressed for the full penalty—sentencing as "ordinary" criminals, payment of costs of the prosecution and of the damage done. This was greeted with hisses and with a statement by the presiding magistrate that he would not even consider such a judgment. Jane and Margaret Murphy were tried and sentenced the same day and the sentence for all four was the same: "a penalty of 40s[shillings], with the alternative of a month's imprisonment, and a further month in default of bail."[18] All but Hanna had been jailed previously for suffragist activities.

Before sentence was passed, Hanna had declared that she was ready to go to jail but insisted, like her father before her, that she must be treated as a political prisoner, a "First Class Misdemeanant." She and the other women sent "memorials" to the lord lieutenant requesting this status immediately upon incarceration. Pressure was also put upon the governor of Mountjoy Prison by Francis Sheehy-Skeffington and others. Before the sixth day of their imprisonment, Francis received a letter informing him that all the women would receive the full privileges requested.[19]

Prison life was not particularly oppressive. The atmosphere may have resembled that of a military camp, as Hanna said, but this was merely because wardresses, keys dangling at their sides, marched about, saluted one another, and dressed in a half-military garb. Actually these women with their hideous Victorian hats were in most cases very sympathetic to the political prisoners and, from time to time, would bring Hanna a mug of coffee or soup between meals, cautioning her to hide the cup if another wardress entered.[20]

Hanna rose at 6:30 A.M. and bathed, had breakfast at 8:00, and exercised from 10:00 to 12:00; lunch was at 1:00 P.M., followed by another exercise period, after which there was an hour of work from 3:30 to 4:30 before tea. Once a day meals were sent from Mrs. Wyse-Powers' restaurant in Henry Street and these were supplemented with prison fare as well as by those steaming mugs of coffee supplied by friendly wardresses.[21] At the time Hanna was released she was planning to have Francis send her a pocketbook, newspapers, a wicker chair, and writing paper. Apparently she was planning to make Mountjoy, as she would say, "a home from home."[22]

Visitors were frequent. Her first one, the prison chaplain, informed her that he remembered her father. "A stubborn man," he said. Not long after, one of her suffragist friends, Mrs. Haslam, came. "Don't think I approve," she cautioned, "but here's a pot of verbena I brought you. I am not here in my official capacity, of course." The Irish Women's Suffrage and Local Government Association felt these violent tactics were "pulling back the cause," she said. "But here's some loganberry jam — I made it myself." Haslam's attitude was like that of many of her visitors and Hanna understood. Her uncle, Father Eugene Sheehy, came — "one of those dear comfortable relations who condone anything in a favourite." Her father visited as well, although as a loyal party member he was disapproving. "He was a stoic father and I responded and respected, though I officially disapproved of his attitude as much as he of mine," Hanna remarked. Her mother, also disapproving, came on occasion.[23]

The most regular visitor was Francis, who was there almost every day and who seemed, Hanna thought, to be enjoying her experience vicariously. Never, she said, was he "amenable to the governor's suggestion to advise his wife to be 'sensible.'" Her son, Owen, only three years old, sometimes came along with his father. On one occasion, he was allowed to go to her cell "to sample chocolates, an unheard-of-concession, because he had managed to fall on the stone floor of the reception room and raised such a howl that the Superintendent said it would never do for him to go out roaring, as it might get into the Press!"[24]

Just before Hanna was sentenced, she had submitted an article called "The Women's Movement — Ireland" to the *Irish Review*, a monthly magazine devoted to Irish literature, art, and science. It appeared in the July issue and was a strong denunciation of the Parliamentary Party and of what she considered the average Irishman. "Now that the first stone has been thrown by suffragists in Ireland," she wrote, "light is being admitted into more than mere Government quarters, and the cobwebs are being cleared away from more than one male intellect." It was right that women, who had always been ready to fight "in the cause of male liberties," should now fight against the problems facing women in Ireland such as "sweating," prostitution, and the "bargain marriage," described by Hanna as "a sordid institution which banishes love from our Irish countryside." Reform could wait no longer; previous methods had failed. With the advent of the militants' so-called "disgraceful tactics," a chapter had ended. "It will be interesting material for the psychologist working out a research-thesis on Female Patience in the 19th century," she concluded.[25]

As Hanna had reminded her colleagues in the courtroom, Prime Minister Asquith was to visit Dublin in July 1912 to publicize the Home Rule Bill that he had introduced in April. By mid-month letters began to appear in the *Evening Telegraph*, signed with pen names like "Home Ruler," warning suffragettes not to demonstrate during the visit. One, signed "A Home Ruler Woman," threatened that if Francis Sheehy-Skeffington "and his suffragist friends begin their dirty tricks and surprises, they may expect to receive at the hands of Nationalists more than what they bargained for." Another, signed "Milesius," urged the police to "use whips on the shoulders of those unsexed viragoes." An *Evening Telegraph* editorial stated that any attempt to disturb the prime minister's visit would be considered a declaration of war on the Home Rule movement and warned "Mr. Sheehy-Skeffington and the little band who share his views" to keep their hands off Mr. Asquith.[26]

Undeterred by the threats, the Irish Women's Franchise League proceeded with plans to give Mr. Asquith a suffragists' welcome. Early in the day, some fifteen women paraded the streets of Dublin bearing placards with such messages as "Home Rule for Irish Women as Well as Men" and "Who is Mr. Asquith?" Later, as Asquith's steamer approached Kingstown, it was met by a small yacht manned by women shouting, "Votes for Women." The demonstrations were peaceful and, actually, the spectators seemed to find the whole affair rather amusing. The situation, however, was soon to change.[27]

Three British women—Lizzie Baker, Gladys Evans, and Mary Leigh—had come to Dublin to demonstrate, much to Hanna's chagrin, as she looked back on the matter. She deplored the fact that they had not left the "heckling" to the Irishwomen, for even the best-intentioned English, she felt, had "blind spots" where Ireland was concerned. Later, there were various interpretations of what took place but Mary Leigh, in a 1965 interview, said that as Mr. Asquith's carriage reached Nassau Street she ran up to it and dropped a small hatchet at his feet. A message attached to it read: "This is a symbol of the extinction of the Liberal Party for evermore."[28] According to Hanna's version, however, the hatchet was thrown and "it skimmed between Asquith and Redmond and grazed the latter's ear."[29] Another version came from Marie Johnson, a member of the Irish Women's Suffrage Society in Belfast at that time, who wrote Andrée Sheehy-Skeffington many years later: "A small axe" missed Asquith but "struck John Redmond . . . on the head. The cry was all over the place that it was one of the militant leaders from England, but it was not so, it was thrown by Helena Moloney [sic], a very extreme Republican, simply anti-British."[30]

That same evening, Gladys Evans and Mary Leigh attempted to burn down the Theatre Royal where Asquith was to speak the following day. They set fire to the curtains in one of the boxes, but this was quickly noticed and extinguished with a minimum amount of damage resulting. A few minutes later, however, there was an explosion in the theater. This, too, resulted in very little damage. The rooms of the two women were searched and, according to police reports, explosives were found. Both were arrested and later sentenced to five years' penal servitude. T. M. Healy, in his *Letters and Leaders of My Day*, wrote admiringly: "I was offered a hundred guineas to defend the Suffragettes in Dublin about 2nd August. Their solicitor tells me the women don't care what sentence they get, or what becomes of them! A fine spirit!"[31]

At this point the public became hysterical and the press carried banner headlines such as "The Virago and the Hatchet" and "Hatchet Outrage." Hanna reported that Mrs. Emerson, secretary of the Irish Women's Franchise League, was seized and almost thrown into the Liffey from O'Connell Bridge. Women attempting to hold a meeting at Beresford Place were mobbed and when they sought refuge in Liberty Hall were turned away. Hanna's mother thanked Providence that her daughter was in jail where she was safe.[32]

The vigilance of the police, though it seemed excessive, did have a certain justification. Confidential information had been received by the Commission of the Dublin Metropolitan Police, the inspector general of the Royal Irish Constabulary, and the chief secretary, that an attempt was to be made to assassinate the prime minister during his Dublin visit. According to the informants, "The instigators of the plot are the advanced section of the militant Suffragists." The attack, it was said, was to be made while the prime minister was being driven through the city from the railway station. The horses would be shot first "to guard against failure"; with the carriage at a standstill, Asquith was to be fired upon.[33]

The Irish Women's Franchise League, at least publicly, washed its hands of the whole affair. Gretta Cousins, in her capacity as honorary secretary, immediately issued a statement to the papers denying that the organization had any connection with the incidents or any knowledge of the presence of the English women in Dublin. "Beyond unity of demand," she added, the league had no association with its English counterparts.[34]

Meanwhile, for the women members of the league confined in Mountjoy, it was punishment not to be able to participate in the Asquith demonstrations. They did, however, wear handmade black mourning rosettes all during the period of his visit. There was great rejoicing when the story reached them of Francis Sheehy-Skeffington's success in getting into the Asquith meeting. With the help of Dudley Digges, a Dublin-born actor who was staying with Constance Markievicz at Surrey House, Francis, with judiciously applied grease paint and powder, became a rather meek-looking little cleric. In the middle of Asquith's speech, the bearded clergyman rose and the well-known voice of Sheehy-Skeffington could be heard shouting: "What about the women of Ireland? What are you going to do for them?" Within minutes the stewards had hustled him out into Poolbeg Street.[35]

When news of the harsh sentence meted out to Evans and Leigh reached the women in prison, four of them went on hunger strike—one was Hanna. Relatives and friends pleaded with her not to take this step but, once again like her father, she was adamant. This was, according to her, "a new weapon—we were the first to try it out in Ireland—had we but known, we were the pioneers in a long line." The thought of going even a week without food was frightening but they did it and found that it was not as bad as they had anticipated. "Eating is a habit the body learns to do without, getting weaker in the process until the desire itself passes," she wrote. The pounding of her heart woke her up in the night and her forehead was so hot that water applied to it evaporated immediately. She soon began to feel lightheaded and her sense of smell became so acute that she could even smell the tea. "One instinctively skips in books the descriptions of food; I never realized before how much both Scott and Dickens *gloat*, and how abstemious are the Brontës and Jane Austen." She slept a great deal and the days passed.[36]

After thirty days, a week of it spent on hunger strike, Hanna was released from Mountjoy. She was, of course, weak as a result of the strike, and being confined to her cell for twenty out of the twenty-four hours each day had not helped either. She was, nevertheless, in good spirits.

Home at last, she was greeted with a notice of dismissal from her post as a teacher of German in the Rathmines School of Commerce. The enrollment for her class the preceding term had been insufficient to warrant the renewal of her contract, she was informed. Since there had been no hint of this prior to her incarceration for political activities, the true reason seemed obvious. But obvious or not, the pages of the *Irish Citizen* hastened to underline it, and soon letters protesting her dismissal began to come in to the paper from people of importance in educational circles. By November a committee had been formed and a petition circulated that stated: "in the interests of education, and to protect the security of tenure of teachers and their rights as citizens," the signatories protest Hanna's "summary dismissal, without sufficient reason."[37] Before the year ended more than 160 people had signed, including the president of the Irish National Teachers' Organisation, the lord mayor of Dublin, the poet George Russell (AE), the political activist Maud Gonne, four members of Parliament, and Alice Stopford Green, the historian.

With Hanna's papers is a rough draft of a statement to the Rathmines School of Commerce Technical Committee, indicating that, because the issue "intimately concerns the general body of teachers under technical committees & the students & patrons of your schools," she was forwarding copies of her letter to the press. In it she stated her case fully. Notification of dismissal had reached her only one week before the beginning of the term when it was extremely difficult, if not impossible, to obtain another position; the drop in attendance toward the end of the previous session had taken place in all classes and in other technical institutions as well where there were night classes at which attendance was purely voluntary; the number of her students obtaining certificates of merit was greater than it had been the previous year; and the inspectors' report had indicated increased efficiency since she had been teaching. A requested interview with the committee had been denied, though for three years she had made every effort to maintain a high teaching standard and to devote herself to the school and to her pupils, as well as to keep herself abreast of the latest teaching methods by taking special courses abroad at her own expense.[38]

There may have been a reason other than her jail sentence for Hanna's dismissal. She was a formidable and open critic of the convent schools' attitude toward the lay teacher. Chief Secretary Augustine Birrell had put forth a plan to improve the position of secondary teachers which advocated a minimum wage for both men and women, a half-year's notice of dismissal, and, possibly, a register for teachers. Hanna considered it fine, as far as it went, and she called upon "sound public opinion" to back the proposal. Under the existing system, the female lay teacher was paid less than half the wage of her male colleague. She was also required to take tests which the religious teacher was not. Only in Ireland, Hanna claimed, was a religious vocation considered all that was needed to qualify for a teaching position. No other "training, mental equipment, or experience" was required.[39]

Hanna knew that the Birrell recommendation was being harshly opposed by Catholic headmasters and others in clerical positions who spoke for the convent schools. Their claim was that the plan would be harder on Catholic schools than on Protestant. Indeed it would, Hanna said, and it should be. In the Catholic schools, the lay teacher followed the convent regime as though she were a nun. She was usually hired on a yearly basis and her employment could be terminated without notice. There was no increase in her salary with added experience. A Protestant teacher, not faced with so much clerical competition, had a better chance of promotion and better pay. Under the Birrell plan, this would be equalized to a certain extent.[40]

Even with all the benefits in the Birrell plan, however, the female secondary teacher would still face the same basic inequalities as before. Though her pay would be increased considerably and her prospects also, she would continue to receive approximately half of what men earned. That none of the male secondary teachers who approved of the plan had "lifted a voice in protest" about this inequity did not escape Hanna's notice. She had heard the excuse given that men had to think about their dependents. Had they never noticed that many women teachers had aged parents or younger siblings dependent upon them?[41]

Hanna could see three ways in which the proposal could be improved. Secondary teachers should receive a pension; there should be some way of limiting the use of unpaid and unskilled teachers; and the principle of equal pay for equal work should be firmly established. She called the plan "the first brave attempt to ameliorate the condition of the most harassed and exploited class in the country—the secondary teacher," but she was careful to note that, when women got the vote, they would see to it that at least the last of the three ways to improve the scheme would be carried out. Even unamended, however, any plan that called for upgrading the present status of both male and female teachers and for establishing a national register should be supported by every educator.[42]

The action of the Rathmines School of Commerce, unjust though it was, had its compensations. Free of the classroom and of the preparations for her evening classes, Hanna was able to devote more of her energies to the Irish Women's Franchise League and to lend a hand with the *Irish Citizen*. She also had more time for writing and for the theater, both of which she enjoyed tremendously. The results of combining both pleasures were apparent almost immediately. In September the *Irish Review* carried Hanna's reviews of three new Abbey Theatre plays—*Patriots* by Lennox Robinson, *Maurice Harte* by T. C. Murray, and *Judgment* by Joseph Campbell. She called Robinson the best of the Abbey dramatists and went on to heap praise on his play, calling particular attention to the irony and "tragedy of the enthusiast who, to his implacable devotion to a cause, sacrifices with the egoism of the zealot fortune, love, reputation, and finally the life of his child, and beholds at last the futility of his life's endeavour."[43] Joseph Holloway, Dublin's compulsive theatergoer, was closer to the truth when he said *Patriots* was "nothing to boast of as a play."[44] This was by no means the only time that her critical judgment proved unreliable. Actually neither Hanna nor her husband was able to keep the necessary distance between political and aesthetic concerns, and as a result, each was given to sometimes embarrassing lapses of artistic taste.

In October, Hanna wrote a piece for the *Irish Citizen*, "The Women's Vote in Western America—A Factor in the Presidential Election," that showed wide knowledge and keen interest in the American suffrage scene. As she saw it, the suffrage movement was becoming global in its influence but it was the American far west that had been "the first part of the world to concede this human right." Women, banding together, were becoming a force to be reckoned with in politics and in elections.[45]

To Hanna's mind, however, the women's movement would not become an important force without militancy being added to solidarity. Before the end of the year, she came out strongly in defense of the militants for what were termed "pillar box" attacks. The inspiration for this method of protest, according to George Dangerfield in *The Strange Death of Liberal England*, originated with Christabel Pankhurst from her hideout in Paris.[46] Small open bottles containing a black fluid that resembled treacle were placed in post boxes, thus damaging the letters. So that there would be no doubt as to why this was being done, the bottles would sometimes be labeled "votes for women" or placed in envelopes addressed to various members of Parliament known to oppose women's suffrage. On occasion, the liquid was simply poured into the boxes. One critic of the "pillar box"

attacks said they savored of "anarchy and the final dissolution of all society." Hanna agreed: "It matters little what name it be called—anarchy,
revolt, upheaval. It is for the public and the Government to recognise that
this is not a riot, but a revolution, and that if society attempts to stand
much longer in the way, society as at present constituted must go."
Thanks to the attacks leveled against the militants, she argued, the women
had taken the only logical step, from breaking government windows to in-
terfering with services such as the post office and the telephone. "Desperate diseases need desperate remedies," she said, "and if the vote is wrested
from Government by methods of terrorism when five and forty years of
sweet and quiet reason produced only seven talked-out or tricked-out suffrage bills, why, who can say it wasn't worth a mutilated letter, a cut wire,
a Premier's racked nerves?"[47]

Her personal protest—on a comparatively minor issue—involved
the university. The *Freeman's Journal* had published a list of graduates of
University College, Dublin, who had been nominated for election to the
governing body and had felt it necessary to add a footnote explaining that
one name on the register—"Johanna M. Sheehy"—was the maiden name
of Mrs. Sheehy-Skeffington. In order to have her name changed on the
register, Hanna would have had to produce a marriage certificate, which
she stubbornly refused to do. After all, male graduates who wished to
have their names changed for any reason whatever had only to make application and the change would be recorded.[48]

This was 1913 and, relieved of teaching chores, Hanna seemed to
have hit her stride. She was writing, speaking, chairing meetings, and, in
addition, bringing up a son and managing a household. She was doing
much more *Irish Citizen* work as well, for, in March, James Cousins resigned as editor of the paper and Francis took it over completely. Comments in Sheehy-Skeffington's correspondence during 1914 show how
prominent Hanna's part became. A letter to Mrs. George Bernard Shaw
says in part: "Let us clear up one misunderstanding. I, who 'run' the *Irish
Citizen* on the technical and business side, am the male member of our
household. My wife (*H.* Sheehy-Skeffington) writes a good deal for the
paper, but her organising activities are devoted to the Irish Women's Franchise League, of which she is Chairman of Committee."[49] To his friend
Maurice Wilkins, he wrote: "I have to go away for a few days this week,
and am leaving the *Irish Citizen* in my wife's charge. As she has no experience of the technical part, could you possibly assist her by going to the
printing works for a couple of hours on Wednesday? Of course you will

not have to do any writing, or to undertake any worrying responsibility; just to help her in putting the pieces of the puzzle together."[50]

Hanna's friends, in and out of the Irish Women's Franchise League, were not unaware of her contribution to the feminist cause. To her great surprise and delight, that spring a group of them presented her with a silver tea service, not only as a tribute to her work in the suffrage movement but also "as a mark of the indignation felt at her dismissal from the Rathmines School of Commerce in consequence of her political activities."[51]

A Harrowing Game

T HE SUFFRAGE MOVEMENT had never enjoyed a good press, but in the spring of 1913 the papers seemed to be waxing increasingly hysterical on the subject. The *Dublin Evening Mail*, early in April, carried a banner heading of "Outrages" over a story about the activities of British suffragists, and the *Irish Independent*, shortly afterward, had a lengthy story headed "The Suffragette Terror," which concentrated on Irish suffrage offenses. A bomb made of loaded bullet cartridges, fuse lit, was discovered in the ladies' lavatory of the Empire Theatre during a matinee performance. In an adjoining room a note was found that read: "Votes for women; life and property not safe till we get it."[1] At once, and understandably, the newspapers attributed the attempt to the Irish suffragettes; Hanna just as rapidly answered the charge in open letters to both the *Evening Herald* and the *Evening Telegraph*. Since the word "life" had been used in the message, she maintained, no suffragist, Irish or English, could have been responsible for the deed. The militant suffragists had repeatedly tried to make clear they were making war upon property and the government but that they respected life. She urged the police to try to trace the bomb to its source. They might then find "the offender in the ranks of those notorious for disturbing Suffragist meetings, and those whose object is to inflame the mob by bogus outrages and engineered explosions." It should have occurred to Hanna that one of the suffragists, "inflamed" by her own propaganda, might have gone a bit too far, but she was uncompromising when making a point. "We protest most emphatically against any attempt to identify our movement with these silly scares, set on foot by the enemies of our cause," she concluded.[2]

The government, like the press, seemed to feel that the activities and statements of those connected with the suffrage movement were becoming intolerable. Current coercive measures having proved ineffective, it took the next step: the introduction of the Prisoners (Temporary Discharge for Ill-Health) Act, immediately labeled the Cat and Mouse Act. Under its provisions, a prisoner could be released temporarily and conditionally by order of the secretary of state, if health, due in whole or in part to conduct while in prison, was such that further detention was undesirable. The prisoner, however, would be instructed to report on a designated date and, failing to comply, could be rearrested without warrant. The sentence remained suspended from the time of release and was resumed upon the prisoner's return.

Beyond question, the legislation was a retaliatory measure to counteract the hunger-strike tactics of the suffragists. Its first test in England came in April 1913. Mrs. Pankhurst was sentenced to three years' penal servitude under the Malicious Damages to Property Act and was released after nine days, so ill as the result of a hunger strike that she was taken to a nursing home. Under the terms of the new legislation, she was to return to jail before the end of April, even though the act had not yet become law. When she refused to do so at the designated time, she was rearrested. Again she refused food and had to be released after a short time so ill that, on doctor's orders, she left the country for a rest cure. Upon her return, no attempt was made to rearrest her.[3]

The first test in Ireland came a month after Mrs. Pankhurst's original arrest. The Parliamentary Party had voted for the measure overwhelmingly and had followed that action by a vote, under orders of the party leadership, against the women's suffrage amendment to the Home Rule Bill. The militants moved quickly. On the eve of a United Irish League meeting at which he was to speak, they painted broad arrows on a bust of Redmond, leader of the Parliamentary Party, and smashed the fanlight in the U.I.L. offices. A fair-sized crowd gathered after the window was broken, but not one person moved to turn the women over to the police. Finally Marguerite Palmer, wanting to make it clear that their action was deliberate and politically motivated, approached a constable with the request that they be arrested. "We're after breaking glass," she said.[4] She got her wish and, along with two other women, was "sentenced to six weeks' imprisonment, in default of paying fines and compensation." After three weeks in Tullamore jail and a five-day hunger strike following denial of political prisoner status, they were released under the Cat and Mouse Act and ordered to return to prison on 2 July to complete their sentences.[5]

The indignation generated by the law's inauguration in Ireland served as a kind of cement for the ranks of the suffrage movement. When, late in June, a protest meeting was held in the Dublin Mansion House with Hanna presiding, it drew an overflowing audience representing all shades of suffrage opinion. Hanna's brother-in-law, Tom Kettle, moved repeal of the act, which he called "a dangerous weapon of political oppression," and remission of the remainder of the sentences of the three women against whom it had been employed. Louie Bennett, a leader in the fight for the rights of the working woman, seconded his motion on behalf of the Irishwomen's Reform League, the Munster Women's Franchise League, the Northern Committee of the Irishwomen's Suffrage Federation, and the Sligo and Armagh Suffrage Societies—all affiliated with the Irishwomen's Suffrage Federation, which she had helped to form in 1911. She made it clear that she was, personally, an antimilitant, though some of the members of the federation were not, but she felt there were times "when non-militants must join their sisters in protest against some cruelty and injustice," and the Cat and Mouse Act was both cruel and unjust.[6]

Countess Markievicz, calling herself a "Separatist and a Republican," said that she belonged to no suffrage society since she was not interested in obtaining a vote for the British Parliament. She was, however, happy to have an "opportunity to express her sympathy with those women who were suffering martyrdom for their cause" and she was, she said, "proud to be a woman: how many men would face the Hunger Strike for any cause on God's earth?"[7] Like Hanna and others in the women's movement, the countess was given to making sweeping statements as to what men would or would not do—generally the latter.

As might be expected, Hanna was among the most vocal leaders of the opposition to the law. Its application to Ireland was, she said at the Mansion House meeting, "an incitement to militancy." Extending the women's sentences over a long period would simply make them "feel that they might as well earn their sentence." She outlined steps to be taken: first, fight for remission of the remainder of the sentences of the three women; after that, take action to have the measure repealed. To the vigorous applause of her audience, she said that the women would not go back to jail. She was right. As a result of widespread resentment about the law, no attempt was made to enforce it in Ireland. At year's end, the three "mice" were still free.[8]

Some months after this protest meeting, in November 1913, James Connolly, a labor leader and friend of all the women's movements, addressed the Irish Women's Franchise League. The women, he said, had taken a surprisingly short time to learn that they could trust no party, and that "if freedom were attained it must be by their own efforts." Little girls were working in factories in Belfast and in Dublin under "revolting and inhuman" conditions. For some forty thousand women workers in Ireland, there were only two factory inspectors and this condition would not change while the women had no voice—that is, no vote. Men, Connolly pointed out, had managed to better their condition at least somewhat through the ballot, while the voteless women continued to work for slave wages under brutal conditions. He left no doubt that he considered militancy a necessity if the franchise were to be obtained.[9] Listening, Hanna agreed completely and, within a month, demonstrated once again that she had the courage of her convictions.

The occasion was a unionist meeting in Dublin at which Andrew Bonar Law, M.P., leader of the Conservative Party, and Sir Edward Carson, the Dublin-born unionist whom Kettle labeled the lawyer with the Dublin accent, were to speak. Early that afternoon, as they were leaving Lord Iveagh's house in St. Stephen's Green, they were met by Hanna and Meg Connery, both armed with leaflets, who approached them from opposite sides. Mrs. Connery was ordered aside by a policeman but was not hurt or arrested. Hanna, however, was grabbed by a Sergeant Thomas and her arm twisted. She said later that "the Sergeant's autograph, one purple thumb-mark and four red angry finger-nails, did not fade from that arm till Christmas."[10] Charged with assault, she was then taken to the nearest police station.

At her trial, Chief Divisional Magistrate E. G. Swifte presided, as he had during her earlier court appearance. First, Hanna showed that she was still visibly bruised and attempted to enter a countercharge against the arresting sergeant but without success. There was general laughter in the courtroom when the sergeant testified that Hanna, whose forehead barely reached his belt, had bitten him and tried to "throw" him. Given the choice of paying bail or going to prison, Hanna chose the latter. She began to serve her sentence of seven days' imprisonment in Mountjoy, but was released after five days, since she had once more gone on hunger strike.[11]

Hanna seemed to be disturbed more by the unfairness of being imprisoned unjustly than by any physical discomfort that she had to endure in prison. To be sentenced on a charge trumped up by a police officer to save himself indicated just how helpless "victims of the law" were.[12] She termed such sentences outrageous and vowed to herself that she would never again go to jail without committing some act that warranted detention, even if it were to "throw a stone at the judge's head."[13] As always, the hunger strike took its toll, however, and Hanna was released from prison in an extremely weakened condition.

Aside from winning her early release, her strike had, of course, given valuable publicity to the suffrage cause, which seemed particularly healthy just then. Societies were growing, new centers were opening, old ones were increasing in strength, and the Irish people generally seemed to be becoming more sympathetic to the women's movement in spite of the politicians.

Gratifying also was what seemed to be a better understanding and increased cooperation between the militant and nonmilitant wings of the movement as well as between labor and the suffragists. Toward the end of the year, a joint meeting of the Labour Party and the Irish Women's Franchise League had taken place which, it was felt, would not have been held even a year earlier.[14] Such cooperation was not new to the Sheehy-Skeffingtons for they had always believed that the labor movement and the suffrage movement were, inevitably, intertwined. They had supported their belief with action as had other leaders of the suffragist movement. When James Larkin, assisted by his sister Delia, Helena Molony and the Irish Trade Union Congress, formed the Irish Women Workers Union in 1911, Hanna, as well as Constance Markievicz, addressed its recruiting meetings without a moment's hesitation. When the labor disputes of 1913 resulted in a brutal lockout, both women plunged into the difficult task of assisting the hungry workers, men and women, by setting up a soup kitchen in Liberty Hall. Other I.W.F.L. members collected and distributed food, and raised funds for clothing and other essentials.[15]

All was not harmonious on the suffrage scene, however. A note of discord was struck when the Women's Social and Political Union in England, headed by the Pankhursts, attempted to make inroads into the suffrage movement in Ireland. There had, earlier, been a serious split in the ranks of the W.S.P.U., caused by militancy of a type that many of its members and members of the Irish Women's Franchise League as well could not condone. Particularly distressing was a policy of arson that had been put into effect in Ulster. The split even disrupted the Pankhurst family, with Sylvia breaking with her mother and Christabel.

The Pethick-Lawrences were among those who left the organization. Though they retained sole editorship and control of *Votes for Women*, it was no longer considered the organ of the W.S.P.U. George Dangerfield, in *The Strange Death of Liberal England*, states that neither Mrs. Pankhurst nor Christabel was particularly distressed by their defection, since each had always disapproved of a male playing a leading part in the organization. Along the same lines, he hints that Mrs. Pankhurst, who did not have much use for men, had also considered it ridiculous for Francis Sheehy-Skeffington, in the guise of a priest, to heckle Mr. Asquith at a nationalist meeting. If men wanted to assist the movement, their involvement should be, she thought, of a more dignified kind.[16]

Christabel Pankhurst was now in Paris planning grand strategy while her mother continued to conduct operations in England. From Paris, Christabel wrote Hanna, in September 1913, that the Women's Social and Political Union was going to make an attempt to gain a foothold in Ireland. Already one of its organizers was established in Ulster; another, Margaret Edwards, would be in Dublin within days and would proceed, Christabel informed Hanna, to set up a W.S.P.U. branch there. She was sure that this "additional Suffrage stir" would be profitable in many ways, hastening to emphasize that the move was made in a spirit of friendship toward the Irish Women's Franchise League and was calculated to further the interests of the entire women's movement.[17]

The results were easily predictable. Not many months later, in 1914, the *Irish Citizen* pointed out in an editorial that the establishment of W.S.P.U. branches in Ireland had been "a regrettable feature of the past year." What few members the British organization had been able to attract would have served the Irish women's movement far more effectively had they joined Irish societies. It was hoped the W.S.P.U. would see that establishing a foothold in Ireland was an impossibility and would withdraw gracefully.[18]

In the end, fate intervened. Before the year was out, war had erupted and the Women's Social and Political Union not only withdrew its forces from Ireland but suspended its activities completely. Mrs. Pankhurst issued a letter calling the suspension temporary. She was sure every patriotic woman desired the country to be victorious and pledged herself to fight toward that goal. As she saw it, the very existence of all small nations was at stake and the status of France and Great Britain in jeopardy. The W.S.P.U. paper, the *Suffragette*, was soon renamed *Britannia* and carried a new banner head: "For King, for Country, for Freedom." Though Christabel and her mother were in complete agreement, Sylvia vowed to continue to fight against the government and against "the war of iniquity, falsely extolled as 'the war to end war.'"[19] This was also the position of the Pethick-Lawrences and the *Irish Citizen*. "War in itself is Hell," an editorial in the *Citizen* stated, and women were urged not to yield to false arguments for its necessity.[20]

Carefully preserved among Hanna's papers is a communication from the Women's War Service over the signature of Emmeline Pankhurst, entitled "A Procession and Deputation to Mr. Lloyd George." Mrs. Pankhurst had not lost her touch: it was a powerful appeal. The nation was in danger of losing its freedom, she wrote. The service that women could render might make the difference between victory and defeat, and she hoped they would be "allowed" to help. A deputation, to be proceeded by "a Great Procession of Women," was being formed to wait upon Lloyd George, as minister of munitions, so that he might hear their "demand for the right to make munitions and render other War Service."[21]

The *Irish Citizen*, expressing dismay at the stand of Emmeline Pankhurst and her followers, denounced as sheer nonsense the women's eagerness to serve the war effort. Apparently these "ex-militants," as the *Manchester Guardian* had termed them, could not see the irony of a deputation being received by Lloyd George and cheering when they saw him standing on the platform beside Mrs. Pankhurst, when just a short time earlier she had taken full responsibility for blowing up his house and had drawn three years' penal servitude for the deed. The humor of a situation in which Mrs. Pankhurst was "demanding" that she and her followers be given instruction in the manufacture of high explosives seemed to escape them.[22]

The Women's Social and Political Union was not alone in being swept up in the war fervor and hysteria, however. The Irish Suffrage Federation, for instance, formed a Suffragists' Emergency Corps, and its members plunged into relief work. The Irishwomen's Reform League formally disassociated itself from the *Irish Citizen* because of the paper's antiwar stand. Clearly one effect of the war was to shatter the always fragile unity of the suffrage movement and the significance of this should not be minimized.

Insofar as the Irish Women's Franchise League was concerned, though, the outbreak of war did nothing to limit its activities. If anything, the leadership's determination to give the winning of votes for women first priority increased. Recruiting for the British Army had begun in earnest in Ireland and, in order to whip up enthusiasm, Prime Minister Asquith was scheduled to speak at the Mansion House on 25 September. Another attempt was made by the Irish Women's Franchise League to bring votes for women to his attention but once again a deputation was refused an audience. Plans were made to station women all along the route to the Mansion House to distribute leaflets and Hanna and Meg Connery took up their posts at the head of Dawson Street. The leaflets having been disposed of, they climbed up on a nearby fountain and began to address the crowd.[23]

It seemed to Hanna that the attitude of the people toward suffragists was undergoing a definite change, for the crowd was not at all antagonistic. "Only one hero attacked us," she said, going on to tell of the uniformed postman who struck Meg Connery on the shoulders and face while she was being held by the police. When Hanna had tried to draw the attention of a constable to the assault, she was ignored. Another constable seized Hanna, and shortly afterward both women were arrested, taken to College Street Police Station, and held until midnight, spending the time wondering what they would be charged with and weighing the possibilities of bail and a hunger strike. Though the women had been told that they could bring charges against the police for "assault and unlawful arrest," they knew it would be useless. "After all," Hanna said, "what can we expect? We are not voters, nor recruits, nor even Belgian women."[24]

Shortly before Prime Minister Asquith's visit to Dublin, Home Rule finally received Royal Assent and, at last, the statute book carried a Government of Ireland Act, though it contained a proviso that excluded the Province of Ulster. No sooner was this enacted, however, than another bill was introduced stating that, because England was at war, the law was not to become effective until the conflict ended.

It had always been apparent to the Sheehy-Skeffingtons that the division in the ranks of women between those who demanded Home Rule first and those who felt obtaining the vote was the more immediate problem had done much damage to the feminist cause. This seemed the right moment to call for unification; the pages of the *Irish Citizen* the right place to do so. Under the heading, "An Appeal to Nationalist Women," a strong editorial, bearing the Francis Sheehy-Skeffington stamp, appeared early in October and argued that, even though Home Rule had been suspended, it was not too soon to start to build a political organization to strengthen sympathy for women's suffrage. Since an amendment to the Home Rule Bill, designed to ease the incorporation of that legislation in Ireland, had been promised for the next session of Parliament, every effort should be made to see that votes for women became part of the amendment. If those women who had put the cause of nationalism first did nothing now to ensure enfranchisement, it would appear that "their concern about Home Rule was merely a cloak for lukewarmness as regards the suffrage case." At the least, these women should now join some suffrage organization and one of the first effects of the passage of the Home Rule Bill should be an increase in the membership of all such societies.[25]

The Sheehy-Skeffingtons saw the struggle for women's suffrage as closely allied to their stand against war and conscription. For the most part, it was not a popular stand. But they were opposed to war, any war, and it seemed obvious to them that Irishwomen, with no political voice, had no responsibility for this one. In the pages of the *Irish Citizen*, Hanna made a strong plea for pacifism and for a continuation of the struggle for the vote. It was so well received that it was reprinted in leaflet form.[26]

Her writing had become as impassioned as her speaking. "War is the favourite method employed by governments hard pressed at home and eager to shelve their responsibilities," she wrote. War propaganda urged women not to insist on their claims at this time of crisis, Hanna pointed out, and she went so far as to call women who heeded this propaganda "traitors to their cause" and to call their "supineness" responsible in large measure for their not having the vote. She concluded: "If male statesmanship after all these centuries has nothing better to offer by way of adjusting differences than a universal shambles, then in Heaven's name let men allow women to lend a hand, not at mopping up the blood and purifying the stench of the abattoir, but at clearing away the whole rotten system."[27] Alice Park, a prominent American suffragist, wrote from the United States asking for more copies of the article and saying: "I have worn the purple, white and green ribbon [of the Women's Social and Political Union] for more than a year; and this week I have laid it aside, and put on the colours of the Irish Women's Franchise League and the United Suffragists combined."[28]

There is a question as to how far the militancy of pacifists can be extended before they are no longer considered pacifists. For many, there also seemed to be a contradiction in the militants' railing against war when they used violent tactics to counteract it. Hanna saw none and had no difficulty explaining her stand. War destroyed life in order to protect property, she said; militants destroyed property in order to enhance the value of life. This being the case, she felt it was her duty as an Irish militant suffragist to make war upon war.

She also attempted to clarify the stand of the Irish Women's Franchise League. Women had not been consulted either "directly or indirectly" with regard to the war or the steps that led up to it. Consequently, they had no responsibility to endorse it or the way in which it was being conducted. For this reason, the I.W.F.L. had been careful, since its inception, to express no opinion concerning the war, to take no part in it, and to continue to agitate for the vote for women. In answer to criticism of the league for not assisting in war-relief work, Hanna argued cogently that it had taken no stand with regard to the 1913 lockout though members had as individuals assisted the strikers. "Our attitude towards war-relief schemes is precisely similar," she said.[29]

It was necessary to defend her position once again when Thomas Haslam, in a letter to the *Irish Citizen*, protested against the antiwar, militant stand of the suffragists. Any cause, Hanna replied, that attempted to rely "on appeals to conscience and to reason" was "one that statesmen will continue to believe in piously, and as piously to ignore." She reminded Mr. Haslam, who had suggested that this was a war of self-defense on the part of England, that every country believed it was fighting a just war and that the enemy was always the aggressor. "O'Connell," she said, "did not achieve Catholic Emancipation by praying for it; the negro slaves were not freed by appeals to the reason or conscience of their owners; . . . Home Rule has not been placed on the Statute Book as a result of an appeal to reason and conscience." If anything could be learned from history, she claimed, it was that only by some show of force did any cause finally reach its goal.[30]

True to their own exhortations, the Sheehy-Skeffingtons continued to battle against the war and conscription through every possible medium— the Socialist Party, to which they both belonged, the labor movement in general, the Irish Women's Franchise League, and the pages of the *Irish Citizen*. Keenly interested in all peace movements, the I.W.F.L. had decided to send a representative to the Women's International Peace Congress to be held at The Hague in April 1915, and Hanna had been chosen as a delegate. The government, though, using the war as an excuse, refused permits to British and Irish women. The protest to this move was so vehement that finally the government consented to issue permits to a certain number "certified to be discreet." Hanna, rarely discreet, was one of those excluded from the list; as a matter of fact, only Louie Bennett was granted a permit from Ireland. Before the time came for her departure, however, the government closed the North Sea to all traffic and kept it closed until the congress was over.

Determined not to take this without protest, the women stormed the

House of Commons and the Home Office for a week—but it did no good. In a further attempt to ensure that they would not be "tricked again,"[31] a public meeting was held in Dublin early in May under the auspices of the I.W.F.L. Louie Bennett attended and, in a lengthy speech which again demonstrated the problems the war was creating in the suffrage ranks, denounced the whole tone of the meeting. The following day she wrote Hanna that she had found the mood there much more anti-England than anti-militarism. She had the distinct impression that, though the participants considered the present war "barbarous and immoral," they felt a war fought for Ireland would be justifiable. In her opinion, this was a "superficial form of pacifism—hardly worthy of the name" and she would take part in no more meetings that "put Irish nationalism above international tolerance."[32]

The *Irish Citizen*, following its policy of presenting all points of view, gave Louie Bennett space in its pages to express her dissatisfaction with the protest meeting. Her article condemned those who countenanced "barbarous methods" to attain the worthy goal of peace for, she maintained, they were only substituting one form of bondage for another.[33] Her stand, while sincere and consistent, must have had the effect of further weakening the whole women's movement, since hers was a powerful voice in women's labor circles.

Scarcely had The Hague Conference furor subsided when Francis Sheehy-Skeffington, who had been speaking against conscription every Sunday for forty weeks under the auspices of the Socialist Party of Ireland, was arrested. Under the Defence of the Realm Act, he was charged with making "statements likely to be prejudicial to recruiting." Denied a trial by jury, he was taken to Mountjoy until his appearance before a police magistrate could be scheduled. Ten days later he appeared before Magistrate Mahoney and received his sentence. It was a harsh one—the maximum penalty in the magistrate's power, in fact—six months' hard labor and six additional months in default of bail. Though he had conducted his own defense capably, it had been to no avail and he rose to accept the verdict calmly, saying: "I will serve no such sentence. I will eat no food from this moment, and long before the expiration of the sentence I shall be out of prison, alive or dead!"[34]

Francis kept his word. Though threatened with forcible feeding, he took no food from the moment hs jail sentence began. Hanna, worried and frightened, began immediately to write and wire family and friends and to protest to the authorities and the newspapers. Stunned and deeply grieved by the severity of the sentence, Father Eugene wrote her—"If only I could take his place!"—and her father, also distraught, wrote: "I hate the idea of that hunger strike and his suicide. The sentence itself reads murder to a frail man like Frank." He would see people in authority to try to get the sentence modified, he told Hanna, but was not hopeful.[35]

George Bernard Shaw was one of the people to whom Hanna had appealed. His reply seemed of such importance to her that she wired him her thanks and asked if she might publish the letter. Feeling was very strong in Ireland against the sentence, she told G.B.S., and she felt that publication of his letter would strengthen the opposition. His immediate reply gave her full permission. He had, he wrote, composed the letter with the thought that she might want to publish it but was convinced that nothing could be done. "The Defence of the Realm Act abolishes all liberty in Great Britain and Ireland except such as the authorities may choose to leave us," he told her. And he went on:

> Therefore if they should decide for any reason to hang your husband, you will not have any practical remedy. Protests are quite useless. The Opposition in the House of Commons will not oppose. The press will not defend public liberties. . . . Under these circumstances I think your husband made a very grave mistake in putting his head into the lion's mouth as he did. Something can be done with a tyrannical Government: nothing can be done with a terrified Government and a cowed people.

He felt that any interference on his part would only make matters worse. He was not afraid of a German victory, he said, and had very little patience with those Englishmen who were. He added:

> If they cannot win at the present odds without putting Mr Sheehy Skeffington in prison for depleting the British army to the extent of half a dozen men or so, they deserve to be beaten. Unfortunately this confidence of mine sends the British alarmists into ecstasies of fright. They commonly allude to me as a pro-German; and if they knew that I sympathized with your husband they would declare that nothing but his imprisonment for life could save England. I can fight stupidity; but nobody can fight cowardice.[36]

Action by the Irish Women's Franchise League took the form of a resolution, sent to Mr. Redmond, protesting the denial of trial by jury to

Sheehy-Skeffington and other political prisoners then confined to Mount-joy, and calling for their unconditional release.[37] Letters, messages, and other expressions of concern and goodwill reached Hanna daily. Louie Bennett wrote offering much-needed help with the *Irish Citizen*. Alice Stopford Green wrote to say that she was taking action so far as all political prisoners were concerned. Letters offering financial assistance arrived as well.

There were also letters, constantly, from J. B. Skeffington. Evidently Hanna was able to respond to them civilly but it must have taken a great deal of self-control. J. B. was not surprised at the harshness of his son's sentence, he wrote Hanna. Francis should have expected nothing less since only "a Monomaniac" would have acted as he had. "How could any sane person praise Germany," he asked, "the most degrading tyranny of mind and body at peace and the most brutal savagery at war?" His bitterness also extended to Hanna, whose jailing and hunger strike had, in his view, given Francis something to try to rival. Instead of restraining her husband, she had merely been setting him a bad example. "How any sensible and educated people could think to prosper by outraging all the powers and influences of the country is a marvel."[38]

The sharpness of J. B.'s words was to a great extent offset by his deeds. He spoke with Irish members of Parliament, urging them to intercede for his son, though he was sure that Francis had antagonized them. He also attempted, without success, to have a doctor other than the one assigned by prison authorities examine him in the hope that he would testify to Francis's ill health and inability to serve his term.[39]

As he had threatened to do, Francis refused food, and his father, convinced that this was the height of folly, was terribly worried. By the third day of the hunger strike, J. B. was certain that his son would not last a fourth. But he greatly underestimated Francis's endurance. Sheehy-Skeffington survived seven days without food (after six he went on a thirst strike as well) before he was finally released, pale, emaciated, and so weak that his cab driver had to help him into the house. His voice, as he attempted to greet his son, Owen, was hardly audible.[40]

Under the Cat and Mouse Act, Sheehy-Skeffington was ordered to return to Mountjoy at the end of June. This was, according to Hanna, the first time the law had been invoked for other than a suffragist offense. As she saw it, in order to complete his year's sentence, he would have to suffer "fifty-two weeks of hunger strike, plus two years, in fortnightly periods, for recuperation." How her husband's repeated hunger strikes, followed by either permanent disability or death, could aid recruiting in Ireland she failed to see.[41] In Francis's mind, there was no doubt as to what course he would follow if forced to return to prison at the end of his reprieve: he would immediately resume his strike. Hanna, though heart-sick, made no attempt to dissuade him, but his father, convinced that the hunger strike was a mean and foolhardy weapon, had no such reservations. "It appeals," J. B. told Hanna,

> to the *pity* and *mercy* of the very foes who hold you in Prison. It says in effect—"Pray don't let me die," save me from myself. It pleases and *gratifies all enemies*. It brings the faster to death's door and makes him unable to judge or to act for himself. . . . We have too little life, health than to waste any. It is criminal folly of the worst kind to make any such attempt on one's life. . . . Is it not the height of folly to worry and destroy one's friends only to please one's enemies and reduce one-self to a nonentity? Surely Life and mind and strength are too precious to throw away.[42]

He urged both Hanna and his son to consider the matter carefully but the question did not arise since no attempt was made to rearrest Francis. Whether this was because of his health or of pressure by his family and friends is difficult to determine.

J. B. had also suggested that his son spend some time in Wales re-cuperating and then go to America, if he could manage to slip by the au-thorities, who would surely be keeping a careful watch on him. As usual, he was helping the Sheehy-Skeffingtons financially and offered to con-tinue to do so. As usual, also, his assistance was sorely needed.

In order to supplement their income, Hanna made an effort to ob-tain assignments as a language teacher in the City of Dublin Technical Schools before the 1915 fall session began. She had been doing some sub-stitute teaching in the Alexandra School in Earlsfort Terrace during the winter and had no difficulty obtaining a letter of recommendation from the headmistress. Calling Hanna an excellent French scholar, she stressed Hanna's keen interest in her pupils' education and praised her technique for getting students actually to think in the language, a point also noted in a letter from the former principal of the Rathmines School of Com-merce.[43]

The decision was made that Francis would, as his father had ad-vised, go to Wales to recuperate and, from there, escape as soon as practicable to the United States. Once in the States, he would attempt to earn money by lecturing and he intended to use his lectures to speak out against the war and against efforts to impose conscription upon Ireland. Hanna, though filled with apprehension, knew she must carry on. She would teach; she would manage the *Irish Citizen*; she would fight for votes for women and against war; and she would attempt to keep her son from feeling his father's absence too keenly.

David Sheehy, M.P., Hanna's father. Self-confident and firm in his convictions, he was a significant public figure in Ireland. (Courtesy of Pan Collins, his granddaughter)

Bessie Sheehy, Hanna's mother. The mother of four girls and two boys, Bessie was the guiding force within the family. (Courtesy of Pan Collins, her granddaughter)

The Sheehys. This family portrait, date uncertain, shows Hanna, Richard, David, Margaret, Eugene, and Mary, standing, left to right; and Father Eugene, Kathleen, and Bessie, seated, left to right. (Courtesy of Andrée Sheehy-Skeffington)

Francis Sheehy-Skeffington. A "Votes for Women" button, which Hanna's husband wore for years, is visible in this photograph. (Courtesy of Andrée Sheehy-Skeffington)

J.B. Skeffington. The black arm band on Francis's father was probably worn in mourning for his wife, who died in 1909. (Courtesy of Andrée Sheehy-Skeffington)

The National Library of Ireland. Entrance off to the left. It was here that Hanna Sheehy and Francis Skeffington often met during their courtship. (Courtesy of National Library of Ireland)

Exterior of Catholic University (University College, Dublin) as seen from St. Stephen's Green. The low building to right of photograph is the chapel in which Hanna and Francis were married in 1903. (Courtesy of National Library of Ireland)

Father Eugene Sheehy (Uncle Eugene), Hanna Sheehy-Skeffington, and her husband (left to right). This 1912 photograph was taken upon Hanna's release from Mountjoy Prison, Dublin. (Courtesy of Andrée Sheehy-Skeffington)

1912 Executive Committee of the Irish Women's Franchise League. Hanna Sheehy-Skeffington, extreme right, was an active participant. (Courtesy of Andrée Sheehy-Skeffington)

11 Grosvenor Place. This was the Sheehy-Skeffingtons' second home and their residence at the time of Francis's murder. (Courtesy of National Museum of Ireland)

Darkness at Easter

HE PEACE and isolation of rural Wales proved to be exactly what Francis Sheehy-Skeffington needed and, recovering rapidly, he was on his way to the United States by the end of July 1915. It was his father's fervent hope that he would stay there, at least until the war was over. The climate, especially in the southern states, he told Hanna, would be good for his son's health. Apparently he thought the political climate would be good for him as well. There, at least, he could write and speak without fear of reprisal.[1]

Hanna, while agreeing that the trip was a good idea, was nonetheless very uneasy. Francis had, after all, left Ireland illegally and there could be trouble when he returned. Of more immediate concern was his health. Although he assured her in every letter that he was "in excellent form in *every way*"—and he wrote her forty-one times during his stay in the United States—she was not convinced. He, in turn, though she was feeling unusually well, was worried about her and urging her "to take things a little less strenuously." He had only praise for her work on the *Irish Citizen*, however, particularly on the editorials.[2] It was probably just as well that she was "driven to death" with work;[3] otherwise she would have had even more time to worry.

Francis's praise for her work on the *Irish Citizen* was not misplaced. In both quality and spirit, the editorials continued as before, taking vigorous stands against conscription, against the Parliamentary Party, and for the vote. One—"No Vote, No Register"—advised Irishwomen "to resist any attempt to enforce a War Register in Ireland and to refuse to give any information or service to a Government that denied them a place on the Parliamentary Register." Another—"What Is a Popular Franchise?"—attacked Redmond and the Parliamentary Party for their opposition to votes for women and began: "Mr. Redmond has again been speaking on national liberties for the whole people to a strictly male audience, as usual, with 'several ladies occupying seats in the gallery.'"[4]

Under the "Current Comment" section, there was no mistaking Hanna's touch. A typical item, labeled "Masculine Waste," cited 200,000 forms issued in connection with the Voluntary Registration Act, of which only 17,000 were completed, with 800 of those spoiled, "a total expenditure on printing alone which 'New Ireland' estimates at £500—absolute waste," and went on to criticize male ineptitude in allowing Canadian flour, meant for distribution to the poor, to lie in a Dublin depot, "rotting."[5] Another item, also typically Hanna's, was called "Queen Mary on Girls' Education." The queen, *Irish Society* had reported, believed that her daughter had made fine progress under the instruction solely of governesses and she said that she had no intention of making any change. She also remarked that, "although Princess Mary has been so very much under feminine influence all her life, she is very nice and pleasant to the opposite sex, and in no way indifferent to their society." The *Irish Citizen* commented: "That 'although' is delightful. Is it usually found that girls bred up under feminine influences dislike, and are indifferent to, the opposite sex? What about boys? Should they, too, have feminine teaching in order to find out how to behave to women?"[6]

Clearly it was difficult for Hanna to "take things a little less strenuously," as her husband had advised. There was young Owen to care for, there was the routine of the household to supervise, and there were the many demands of the Irish Women's Franchise League and, above all, of the paper. There was also her own temperament: she was a woman who placed rigorous, sometimes unreasonably rigorous, demands on herself. A perfectionist driven by feelings that she was not doing enough for family, friends, or one or another of her many urgent causes, she was capable, despite a recurrent cough, of extended periods of intense activity. These stretches of seemingly boundless energy and drive often ended, however, in profound weariness and occasionally in frustration and acute depression. Francis was worried about her now, though he never seemed to grasp the pattern of her behavior. Late in October, searching for an answer to one of her bouts of melancholia, he wrote her: "I'm sorry to hear of your being depressed again, Hanna sweetheart; I thought from your last that you were in good form again. For fear cash may have something to do with it, I am enclosing 20 dollars (about £4), in the hope that it may help you to tide over!"[7]

Hanna never questioned Francis's devotion or thoughtfulness but

there must have been times when her husband's similarity to his father depressed her as well. In one letter he admonished her for not telling him
whether or not she had received certain letters and for not acknowledging
"everything specifically" as he did[8]—his letters were not only dated but
numbered. He also criticized her method of punishing Owen by sending
him to bed, which he thought "a more objectionable punishment than
beating." He added—it may be hoped humorously—that she was apparently unable to manage the boy but would just have to get along as best
she could until he returned.[9]

Francis's health continued to be excellent and his tour a great success. In fact, the *Irish World*, an anti-Redmond Irish-American paper, had
offered him a lucrative journalistic position. Though flattered by the offer, he never seriously considered accepting it. Both Sheehy-Skeffingtons
loved Dublin and Ireland too much ever to want to be away from them for
long.

By mid-November Francis was beginning to count the days until his
return home.[10] Hanna was delighted at the prospect, too, but her happiness was tempered by increasing anxiety over what would happen to him
upon his return. Thanks to the Cat and Mouse Act, he was in grave danger of being arrested as soon as he set foot on British soil. His letters attempted to allay her fears about Dublin Castle's plans for him. He was, he
told her, far more worried about her than about himself since, as usual,
she was the one who suffered the most for his sins.[11]

The days were passing quickly for Hanna; she was booked weeks in
advance for speaking engagements and deeply involved in the details of
planning and organizing Irish Women's Franchise League activities. She
spoke not only at the regular Tuesday-evening meetings of the I.W.F.L.,
at many of which she presided as well, but also at the special Sunday
meetings in Phoenix Park, where she always arranged to have the *Irish Citizen* sold. One of the most successful of the latter gatherings was held to
encourage Dubliners to protest the "unwarranted and unjustifiable abuse
of the liberties and rights of Irishmen and Irishwomen" who had been imprisoned under the Cat and Mouse Act. The attendance was the largest
seen in the park in many years and it goes without saying that Hanna was
one of the speakers.[12]

Finally Francis was on his way home. He had booked passage on the
St. Louis, leaving New York 11 December 1915, and was scheduled to land
in Liverpool on the 19th. Barring incident, he would be home before
Christmas. He was prepared for all eventualities, he wrote Hanna, and he

instructed her to publicize his arrival time thoroughly. As a matter of fact, though he was apprehended immediately upon landing in Liverpool and taken to the Bridewell, he was released within hours. His personal effects, however, were held and not returned to him until late February. What Hanna dreaded most—his jailing and inevitable resumption of the hunger strike—did not take place. All seemed well and, to her great delight, their little family was reunited for the holidays. But within months events would occur that were far more tragic than any she had imagined.

Francis was feeling exceptionally fit and, with scarcely a day's delay, he was addressing a meeting in the Rotunda. The audience was large and he was at his best, speaking for more than an hour. He was in equally good form in January 1916, when he spoke at length before the Irish Women's Franchise League at Forresters' Hall with James Connolly presiding and Hanna participating in the discussion.[13]

On Tuesday evenings Hanna, as usual, was on the platform at the regular Irish Women's Franchise League meetings. On 11 January she presided over a meeting that reviewed the activities of the past year; a week later, with Meg Connery presiding, she joined in the discussion following a talk by Professor Houston on "What Women Can Do to Increase the Food Supply"; late in the month she was on hand to discuss a paper given by Mrs. Richardson on St. John Ervine's novel, *Mrs. Martin's Man*, whose heroine, most felt, assumed far too meek a role in her relationship with a "worthless and unfaithful husband."[14] Her efforts were tireless. The previous year, for instance, she had participated in or had helped to plan virtually all I.W.F.L. activities: sixty suffrage meetings in Ireland, both indoor and outdoor; campaigns in two by-elections in Dublin; a series of meetings in Clare that for the first time introduced the suffrage issue there; the monitoring of court cases concerned with women's interests; and assistance to any movement that sought to better working conditions for women.

In January 1916 Hanna, never satisfied, sent an urgent plea to all members of the Irish Women's Franchise League asking that activities be stepped up. She pointed to indications that the issue of votes for women would be brought up quite soon in relation to a proposed bill extending the voting privileges of men. "Unless we are ready for an active campaign to combat this attempt on the part of the Government to ignore women's claims for citizenship," she wrote, "the labour and sacrifice of years may be frustrated and our cause put back for generations."[15] Her plea was supplemented, in the early months of 1916, by inspirational editorializing in the *Irish Citizen.* "Current Comment" for April found clear signs that "feminism, conscious or unconscious," was gaining strength; for example, the *National Student*, a student publication at University College, Dublin, was adopting a "strongly feminist tone." "Comment" added: "Even the United Irish League is waking up, and has founded—in London!—a Women's Branch, to keep political work going while the men are at the war!"[16]

So far as the feminist movement in Ireland was concerned, the *Irish Citizen* had been playing and continued to play a major role. The paper, just as Sheehy-Skeffington and Cousins had hoped, carefully observed the contemporary scene and called attention to examples of antifeminism when it detected them. "In Ireland," it noted in May, for instance, "the only anti-feminist manifestations to be recorded are those of an organ of complacent coxcombery called 'The Irishman,' the fatuous attitude of which towards women is of a piece with the rest of its pose." The paper went on: "Archbishop Crozier's calm suggestion that no woman should be allowed to get married without a knowledge of cookery is a parallel imbecility."[17]

The archbishop's remark was a blatant example of sexism but, in a covert form, sex discrimination was practiced by groups like the Irish Volunteers and condoned by others like Cumann na mBan. The *Irish Citizen* did not fail to point this out:

> Cumann na mBan . . . continues to work for the Irish Volunteers in a purely subordinate capacity, without any voice in the control of the organization, without any official declaration from the Irish Volunteers that the 'rights and liberties' for which they stand include the rights and liberties of women, without even themselves making an official declaration that they interpret the Irish Volunteers' programme in that sense. Mr. John MacNeill, speaking on April 9th, laid considerable stress on the work women could and should do for the Volunteers, but did not, we are informed, say anything about what the Volunteers intended to do for women; indeed, why should he, when the women themselves offer their aid unconditionally? There is only one word for this attitude of unconditional subordination to men's movements: it is slavish.[18]

So the early months of 1916 passed for Hanna and it was April, with Easter Week and the Rising rapidly approaching. Her sister Mary's husband, Tom Kettle, was wearing a British uniform as was Cruise O'Brien,

Kathleen's husband. Culhane, Margaret's husband, had been ill for some time and early in 1916 he died, leaving Margaret, at thirty-five, a widow with four children. Providentially, the sisters were closer together than ever. And soon Hanna was to need their support more than she ever had.

Though they did not know precise details, the Sheehy-Skeffingtons must have known something of a projected rebellion: years later Hanna gave her son an account of some of the events that took place prior to it and of her feelings about the Rising itself. She told him of a plan to have a German ship, the *Aud*, bring arms to Ireland. The ship got as far as the bay of Kerry, where it was intercepted by the British, and, rather than have the arms taken, blown up by order of the commander. The Rising was to coincide with the scheduled landing of the ship on Good Friday but, after its loss, some of the Volunteers wanted the event postponed or dropped completely while others, such as Connolly and Pearse, wanted to push ahead regardless. The latter prevailed, "with the result," Hanna noted, "of complete confusion & loss." Still, she said, "I think Connolly was right to go on once they got so far." While her remark may represent a position she took long after the event, this seems less likely in the light of the further comment that her husband "thought otherwise, feeling that any rising was foredoomed."[19] There is the possibility that Francis and Hanna were discussing a rising in the abstract, but talk it over they certainly did.

Another fact points to a certain amount of foreknowledge of the rebellion. James Connolly and Francis Sheehy-Skeffington were very good friends. (While awaiting execution, Connolly, not knowing that Francis was already dead, asked that he be made Connolly's literary executor.) They must have seen and talked with each other during that period and the Sheehy-Skeffingtons would have been sympathetic with the aim of establishing an independent Irish republic. But they would without any doubt have rejected the philosophy of the leaders of the Rising, which Dorothy Macardle described as a belief in "the necessity for blood sacrifice to give life to the nation's cause."[20] The spilling of blood they always found abhorrent, no matter how just the cause.

Easter Sunday morning, 23 April 1916, Sheehy-Skeffington, reading the *Sunday Independent*, was puzzled by a notice issued the previous day by Eoin MacNeill, the head of the Irish Volunteers. The wording troubled him. "Owing to the very critical position," it began, "all orders given to Irish Volunteers for to-morrow, Easter Sunday, are hereby rescinded, and no parades, marches, or other movements of Irish Volunteers will take place."[21] Unable to come to any conclusion, he decided to go to Liberty Hall to see if he could learn more about the situation. There he found the military council of the Irish Republican Brotherhood—Sean MacDermott, Tom Clarke, Padraic Pearse, and James Connolly—in secret session. William O'Brien, Connolly's closest friend and his colleague in the labor and socialist movements, was hanging about but, though he said later he was well aware of what was going on, could give Sheehy-Skeffington no concrete information.[22]

The following morning, Easter Monday, Sheehy-Skeffington went into town once more. What he found, he told Hanna that evening, was a full-blown insurrection in progress. Headquarters had been set up in the General Post Office, and throughout the city there was the sound of rifle fire. Dublin Castle had been attacked by a small unit of Volunteers and Citizen Army men and here he became personally involved. With volleys and counter volleys sweeping across Cork Hill, he saw a British officer fall wounded near the Castle gate. Somehow he managed to commandeer a chemist to go with him to try to help the wounded man, but by the time they reached the gate he had been taken inside. Only a pool of blood remained.[23] Hanna, furious at the risk he had taken, scolded; but his argument—he could not let anyone bleed to death if there were even a remote possibility of saving him—silenced her.

Leaving the Dublin Castle area, he made his way toward the General Post Office. O'Connell Street was bedlam. The police had abandoned it and the surrounding area in fear, and looters were everywhere. Since it was a bank holiday, the shops were closed but shrieking crowds were kicking in store windows and merchandise was being passed from hand to hand. Occasionally one of the Volunteers would shoot over their heads but no one paid much attention. Shocked, Francis went on to the G.P.O. to report the situation. He found Connolly set up in a headquarters office, directing secretaries and typists. Well aware of the looting taking place, Connolly saw no way to stop it. It was the least of his worries, he indicated. One of the Volunteers who had attempted to control it even found the situation rather amusing. He had never seen so many industrious Irishmen, he said.

Sheehy-Skeffington was not amused and by the time he reached home, he thought he saw what steps might be taken. A Citizens' Defence Force could be organized and at least some attempt made to control the looters. Immediately he and Hanna sat down to draw up a statement to be posted in strategic spots the following day. The final version read: "When there are no regular police on the streets, it becomes the duty of citizens to police the streets themselves and to prevent such spasmodic looting as has taken place in a few streets. Civilians (men and women) who are willing to cooperate to this end are asked to attend at Westmoreland Chambers (over Eden Bros.) at five o'clock this (Tues.) afternoon."[24]

Hanna's reaction to all this was a determination to go to the General Post Office the following day to see what she could do to help. In the morning they went into town together: Hanna on her way to the G.P.O. and Francis on his way to post the notices and to buttonhole likely prospects for his defense force. They planned to meet for tea at the Westmoreland Chambers (headquarters of the Irish Women's Franchise League) after 5:30 P.M. All around her, Hanna saw the results of the first day of the insurrection. Looting had apparently continued during the night for the destruction was much greater than Francis had described it. Shops had been set on fire and were still burning. Near the post office, people were sitting about as though in a park comparing and swapping their loot.

Apparently she was needed at the G.P.O. for, once there, James Connolly, commander of the Republican forces, sent her and several escorts to the College of Surgeons with food and despatches.[25]

Hanna was only one of the many women who participated in the Rising. When plans were made, Cumann na mBan units were assigned various posts to serve in a first-aid and commissary capacity. In their biography of Eamon de Valera, the Earl of Longford and Thomas P. O'Neill maintain that none of the women reported for duty because they were unhappy with de Valera's decision not to see them.[26] A member of the Ingnidhe Branch of that organization, however, Sheila Crenan, said that half of her branch were mobilized for Upper Mount Street. They waited there under their captain, Eileen Walsh, for orders from de Valera, but he failed to get in touch with them although they had offered their services unconditionally and, in particular, had not asked to be armed. When an emissary was sent to de Valera for instructions, he reported back that de Valera "could not be bothered with the women." At that point, according to Sheila Crenan, some of them got in where they could and others went home.[27]

Throughout the week of the Rising, Cumann na mBan and other nationalist women provided first aid, acted as couriers in extremely dangerous situations, and offered food and shelter where needed. Constance Markievicz, serving as a staff officer, commanded a batallion at St. Stephen's Green. Dr. Kathleen Lynn, for many years an uncompromising Republican, acted as medical officer for the Rising and her associate, Madeleine ffrench-Mullen, was in charge of the Red Cross and the commissariat. Margaret Skinnider led a squad of men against a machine-gun post in St. Stephen's Green and was seriously wounded. And the list could go on. It is not surprising that there were more than seventy women among those arrested after the surrender.[28] It was in the spirit of all of these that Hanna went to the General Post Office on that fateful second day of the Rising.

Sometime after five, she went to meet her husband for tea. He had managed, he told her, to enlist the help of many civilians and priests, had posted a few guards, and had prevented a few shops from being looted. They were together for a little more than an hour when Hanna decided that it would be wise to go home. The sound of rifle fire was growing louder; the trams were no longer operating so she would have to walk; Owen was at home and might be worried; and, all in all, she was growing apprehensive, she told Francis. He would wait about for a bit, he said, in the hope that more recruits for the antilooting force might appear.[29]

Hanna never saw her husband again—alive or dead. On his way home that evening he was apprehended near the Portobello Bridge, taken to the nearby Portobello Barracks, and the following morning, Wednesday, without hearing or trial, brought before a firing squad and shot. That morning, puzzled that Francis had not returned home, Hanna went into town to seek information as to his whereabouts. The sun was shining, people were milling about trading stories about the fighting but, as Hanna went from group to group, she heard nothing but vague rumors. He had been arrested but nobody was sure where he was being held. She was even told that he had been executed but, of course, she knew better. How could he be executed when there had been no trial? It was easier to believe that he had been accidentally shot but then why had she not been informed? Fearfully, she returned home and did her best not to communicate her fears to Owen.

Thursday morning she began her round of inquiries once more. She was sure now that something dreadful had happened to Francis, for she knew that he would have sent some word to her if at all possible. The fighting was growing heavier in town; the sound of rifles and machine guns was almost constant. English reinforcements had begun to pour in and the previous day Liberty Hall had been shelled. Sick with fear for her husband, her inquiries once again unsuccessful, Hanna returned home.

On Friday morning Hanna's sisters, Margaret Culhane and Mary Kettle, decided to go to Portobello Barracks to see if they could obtain any

information about Francis. There they talked with a Captain Bowen-
Colthurst, who denied any knowledge of their brother-in-law. Puzzled by
the vehemence of his denial, they nevertheless accepted his story since
they had no intimation then that a murder had even been committed, let
alone that he was the one who had ordered it.[30]

It was this same afternoon that Hanna was informed by a reliable
witness that he had seen her husband's body in the mortuary of Portobello
Barracks, but he could tell her no more. Hastening to the barracks, she
talked with the military chaplain and appealed to his humanity to tell her
something of her husband's fate. His account left her unsatisfied and,
when she asked to reclaim her husband's body, he told her that Francis
had already been buried.[31] It would be many weeks before Hanna knew
all the details and then only after her husband's murderer had, thanks to
her efforts, been court-martialed.

The horrible day was not yet over for Hanna. Shortly before seven,
a party of British soldiers, led by Captain Riversdale Bowen-Colthurst,
raided her home. The house was surrounded by some sixty to one hundred soldiers who, after firing a shot through the front window, burst into
the house with fixed bayonets. Except for her maid, Hanna and Owen
were alone and she was putting him to bed. They were ordered to put
their hands up, escorted into the front room, and told not to move. Some
of the men remained to guard them, some were stationed outside the door
of the room, and some were on their knees in the garden, their rifles at the
ready. When they left some three hours later, a guard remained outside
throughout the night.[32]

Once the soldiers were gone, Hanna looked about. The house had
been ransacked and the soldiers had taken away with them German and
Russian books that Hanna had been using as a teacher of languages. About
the German books, she had heard one of the soldiers say to an officer,
"Apparently, sir, he was in correspondence with the Kaiser." They must
have brought a key to her husband's study with them for papers had been
taken from that room, which was always kept locked—Francis objected to
having it dusted. Hanna said later that they found no ammunition. What
she could not know was that the only "ammunition" they were searching
for was some document or documents proving her husband's threat to
the government. Those papers found on him when he was arrested—a
picture of his son, a membership card in the Irish Women's Franchise
League, and the antilooting poster—had incriminated him in no way
whatsoever and they were growing desperate for evidence.[33]

For Hanna, grief-stricken, this must have been the final indignity. Typically, she came up fighting, determined to give some meaning to the senseless tragedy. She would begin by exposing the role of the British military in her husband's murder. Her campaign began with a visit to John Dillon, M.P., the only one of the Parliamentary Party leaders who had actually experienced the Rising, having been unable that week to leave his house which was very close to the General Post Office.[34] With the hope that he would help in making the facts public, Hanna gave him the details of her husband's death and implored him to demand that Prime Minister Asquith hold a full inquiry into the case. Hanna never forgot Dillon's reaction to her visit for she had never seen a man, outwardly rather cold, so moved. "The old rebel in him was again alive, defiant," she wrote many years later.[35]

Just a few days afterward, John Dillon made a historic speech in the House of Commons that did a great deal to damage British prestige and to restore to honor the Irish insurgents. He took up the question of the executions then taking place in Ireland after secret military trials. As he spoke, thirteen men had already been executed and two more were scheduled to be executed the following day. "We, I think, were entitled to be consulted before this bloody course of executions was entered upon in Ireland," he said. "God knows the result of flouting our advice, as it has been flouted in the conduct of Irish affairs ever since the Coalition Government was formed, has not been a brilliant one. I think that in this matter we were entitled to be consulted."[36]

The murder of Francis Sheehy-Skeffington, Dillon pointed out, must have been known to at least three or four hundred military men and to much of the city of Dublin, yet Mrs. Sheehy-Skeffington had been told nothing of it until her husband had been dead for several days. How could the military authorities in Dublin say they knew nothing of what had happened until 6 May? There seemed no doubt that had Sheehy-Skeffington not been such a prominent citizen the case would have been covered up successfully. He had been asked by the widow of the murdered man, Dillon said, to request a complete and public investigation and he was confident that the prime minister would agree that this was "a matter of elementary justice."[37]

To Hanna, Asquith's reaction to the speech seemed not only ludicrous but incredible. The prime minister said: "I confess I do not and cannot believe it. Does anyone suppose that Sir John Maxwell [in command of the British forces in Dublin] has any object in shielding officers and soldiers, if there be such, who have been guilty of such ungentlemanlike, such inhuman conduct? *It is the last thing the British army would dream of!*"[38]

Badly shaken by her husband's death, Hanna needed and received the support of family, friends, and the hundreds of people whom neither she nor Francis had known personally but who were grateful for his help, his encouragement, and the role he had played in the feminist, socialist, and pacifist movements. Since Mary's husband, Tom Kettle, was at Newbridge Barracks as a recruiting officer and Margaret was recently widowed, they were able to be at Hanna's side.

Of all those who came to Hanna's assistance during her terrible ordeal, one was especially important. It was, of all people, the officer who was in charge of the Portobello Barracks' defenses at the time of her husband's murder—Sir Francis Fletcher Vane. Born in Devon, the son of an Anglican father and an Irish Catholic mother, he had served in the regular British Army at the time of the Boer War and, at that time, had protested the internment of women and children and the deplorable conditions under which they were detained. Understandably not very popular in military circles, he retired but reenlisted when war broke out in 1914 and was recommissioned. At the time of the Rising he held the rank of major in the 8th Battalion of the Munster Fusiliers.[39]

Hanna saw Sir Francis for the first time when he visited her to apologize in the name of the military and to give her details of the murder as he knew them. She saw a man about fifty-five years old, red-faced, moustached, with a narrow tuft of beard.[40] He was obviously ill at ease. Though Hanna was unable to control her coldness—two raids on her home as well as her husband's murder had left her with more than a little distaste for the British uniform—she listened quietly. On the third day of the Rising, he said, he had taken a unit to place an observation post on the Rathmines Town Hall tower. Upon his return from that mission, he had been told of the shooting of her husband and also of Thomas Dickson and Patrick MacIntyre, two newspapermen, both quite innocent, who had been apprehended with him. Sir Francis was informed, too, that it was Captain Bowen-Colthurst who had taken the three men from the guardhouse that morning and ordered them shot.[41]

As Sir Francis explained, he had known very little about Captain Bowen-Colthurst, but on the second day of the rebellion he had gone into the mess hall to get a sandwich and had found Bowen-Colthurst sitting there, his elbows on the table and his head in his hands. When Sir Francis entered, Colthurst turned to him and said, "Is it not dreadful . . . to have to shoot Irishmen?" Vane agreed heartily but was somewhat puzzled by the man's intensity. When, the following morning, he learned that Bowen-Colthurst's orders had been duly carried out, he went immediately to Major Rossborough, in charge of the Royal Irish Rifles, to express his disapproval and horror. He found Rossborough deeply worried and well aware of what had taken place. Vane pointed out that the murders would have a serious effect on public opinion—both in the United States and the colonies—but Rossborough felt that he could do nothing unless ordered to do so by his military superiors. Vane could see Rossborough's position since most of the officers in his regiment favored the harshest of measures against the Irish. He told Rossborough, however, that unless Bowen-Colthurst were confined to quarters, he, Vane, would not be responsible for the defenses. If this continued, he said, they would have all of Ireland against them—not just the rebels. Rossborough had given his word and instructed Vane to brief the officers as to their duties and responsibilities under martial law.[42]

How true Rossborough was to his word and how ineffective Vane had been, Hanna could see for herself, he said. Just two days later her home had been ransacked and Bowen-Colthurst had led the raiding party. On the following Sunday, without Vane's knowledge, a party of Royal Engineers had been sent to repair the bullet-pocked wall against which her husband and the two newspapermen had been shot. One day later Vane was summoned to the orderly room and told he would be relieved of his duties and that Bowen-Colthurst would replace him. Protesting that a more responsible officer should assume his duties, he was assured that Bowen-Colthurst would be fine. Vane then went to the general in charge of the Irish Command, was unable to see him, but did talk with the chief intelligence officer. This man, in addition to refusing to do anything about the situation, intimated that they were well rid of men like Sheehy-Skeffington. Now thoroughly disillusioned, he asked for eight days leave, Vane told Hanna, and, on 2 May, went to the War Office in London where he talked with the undersecretary for war and also with John Redmond, the Parliamentary Party's leader. Both were shocked. Before the day was out he was summoned to 10 Downing Street, where he talked with Lord Kitchener, who assured him that Captain Bowen-Colthurst would be placed under arrest. He then returned to Ireland and came immediately to see her.[43]

Vane's complete sincerity was readily apparent. Hanna rose, shook his hand, and told him that she realized that, had it been in his power, her husband's murder would have been prevented. He could be sure, she said, that she did not intend to let the matter rest there. What Vane saw was a courageous, determined woman and one he wanted desperately to help. His feelings are evident in a letter from his wife to Hanna. After apologizing for intruding upon her at this difficult time and expressing her sympathy for Hanna and her son, she went on:

> My husband has written to me so often about you and tells me he thinks you a great and noble woman. The hideous and awful mistake, made by that mad officer, cannot be scarcely forgiven, but perhaps with your great heart you will in time to come, when the first shock has somewhat passed, find that you are even able to forgive him— You must realize that it was not done by any one in authority as no one knew of it, and my husband has been filled with horror and has felt this most painful tragedy, acutely. Can it be any consolation to know that you have the greatest sympathy from thousands of people? . . . God alone can help you to bear the whole misery that you are going through, and I am sure that Sir Francis will be a great comfort to you, and help you in every way—that is possible. He is a chivalrous man, and he has felt most deeply for you. Believe me, dear Mrs. Skeffington, with much sympathy, Yours sincerely—Anna Vane.[44]

On 22 May, Hanna moved from 11 Grosvenor Place to a two-story house at 43 Moyne Road, Ranelagh. She was leaving behind a house filled with many happy memories but also with indelible memories of British uniforms and bayonets.

Aftermath of a Murder

EWER THAN five months after Hanna's husband was murdered, her brother-in-law, Tom Kettle, was killed in the battle of the Somme. The glamorous, talented Kettle, whose charm and wit captivated the entire family, had been wearing the British uniform since 1914 as a recruiter. He had gone on active duty after the Rising but not, contrary to common belief, because he no longer cared to live after the execution of Sheehy-Skeffington and the leaders of the rebellion. In fact, according to his biographer, J. B. Lyons, he had told a friend that he expected to emerge unharmed and had written his brother that he wanted very much to live and to devote his life to the cause of an enduring peace.[1] Mary Kettle was now the third sister to become widowed in less than a year and she, like Hanna, was left with one small child, Betty.

The precariousness of life was now more apparent to Hanna than ever, and because of Owen she decided she must put her house in order. During her husband's incarceration in 1915 and his subsequent stay in the United States, Maurice Wilkins, schoolmaster, writer, would-be poet, and close friend of the Sheehy-Skeffingtons, had been extremely helpful in getting out the *Irish Citizen*. Hanna now turned to him with the request that he act, with her sisters, as co-executor of her will. "Touched and honoured," Wilkins accepted. If she thought, he added, that Francis would have approved her decision, as she obviously did, he would say no more.[2]

Whether Hanna thought she was conducting her affairs as her husband would have wished because she knew him so well or whether she felt she was being guided by him is a question difficult, if not impossible, to resolve. It arises because, as a result of letters from Gretta Cousins, now in India, Hanna was doing some thinking along spiritualist lines. Though no longer in Dublin, Gretta's close friendship with Hanna had continued.

After Francis's murder, her letters became quite frequent and revealed a warm sensitivity that Hanna must have found deeply moving.

At one time, it will be remembered, Cousins had been a practicing medium. Still preoccupied with the occult, she wrote Hanna during the inquiry to say that she was sure Francis was helping Hanna to get through her terrible ordeal and that she knew he was "more keenly interested in the progress of events than anyone."[3] A fortnight earlier, she had been "walking on a quiet path from the sea," Gretta said, when she felt Francis Sheehy-Skeffington's presence beside her. He told her he was happy that at last he had found her "in a receptive mood" and went on to say that he was "still all alive & more acutely conscious than ever," although "not on that account assured of permanent immortality." That was "so like him," Gretta wrote.[4]

With this letter, Gretta enclosed another which she said Frank had guided her hand in writing. "Great affection poured through me from him to you both & I felt him sending special love to your sister Mary too." This, apparently the third letter written through her, she termed a "wonderful experience." Gretta said that her arm was "aching with the force Frank used in shoving the pencil from the left." He had tested her, she felt, by forcing her to write the letter "F" as she would not ordinarily have written it. "He insisted," she wrote Hanna, "on going back and crossing the cross line in it, a thing I never do or think of doing." Finding it difficult to remember what Francis's signature was like, Gretta checked back on one of his letters and found his signature with the "F" exactly as he had forced her to make it.[5]

The letter she presumably enclosed does not appear to have survived but two others she sent to Hanna, purportedly written by Francis through her, do still exist. In one, dated 1 May 1917, he complained of the difficulty in expressing his longing and love for his wife through a third party. A second, undated, is written in a broad scrawl and there is evidence that it was composed while Hanna was in the United States—late 1916 to mid–1918. In it, Francis said that he believed it was harder for her to bear their separation than for him because he could see and be with her whereas she felt cut off from him. He went on:

> Within these last months I have so often stood beside her as she spoke in meetings against militarism or I have sat in a chair in many a parlor while she has been talking to kind friends of my murder and I have watched her with proud eyes and longed so intensely to tell her out

loud when she was alone how splendidly she is carrying on my life work. I often want to give her my old caresses, and *I want to correct Owen too*, but I am so thankful to be able to be near them at all that I take my limitations philosophically. . . .

The pain of last year is a little softened, and all our martyrs are working by might and main to oppose feelings of hatred and bitterness in Ireland for they are fatal to a country's best interests. The future of both Ireland and Woman's Suffrage is considerably brightened.[6]

If Hanna's bitterness was tempered at all by that last paragraph, there is no concrete evidence to prove it.

Since she and her husband had been so intellectually attuned, she must have known Francis's views on the occult. He had expressed them in a letter to Edward Martyn in 1913 when he was appealing to Martyn to attend a gathering in honor of Mr. and Mrs. Cousins, who were leaving Dublin. In it he said that, although he admired the Cousinses very much, this did not necessarily mean they were in absolute agreement. "For my own part," he wrote, "I have no intention of identifying myself with the theosophic and spiritualistic associations of Mr. and Mrs. Cousins."[7] Yet it would be only natural that Hanna, certainly during the early years after her husband's murder, should want to grasp at the possibility that, in truth, Francis was with her always. There are several indications that she might have believed this.

Hanna's good friend, Deborah Webb, had written her in June to say that a cousin had received "a little communication—the full name, I think, of F.S.S. and not much else." She wondered if Hanna might like to have a "sitting with him some time when there might be more chance of a good communication."[8] Hanna had agreed and the séance was held early in August. The result of this experiment is a document in Hanna's papers that professes to record a conversation involving Francis, Hanna, and Thomas H. Webb, Deborah's cousin.

According to the transcript, Thomas Webb received an answer in the affirmative when he asked the customary, "Is there someone here?" The voice said that he had come to speak to his wife directly and that she was Mrs. Sheehy-Skeffington. When asked if Hanna was "claire-audient," the reply was "Yes." "Don't stop cremation," the spirit instructed, when asked about the "mode of burial." (At this time Hanna was considerably upset by her father-in-law's action in having her husband's body removed from Portobello Barracks and buried in Glasnevin, in consecrated ground, without her consent.) Further questioning elicited the information that Francis would like cremation to take place if there was an opportunity, that he was glad to be free of his body, that he could see the people present in the room, and that he was at his wife's right hand. When asked if he saw her constantly, he said that he did. The spirit was then asked what had "struck" him most when he "passed over," and he replied: "Cheerfulness" and "great joy & peace." The sitting concluded with the spirit promising to come again.[9]

Urged by Gretta Cousins, Hanna was also in touch with a Dublin member of the Theosophical Society, a Mr. Leslie Pielon, whom she had given, as directed, one of Gretta's letters. He found it, he said, most interesting and saw no reason to doubt its validity. He knew Gretta very well, respected her "keen logical mind," and knew that she was tireless in her search for truth and abhorred self-deception. Testimony to the possibility of communicating with those who had died was now worldwide, he continued, and it seemed to depend to a great extent on the ability of those who "received." Since Gretta was highly experienced, he felt the accuracy of her messages would be almost a certainty, though he admitted that the content "must be coloured to a certain extent by the mental idiosyncrasies" of the medium.[10]

It should not be assumed that Gretta Cousins wrote only of her communication with Hanna's husband. This militant suffragette, who had been jailed in both London and Dublin and who had, in India, instituted all-women conferences, fought against forced marriages and premature motherhood, protested bills curbing Indian rights to free speech, and been elected the first woman magistrate in India, filled her letters with news of the role of women in India and of her work there. Interest in the occult was only one side of Gretta Cousins.

This was even more true of Hanna: her main purpose was to see that her husband's murderer was brought to justice and, at last, she achieved some measure of success. As Prime Minister Asquith had promised, early in June Captain Bowen-Colthurst faced a court-martial. The room in which it took place was in Richmond Barracks and all signs of its customary use had been removed. Large, high-ceilinged, square, with barred windows and a skylight the only sources of illumination, the room was filled to capacity. In addition to the military, some one hundred others attended, including a number of women. Admission was by ticket only. The officers, uniformed and rigid, and the other officials making up the court were seated around a square, green-baize-covered table, and immediately behind them on three sides sat relatives and others vitally concerned with the case. Hanna, naturally the center of attention, sat perfectly still, a pale figure of tragedy, tense and completely absorbed. Throughout the proceedings, J. B. Skeffington, her father-in-law, sat with her, as did her uncle, Father Eugene. For much of the time her sisters were with her as well.[11]

To the charge of murder of three persons—Francis Sheehy-Skeffington; Thomas Dickson, editor of a paper called the *Eye Opener*; and Patrick MacIntyre, editor of another paper, the *Searchlight*—Bowen-Colthurst pleaded not guilty. Called to testify were the arresting officer, the adjutant at Portobello Barracks, and officers who had witnessed the executions and the events leading up to them. The chaplain, who had seen the bodies in the mortuary, also testified. Counsel for the defense was to plead not guilty by reason of insanity.[12]

The brilliant and eloquent barrister, T. M. (Tim) Healy, M.P., with his pince-nez and rich Cork accent, followed the case for Hanna, undoubtedly at her father's urging, but as was usual at such proceedings, he did not intervene. In attempting to judge for himself the validity of the defense's plea of insanity, he took particular note of two points: Colthurst had become a "Bible convert in India" after having led a rather "wild life"; and in 1914, during the retreat from Mons, he had refused to withdraw and had instead ordered his men forward toward the advancing Germans. It was Tim Healy's impression that Colthurst was not "shamming madness."[13]

The extent of Hanna's suffering as she listened to the details of her husband's murder can only be imagined, but all accounts agree that only once during the proceedings did she lose her composure. A young second lieutenant, William Price Dobbyn, under questioning by the presiding officer, said that, upon hearing shots, he had gone out into the courtyard and had seen three bodies on the ground. It had seemed to him that one of them, whom he recognized as Sheehy-Skeffington, was still moving. He had gone into the orderly room, reported what he had seen, and asked what should be done. He was told to go out and shoot the man again and he testified that the order had been given by Bowen-Colthurst. "What did you do then?" the presiding officer asked. "I stood by four men of my guard, and I complied with the order," Dobbyn said.[14] It was then that Hanna turned ashen, cried out, and seemed on the point of collapse.

When, however, an officer of the Royal Army Medical Corps approached Father Eugene to ask if Hanna might like to leave the court, she answered for herself: "I will not leave this court except by force."[15]

It was always Hanna's firm conviction that the court-martial had been carefully orchestrated to allow for the verdict that was finally pronounced: Bowen-Colthurst was insane when he committed the murders. The testimony of Lieutenant Morris, the officer who had arrested Francis, for instance, made the point over and over that the accused had seemed extremely agitated and excited. He testified that on the afternoon of the executions Captain Colthurst had "made a very ridiculous set speech" in which he said that Sir Francis Vane was a Sinn Feiner and a pro-Boer. "He did not seem to be right in his head," Lieutenant Morris said, adding that Colthurst had also wanted Sir Francis Vane shot or, at the very least, banned from the barracks. The lieutenant went on to state that in his opinion Colthurst could not distinguish legal right from legal wrong.[16]

The finding of the court-martial was issued on 10 June. Bowen-Colthurst was found guilty of the murders of Sheehy-Skeffington, Thomas Dickson, and Patrick MacIntyre, but also found insane at the time he committed the acts. Upon receiving this finding, the king directed that Bowen-Colthurst "be detained in a criminal lunatic asylum during his Majesty's pleasure."[17] He was confined to Broadmoor, in England, an asylum for the criminally insane, and after some eighteen months (accounts differ) released. Not long after, he moved to Victoria, British Columbia, where he lived until his death in 1965, at the age of eighty.[18]

Was Bowen-Colthurst in fact insane? The answer of course turns on the troublesome, perhaps insoluble, problem of defining insanity with precision. The weight of the evidence, however, would seem to suggest that the finding of the court-martial had been just. The reasons Bowen-Colthurst cited for his action in a statement given to Major Rossborough at the latter's request seem totally illogical. He claimed that when he examined the documents found on the three prisoners he could see that the men were all "dangerous characters." This was patently untrue, since two of the men were British sympathizers and the most revolutionary document on Skeffington was his antilooting statement. Bowen-Colthurst also stated that his reason for requesting an armed guard of six men with loaded rifles was so that they could keep an eye on the prisoners; his reason for taking them into the courtyard was that the guardroom did not seem suitable for interrogation. Once in the yard, he had decided that there was a reasonable chance that they would try to escape and, since they were dangerous characters, he had called upon the guard to shoot them.[19] The courtyard was surrounded by a fourteen-foot-high wall, and it would have been absolutely impossible for any prisoner to escape. Either Bowen-Colthurst was an out-and-out liar or he was, indeed, unable to distinguish reality from illusion.

In regard to Bowen-Colthurst's condition, the testimony of two medical men at the court-martial is significant. One was a Dr. Parsons, physician to the Royal City of Dublin Hospital; the other a Dr. Leeper, who stated that he held a certificate for knowledge of mental diseases and that he was medical superintendent of St. Patrick's Hospital, Dublin. Dr. Parsons testifed that he had examined Bowen-Colthurst several years earlier when the latter had returned from the front, and had found him to be in a state of nervous exhaustion and unfit for duty. Any strain, the doctor felt, would have resulted in a complete breakdown, probably mental. He had last seen the accused, he continued, on the previous Friday and had found him excited, restless, and apparently unable to understand the gravity of the present charge. Bowen-Colthurst told him that on the morning of the executions, he had gone to bed at 3 A.M. and had read his Bible. One particular passage had impressed him: "And these my enemies which will not have me to rule over them, bring them forth and slay them." He had interpreted this as a command to slay those men who would not accept His Majesty's rule. When Dr. Parsons was asked what the state of the prisoner's mind was at the time of the murders, he replied that it was his opinion that the accused's "condition was far from normal, and that he was unbalanced." He did not feel that Bowen-Colthurst could be considered responsible for his actions since manifestations of remorse were not present as they would be in a sane person. Clearly the man felt that he had done the right thing. Dr. Leeper's testimony was virtually the same. In fact, he felt that the accused "was on the eve of a complete breakdown."[20]

Another more recent opinion as to Bowen-Colthurst's sanity appeared in a 1981 article by Dr. W. D. Henry, "The Case of Captain Colthurst," published in the British medical journal, the *Practitioner*. Dr. Henry, a psychiatrist, makes it clear that he was unable to examine the Home Office papers on the case since they are not open for inspection for one hundred years from the date of the court-martial. But, based on public documents and particularly the testimony of Lieutenant Morris (in which Morris had said that Colthurst made a speech calling Sir Francis Vane a Sinn Feiner and a pro-Boer and saying that he should be barred from the barracks or shot), Dr. Henry draws this clinical picture: "Captain Colthurst had a personality disorder of the schizoid type, a well recognized entity in psychiatry. The person with a schizoid personality does not actually suffer from schizophrenia, the most serious of the psychiatric illnesses, but some of the more marked attributes resemble symptoms of schizophrenia in a mild, modified way."[21]

Dr. Henry describes this schizoid type as cold, unfeeling, introverted, and isolated. His behavior would often be eccentric and his ideas bizarre. He might be considered merely eccentric but, under stress, occasionally could develop "an acute psychotic state." Colthurst's "acute psychosis," the psychiatrist wrote, "took a form not unlike paranoid schizophrenia with delusions which caused him to see his innocent victims as dangerous rebels who had to be destroyed, and himself, in a rather grandiose way, as the duty-bound agent of God and the King who must destroy them." Dr. Henry expresses surprise, as did many laymen at the time, at the rapidity with which Bowen-Colthurst was released from Broadmoor. It may have been, he speculates, because people with this disorder recover rapidly when stress is removed.[22]

As soon as the proceedings were over, Hanna, dissatisfied with both the court-martial and the verdict, bombarded the press and members of the House of Commons with letters in an attempt to have a full-scale inquiry instituted. The mood of Dublin was with her, shaped by revulsion over the murder of Sheehy-Skeffington and the execution of the leaders of the Rising, and her appeal for an inquiry into her husband's murder was receiving a favorable response from many sources. A letter from Philip Snowden, chairman of the Independent Labour Party and at that time a member of the House of Commons, was typical. He extended sympathy on behalf of his wife and himself, said he was "distressed beyond measure," and offered to help in any way he could to have the matter cleared up and the guilty punished. "Let us hope that his murder has watered the soil of liberty," he wrote. Another member of the Labour Party, W. C. Anderson, stood ready to do anything in his power to get a fair inquiry. Even though he thought the matter would be raised by some of the Irish members of Parliament, he intended to raise it personally. Her husband's murder, he assured her, had been received "with horror and indignation" by the entire labor movement and especially by those who were well acquainted with him and his work.[23]

Yet, even with the changing climate in Ireland and the support she was receiving from politicians and close friends, Hanna saw no sign that she was accomplishing her mission. Time was passing and the government seemed to be no closer to launching a full-scale investigation. She decided next to address an open letter to *New Ireland*, bringing her story up to date. Early in May, she stated, Mr. Asquith had promised John Dillon that a full public inquiry would be held, but that promise had not been kept. Instead a secret inquiry was made, followed by a court-martial to which attendance was limited and at which she was not permitted legal representation. The prime minister had excused his failure to keep his word by saying that he could do nothing until the court-martial was over. Since its conclusion he had failed to respond to any inquiries into the matter.[24]

The Pethick-Lawrences, in constant correspondence with Hanna, urged her to come to London. She would accomplish nothing without personal contact, in their opinion, and others in the suffragist movement made the same point. Finally, early in July, Hanna came to the conclusion that they were right. Once there, she pestered editors and any member of Parliament who would consent to see her. As usual, her personal contacts met with success and, also as usual, she did not waste a moment. On 19 July, she was summoned to meet with Mr. Asquith.

Because she wanted to be sure she had a witness, Hanna persuaded Muriel Matters, a prominent suffragist, to accompany her. Asquith's secretary was present, and the four sat at a green-baize table upon which Asquith kept tapping his fingers nervously. Not once, she said, did he look directly at her. He expressed regret that he was not going to be able to keep his pledge to conduct a full inquiry but said that he was sure such a sworn hearing would be refused by the House. He then asked if she would "be satisfied with an inadequate inquiry," since it was the best he could do. She replied that she would not, of course, be satisfied with any inquiry that he told her in advance would be "inadequate" but that she assumed she would have to accept it. He then, according to Hanna, brought up compensation and assured her that it would be "adequate and even generous." She was not unprepared for this since she had already been approached unofficially with indirect proposals of this nature. The only acceptable compensation, she told him, was the fulfillment of his promise to hold a full public inquiry into her husband's murder.[25]

One of those who found her attitude incomprehensible was J. B. Skeffington. He strongly urged her to accept compensation and, in his customary methodical fashion, listed nine points, headed "Reason for Compensation," setting forth his position. He argued that compensation was "an ancient Irish means of reparation;" that to view it as "Blood money" was an error since the term "means payment to Traitor who be-trays or Assassin who slays the victim;" and that if she personally did not want the money it could be used to support projects her husband had be-lieved in or to establish a scholarship in his memory. Several of his other points were concerned with Owen's future and the possibility that she might die. To one he added: "I too may not live long, especially as my health has suffered severely from this atrocious murder." He urged her to accept a lump sum rather than a pension.[26] Hanna, however, was ada-mant. She resisted J. B.'s pressure and that of all others, and eventually Asquith acquiesced. By early August Hanna knew that, though still un-scheduled, a full-scale inquiry would take place.

Exhausted by the ordeal of the court-martial and her fight for a full inquiry, Hanna nonetheless took time to intervene in the case of Sir Roger Casement, an Ulsterman who had actually attempted to secure a post-ponement of the Rising. He was arrested, accused of being a paid German agent, tried, convicted of treason, and sentenced to death; this caused ha-tred of British rule and contempt for the Parliamentary Party to reach its peak among the people of Ireland. In a letter to the prime minister, plead-ing for mercy for Casement, Hanna said:

> As the wife of one whose life was taken by the Military wrongfully, and without trial, during the recent rising, and as the victim of many wrongs yet unredressed, I feel that I have the right to approach you to ask you to prevent any further shedding of the blood of my country-men by sparing the life of Sir Roger Casement, now under sentence of death.
>
> Though he may be deemed guilty technically under British law, I hope you will exercise wisdom and humanity by seeing that in his case, at least, the extreme penalty is not extracted. In expressing this wish I am conscious that I am speaking in the name of my mur-dered husband, who abhorred the taking of life under all circum-stances, and that I am voicing the sentiments of the majority of the Irish people.[27]

The intense strain on Hanna was taking its toll, however. In mid-August her sister Kathleen wrote to express her concern. "What you say about your heart worries me," she said. Her husband, Cruise O'Brien, thought it was "probably muscular strain," but Kathleen suggested that she consult her doctor. She added: "I know, old girl, that you don't care anything for life just now and that you long to be rid of it all; but then we others are selfish and we don't want to lose you too."[28] She misjudged her—Hanna wanted very much to live. She had decided that, once the inquiry was out of the way, she would take her story to the United States. Robert Lynd, a journalist and friend of the Sheehy-Skeffingtons, had once called Francis "an interrupter of the somnolent."[29] It was a role that Hanna was ready and eager to assume.

The full inquiry finally began on 23 August but beforehand there had been much correspondence and many consultations with Hanna's solicitor, Henry Lemass, with potential witnesses, and with Tim Healy, who was to serve as her counsel. The latter was far from optimistic about the depth of the hearing but, he wrote Hanna, they could only do their best. His 1929 book, *Letters and Leaders of My Day*, however, indicates that on the whole he was satisfied with the proceedings and the results. He felt that Sir John Simon, who presided over the inquiry, served admirably and, though the military was visibly nervous about what additional scandals might be uncovered, held firm in his rulings.[30]

Once more Hanna had to listen to the tragic details of her husband's execution. Pictures appearing in the newspapers show that, as before, her sisters were at her side. As she had previously, she received support from an extraordinary number of individuals, before, after, and during the inquiry. One letter, which she received in August, she found particularly significant. It was from the writer, St. John Ervine, who had seen her husband on both Easter Sunday and Tuesday. He was able to state categorically, therefore, that Francis Sheehy-Sheffington had been opposed to the Rising. Writing her from his home in East Devonshire, Ervine said that he would not be able to attend the inquiry, as much as he wanted to, because he was going into the army in October and had to finish a novel before doing so. He planned to join an Irish regiment for, after watching "the cheering Cocknies outside the jail" when Roger Casement was being hanged, he could not bear to be with Englishmen. One thing that he found himself unable to comprehend or to accept was why none of the other officers, knowing that Bowen-Colthurst was unstable, had prevented him from carrying out the executions.[31]

Had St. John Ervine been able to attend the inquiry, he might have understood the action of the other officers to a certain extent. The testimony showed that they were in a state of complete shock at the rapidity with which the executions were carried out. One member of the firing squad testified that when he entered the courtyard the three men were already lined up against the wall. Bowen-Colthurst's command to load and fire came immediately. After firing and seeing the men fall, he left the courtyard. As he did, he saw Lieutenant Dobbyn go in, put his hand to his head, and say "Oh, my God!" A few minutes later, the witness said, four men were called back, he being one of them, and were told to fire once more "at a certain man." He had had just time enough to clean his rifle.[32]

All through the hearing, Hanna was conscious of the reluctance of the military to reveal details. Some thirty years later she wrote that what had shocked her more than anything about her husband's death and its aftermath was "the automatic and tireless efforts on the part of the entire official machinery, both military and political, to prevent the truth being made public."[33]

On the third day of the hearing, Hanna was called to testify. Stating first that, so far as she knew, her husband had belonged to no "dangerous society" and that he had been a strong pacifist even during their college days, Hanna was compelled to relive Easter Week: the anxious days that followed the last meeting with her husband, the moment when she received the news of his murder, the trip to Portobello Barracks to try to learn details and to recover his body, and the trauma and degradation of the raid on their home. Many of her possessions had never been returned to her, she told the court, and only after Sir Francis Vane's intervention had she been given her husband's ring. There was much, also, that she still did not know; for example, had a doctor seen her husband after his execution?[34]

Further evidence was brought forth at the inquiry that, although it did not directly involve Bowen-Colthurst, strengthened Hanna's case against the military. A second raid on Hanna's home had taken place on the Monday following the first and this was duly recorded in the commission's report. Neither Hanna nor her son had been home at the time— only a temporary maid servant. It appeared that Hanna's regular maid had been so terrified by the first raid that she had left. The temporary maid had been arrested, taken to the Rathmines police station, and held until the following Saturday, when Hanna's sisters had been instrumental in having her released.[35]

The Simon Commission's report, issued on 29 September, had brought out a great deal of evidence beyond that produced at the court-martial and the tone throughout had been conciliatory toward the families and the friends of the victims. Because Bowen-Colthurst was declared insane earlier, however, he was not permitted to testify and to some it seemed that the inquiry was not broad enough and that it dealt with the "tragedy in the kid glove manner."[36] Sir Francis Vane was one of those who were dissatisfied. Writing to Hanna some weeks later, he told her that he believed the report suffered from the narrowness of its frame of reference and that it should have stressed the obvious fact that the Castle was well aware of the details of the tragedy little more than an hour after it happened. He went on to say that he was made "positively ill" by the travesty of placing most of the blame on one officer and whitewashing others. The officer, for example, who had seen to it that the wall against which her husband was shot was repaired and who had given Bowen-Colthurst a promotion and allowed him to conduct a second raid on Hanna's house was "whitewashed" by the commissioners. He found the hypocrisy of the officials "loathsome" though he was ready to grant that the report opened the way for a more complete investigation.[37] Tim Healy saw it as accomplishing rather more than this. He felt that, after the Sheehy-Skeffington disclosures, there would be very little respect for martial law or for decisions made by soldiers.[38]

Hanna, like Sir Francis, saw the inquiry as not entirely satisfactory. It seemed to her that it did, however, establish the truth of some important points: Bowen-Colthurst had been promoted after her husband's murder; there had been no disciplinary measures taken against the other officers involved; Sir Francis Vane, because of his interference in the case, had been dismissed; and the raids on her home had been made in an effort to incriminate her dead husband after the fact by finding some evidence that would help to justify his murder.[39]

Before, during, and after the inquiry, Hanna harassed the military authorities. She had decided that, although it would cause her great pain, she wanted to visit the guardroom at Portobello Barracks. Her request had been granted with the assurance that she would be given privacy during her visit. Earlier she had approached Dublin Castle, accompanied by Sir Francis Vane, to attempt to have returned to her those articles taken from her home during the Friday evening raid. This she succeeded in doing while the court-martial was in progress. One of the bundles contained Francis's jacket, with bullet holes in the back—probably made during the second volley when he was lying on the ground. Much of the material was in filthy condition, and many items were never returned.[40]

One direct result of Hanna's badgering of the authorities was further harassment by Dublin Castle. Some months after she took rooms at 43 Moyne Road, Ranelagh, a police constable came to see her landlady, produced a book of rules, and asked her if she realized that she had to register her lodgers. Informing him that she always had, she showed him the necessary forms, two of which had been filled out by Hanna for herself and Owen. Sensing his antagonism, the landlady said that if he needed any further information he could obtain it from Mrs. Sheehy-Skeffington's father, David Sheehy, M.P. She was the person liable, he informed her.[41]

Hanna's landlady was worried and that evening went to the police barracks to report the incident. Four days later, she was visited once more by the police, who this time asked to see Hanna. Told that she was not there, they asked if she had any furniture or if she had taken any luggage with her, and added that they were to be informed at once when she returned.[42] When Hanna heard the landlady's story, she wrote immediately to Mr. Dillon, who replied that he would have the matter debated in the House of Commons. On 26 October, T. P. O'Connor, M.P., at Dillon's request, put the following question to the House:

> To ask the Chief Secretary to the Lord Lieutenant of Ireland, whether it is with his consent and sanction that Mrs. Sheehy-Skeffington has been subjected to police espionage and persecution since the murder of her husband; whether recently, when Mrs. Skeffington was absent from home on a short holiday, her lodgings were visited by detectives, who cross-examined her landlady and threatened her with penalties for not knowing and revealing Mrs. Skeffington's address; whether the police officer who directed these operations was Sergeant M'Gahey, who is in charge of the aliens department; and whether it is proposed to continue this system of persecution.[43]

Before the question was introduced, Hanna had been informed by the chief commissioner of police that the "visits" to her home had been made under the Aliens' Restriction Act. Her landlady had not complied with its provisions, he wrote, and when questioned he said that she was acting under advice given her by "others." After the question was put, however, the same man informed Hanna that the "visits" had been made without the permission of the authorities and that no instructions had been given to inquire into the movements of her or her family.[44]

It had taken Hanna little more than a fortnight from the time her landlady was first approached to have her situation aired in the House of Commons. Her success in having the findings of the Simon Commission published was almost as rapid. In the interest of giving further publicity to her husband's execution, she had approached the prime minister but her request for publication of the findings had been refused. By early November, though, a letter from 10 Downing Street stated that the matter was being reconsidered and by the end of November she was informed that arrangements were being made for publication.[45]

She was much less successful in dealing with her father-in-law. She had been shocked at the time of the court-martial to learn that, without her permission or her knowledge, J. B. had had her husband's body exhumed and buried in Glasnevin. Now, early in November, she was informed by her solicitor, Henry Lemass, that he had received a letter from the secretary of the Rebellion (Victims) Committee stating that J. B. had entered a claim for compensation on behalf of his grandson. Her solicitor had duly informed the secretary that Mr. Skeffington's application had been made without her sanction and "in direct opposition" to her wishes.[46]

It could not have been easy for Hanna to abide by her resolution. Late in August, at about the time of the full inquiry, her husband's will was probated, his estate consisting of only £550. Needless to say, the sum could do very little toward sustaining mother and son. There would be her teaching salary: the Technical Education Committee had reappointed her for the next term to teach afternoon classes in French and German at Rutland Square and evening classes at Kevin Street school with a salary slightly higher than previously. Other than that, however, there would be no steady income. She was, nevertheless, firm in her refusal to accept any compensation from the British and neither J. B.'s pleas nor his clandestine efforts moved her.

At Hanna's request, Henry Lemass wrote the prime minister reiterating her stand in order to avoid any misapprehension. His client, he said, had never had any idea of accepting compensation and her determination had been further strengthened by additional facts that were coming to light. Though friends and legal counsel had urged her to consider compensation at least for her seven-year-old son, she had decided to accept no money for him either.[47] It was a decision reached after weighing all the arguments carefully and one made with complete confidence that she was doing Owen no wrong. She was just as confident her decision was one her husband, equally principled, would have applauded.

A Journey Alone

EFORE the terrible year ended, Hanna was on her way to the United States to lecture. Some had advised delay because of her health, the attitude of the government, Owen's extreme youth, and her commitment to the *Irish Citizen*. Her own instinct, however, was to move quickly as she had with the court-martial and the full inquiry. In making her decision, she was abetted by her husband's good friend J. F. Byrne (Cranly in *A Portrait of the Artist*), then living in the New York City area and working for the *Wall Street Journal*. In mid-October he wrote Hanna that he had consulted with a number of people on the subject and it was their feeling and his that she should come to the States without delay. His wife Alice added: "So hurry up and don't disappoint us."[1] Hanna didn't.

She had two major objectives in mind when she set out: to draw attention to the brutality that she believed the British were employing in order to suppress opposition in Ireland to conscription as well as to the war; and, equally important to her, to make it clear that Francis's death was not brought about simply by the deed of an insane soldier but "deliberately planned" by Dublin Castle, a point of doubtful validity.[2] These were objectives of such moral urgency that she had refused to be deterred when the British denied her application for a passport. Though informed, authoritatively, that there was a possibility of obtaining one if she agreed not to discuss the war while in the United States, she would make no such promise, choosing instead to circumvent the government's effort to prevent her from traveling or speaking out. Upon arrival in New York, she declined to say just how she had managed to make the journey undetected, but a number of years later she revealed that, after thoroughly studying the life of a Scotswoman who had recently become an American citizen, she had assumed her name and identity and had played the role with confidence.[3]

Hanna's lecture tour was arranged through the Friends of Irish Freedom, a New York-based Irish-American organization formed in March 1916 and dedicated to bringing about national independence for Ireland. Her first major lecture was in Carnegie Hall on 6 January 1917 and was, as the flyer circumspectly read, "arranged by a Committee of friends." The meeting was chaired by Bainbridge Colby, the eminent lawyer who, with Theodore Roosevelt, had left the Republican party in 1912 and founded the National Progressive party. Writers Padraic Colum and his wife Mary were on the committee as were such other prominent Irish Americans as John D. Moore, Thomas H. Kelly, W. Bourke Cockran, Robert Ford, Anna M. Sloan, and Hanna's friend J. F. Byrne.

Interest in the tense situation in Ireland was high just then. An Irish fair was in progress in Madison Square Garden when she arrived and she found posters announcing the execution of James Connolly tacked up all around the city. Press coverage was therefore extensive both before and after her lecture. Of course, the newspapers had a fine story—young widow, seven-year-old son, husband cruelly murdered. In publicizing the meeting, the *Gaelic American* went so far as to label it the "duty" of all Irishmen—and women—in the New York area to accept personal responsibility for its success.[4]

The Carnegie Hall lecture was a fine beginning for Hanna's tour. Addressing a packed hall, she assured her audience that Ireland's desire for freedom would never be crushed. "Irishmen will die at home rather than be conscripted to fight for England," she said, "and when the day of settlement comes—may it be soon—Ireland will have proved her right to a place among the nations."[5]

There was, nevertheless, some criticism of the advisability of a tour such as Hanna was to make. By April 1917 the United States had entered the war and, even before that, a patriotic fervor had spread throughout the land. The *Boston Herald* was not alone when, shortly after she arrived in New York, it published an article condemning those who, in the paper's opinion, chose to "exploit" Hanna. Furthermore, her statement that her husband's death had been inspired by Dublin Castle seemed to be without proof. Her friends would be well advised to let her try to forget the tragedy, the paper said.[6]

The second stop on Hanna's itinerary was Boston. She must have been eager to explore the city, for scarcely a year had gone by since her husband, on lecture tour in the United States, had written her about it in glowing terms. Advance publicity was excellent and over three hundred people crowded stately Faneuil Hall to hear her, some coming as early as 3 P.M. and waiting four hours until the doors opened. The controversial Mayor Curley introduced Hanna, slender, pale, dressed in a black gown with white lace at the throat. Once more she told her story, quietly and calmly. As she talked, it seemed to one reporter that the audience was more moved than the speaker. If they had expected "a tear-stained, broken-voiced messenger from the other side," they were disappointed.[7] In response to a plea by Mayor Curley before the meeting closed, a substantial sum of money was collected.

If the newspaper accounts are accurate, Hanna, as she sometimes did, was making many statements that were without factual basis. She was asserting that Germany was going to win the war, and, at one point, was reported to have remarked that people were beginning to realize Englishmen were "hopeless cowards."[8] Apparently, she also said that conscription and another massacre were in store for Ireland in the near future and that "the gaunt figure of famine" would soon be menacing the countryside.[9] This was neither the first nor the last time that Hanna, consciously or unconsciously, sacrificed accuracy for effect.

Lecture tours seem designed to test the endurance of lecturers and Hanna's was no exception. From mid-March to mid-April alone, she spoke in Boston, Roxbury, and Fall River in Massachusetts; in Palm Garden, Port Chester, Ascension Church, Niagara Falls, and Buffalo in New York State; in Youngstown and Cincinnati in Ohio; in Milwaukee, Wisconsin; and in St. Louis, Missouri. By the time she spoke in Buffalo early in April, she was showing signs of inner tension and a growing weariness. One press report mentioned that although her delivery was simple and devoid of mannerisms, she did have a nervous habit of twisting her wedding ring and that her "mouth, deeply lined from the nose, did not relax in laughter" during the entire evening.[10]

The themes of Hanna's speeches were unvarying. She talked of British militarism in Ireland—the attempts to recruit or to impose conscription—and of the events that transpired during Easter Week. She did not, in those speeches, seem to take into consideration that she was in a country now at war on the side of Britain and that she was in that country illegally. She was well aware of it, however. As a consequence, correspondence preserved from this period has dates, places, and very often names torn off. Friends and relatives who wrote from Ireland addressed her in

various ways but never by her own name. Her father was the most inge-
nious, often addressing his letters to "Mrs. Mary Hanna," beginning them
"My dear Mrs. Hanna" or "Dear Mary," and signing them simply "David
Sheehy."

By the spring of 1917, it became evident to Hanna that it was no
longer advisable to have Owen with her. Her time was completely filled
by speaking engagements, writing projects, and constant travel. Owen,
she felt, needed a more stable environment and also to continue his studies. Accordingly, in the spring of 1917, she sent him to stay with Lydia
Coonley Ward at Hillside Farms, Wyoming, New York. Mrs. Ward was
delighted with him and found him no bother at all though she was convinced that he found school work distasteful.[11] Owen himself confirmed
her opinion in a letter to his mother. "I dont Like School a Bit," he said,
with no regard to rules of punctuation or capitalization.[12]

Friends had been talking with Hanna about a school in Santa Bar-
bara, California, called Boyland which, in the fall of 1917, was to become
a Montessori Method school. This seemed an intelligent solution for her
problem and Owen's as well and in September she enrolled him there.
It was a wise choice. From California friends who visited him, Hanna
learned that the school was excellent and that Owen was doing well and
making friends. From his teachers, she learned that he was "having the
time of his life" but that he did not write well and was sensitive about it.[13]
His letters to his mother, bristling with misspellings, reveal that the problem was not exaggerated. Though for Hanna separation from her seven-
year-old son must have been painful, it was nevertheless necessary for his
sake and for hers.

With the United States now in the war, there were attempts to censor Hanna's speeches. Plans were underway for a Dallas, Texas, appearance when a William J. Moroney wrote Hanna offering to assist with arrangements if she would not speak on politics but confine herself to raising
funds for the Irish Relief Fund. He was not, however, willing to have
Irish independence made a condition for the cooperation of the United
States with Great Britain and her allies. He added, graciously, that he and
his family would be delighted to offer hospitality to Hanna and her son
while she was in Dallas.[14] Exactly what Hanna replied is not known but
its gist can be inferred from Mr. Moroney's next letter, some two weeks
later. "I am opposed," he wrote, "to any agitation now calculated to divert
attention here from our principal business, or to impair the co-operation of
the American and British governments in prosecuting the war. . . . " He

added, "Please forget my offer of hospitality, which appears to have been misinterpreted."[15] Arrangements had been made for Hanna to speak at the Marlborough School in Los Angeles but this also met with opposition. A letter from the principal informed her that she would not be welcome.[16] Hanna's writings suffered from censorship as well. She had submitted an article to the *Nation* that its publisher, Oswald Garrison Villard, liked but felt he had to reject because of the "present mad temper of the people." Now that the country had entered the war, he said, his magazine had been flooded with abuse.[17]

Hanna was successful, however, in having her *British Militarism as I Have Known It* published. A digest of the speeches she was giving in the United States, it received wide circulation and was apparently very well received since, before the end of 1918, it was reissued as part of a pamphlet called *Democracy in Ireland Since 1913*. This collection included "A Forgotten Small Nationality," by Francis Sheehy-Skeffington; the verbatim report of the Simon Commission inquiring into her husband's murder; *British Militarism as I Have Known It*; and a Postscriptum by Hanna, dated 2 April 1918, which was headed "The Release of Sheehy Skeffington's Murderer."[18]

Only a year after Hanna's arrival in the States, news began to reach her of a campaign to have Bowen-Colthurst released from Broadmoor. A letter in the *Times* signed "M.D." protested the cruelty and injustice of trying a "fine soldier and loyal servant of the Crown" as a "common murderer" and passing sentence on him as a "criminal lunatic." He should have been sent, the writer argued, to some place where his war-shattered nerves could mend.[19] The *Spectator* also appealed for the release of Bowen-Colthurst and for the absolution of Dublin Castle from all blame. The *Irish News* countered with the point that it was carrying Irish chivalry too far to give amnesty to a man who had "murdered . . . good Irishmen in cold blood." His detention in Broadmoor made for a safer community, the paper contended, and they wished that he had "the congenial company of the other ornaments of British rule whom the 'Spectator' is so anxious to keep in power in Dublin Castle."[20] There seemed to be no lack of rhetoric on either side.

While Hanna was still in the United States, Bowen-Colthurst was released to a private hospital. Though Hanna had always considered him simply "a tool and a scapegoat of the higher authorities" and had never desired that his life be taken in retaliation for his crime, she did consider it significant that his release should coincide "with the renewed attempts on the part of the authorities to stir up trouble in Ireland." It seemed to her that, with the country now under martial law, his release would encourage other bloodthirsty officers to feel that they would be granted immunity for their deeds.[21] Hanna had little time to brood about Bowen-Colthurst, however. In retrospect, she could be satisfied with what she had accomplished during some nineteen months in the United States. Of all those who had come over from Ireland in the hope of galvanizing American support for Irish freedom during that period—Nora Connolly, Liam Mellows, Padraic Colum, and others—she was perhaps the most effective. Her lectures before civic groups, university students, peace groups, socialists, suffragists, and Irish-American societies were heavily attended and, for the most part, well and favorably publicized. Also, her health was better than ever and, high on the list of things to be thankful for, Owen was well and happy at Boyland. She was beginning to think in terms of going home, but first there was to be a meeting with President Wilson.

Early in January Hanna had received a petition from the Irishwomen's Council of Cumann na mBan with the request that she deliver it personally to President Wilson. It must have been smuggled over, for it could not conceivably have been approved by the censor. The petition appealed to the president and to Congress on the basis of the administration's open-mindedness regarding women's rights and the president's recognition of the justice of Ireland's request for political freedom. Because the United States had expressed its desire for a war settlement that would protect the rights of small nations, the petition asked the government to call for political independence for Ireland—for an Irish republic. Such a republic, it stated, would give women full recognition. The petition was signed on behalf of Cumann na mBan by all the members of its council, including Constance de Markievicz, Kathleen Clarke, and Jennie Wyse-Power.[22]

Hanna, although feeling it was presumptuous to request an interview with the busy president, nevertheless did so. With the assistance of intermediaries, her request was granted and, on 11 January 1918, accompanied by a delegation, she called on President Wilson. The delegates came from Massachusetts, Connecticut, New Jersey, and New York and, according to a list that Hanna drew up and preserved, they were thirty-six strong, with Nora Connolly and Padraic Colum among them. The actual interview, however, had to be private and off the record.

It seemed highly significant to Hanna that the president was willing to grant an interview to someone whose Sinn Fein connection was well-known and to accept a document not passed by the British censor. She interpreted this to mean that he had been given hope, if not a definite pledge, that the Irish question would be satisfactorily settled. Finding him very courteous and eager to acknowledge his Irish blood, she felt he was genuinely interested in the petition.[23]

Hanna stayed on in Washington after her interview with President Wilson to further plead Ireland's cause with senators and congressmen, and was received everywhere with a friendliness that she termed "more democratic and kindlier than the Tory clubdom of the British House of Commons." She was delighted also with what seemed to her a much more liberal attitude toward women on the part of the American lawmakers. The whole experience she found heartening.[24]

Hanna had hoped to leave the United States as early as March 1918, but there were many delays. With the Washington meeting out of the way, she went to California for Owen and, while in that area, spoke in San Francisco on behalf of Tom Mooney, the Irish-American labor agitator, who had been involved in bomb killings during a San Francisco Preparedness Parade in 1916 and sentenced to death. A grateful secretary of the International Workers' Defense League, involved in the Mooney defense, urged her, upon her return to Ireland, to "convey our gratitude to the Irish people for their noble sacrifice in missing you in their hour of trouble, so that you might raise your voice in other lands for the cause of freedom."[25]

There were those, however, who would have preferred to have her raise her voice somewhere else. One was W. C. Moore, a Wall Street market expert. In a "Wall Street Man's Letter to Mrs. Skeffington," which appeared in the *Evening Call*, he accused Hanna of attempting to "stir up a rebellion" in the States as she and "other traitors" had done in Ireland. He did not know whether she was "an ignorant fanatic" or whether she had been hired by "Bill the Kaiser," but he did know that she was not welcome in the United States. In fact, he did not think that she would be welcome in any country. "If such creatures as you and those that you associate with do not cease your activities," he wrote, "the chances are the good people will take you in hand and string you and the others of your ilk to a lamppost."[26]

Returning from California, Hanna filled various speaking engagements in New Jersey, New York, and Rhode Island. There should be no slackening in the Irish-American's fight for Ireland's freedom, she said, and she attacked those she called "near-Irish" who felt that justice for Ireland was treason to the United States. "If that is so," she said, "& if all who lend an ear to us are traitors then Pres. Wilson must be one for he has received our appeal."[27]

On 27 June she was finally on her way home. Much had happened during her absence. For one thing, she was returning to a vastly different family situation. Almost a year earlier, on 15 July 1917, her uncle Eugene had died. Hanna's father had written her that death had come unexpectedly though "he had been growing weak for some months, physically and mentally."[28] The family realized that it was Hanna who would miss Uncle Eugene the most. An undated letter, from which the signature had been torn but which was apparently written by Margaret, mentioned how much he had loved Hanna and how proud he had been of her always, adding that he had been speaking of her at the very end. Her mother had died also. Bessie and David Sheehy had been living with Margaret Culhane for some time and, in January 1918, Bessie had died after a relatively short illness. The family had been quite unprepared for the void her death left and David, especially, seemed unable to cope. His daughters were urging him to try "London and politics as a tonic." During the last months of her life, Bessie had talked a great deal about Hanna and worried about her; while longing for her return she was apprehensive about submarines and other dangers.[29] Not all the changes in the family were sad, however. Kathleen Sheehy O'Brien had had a baby in November— Conor Cruise. Mary Kettle had written Hanna that he was developing "from 'infant' to 'Baby' & is worshipped in every stage," and Hanna was looking forward to seeing him.[30]

She was returning to a vastly different situation in the country as well. Shortly before she left Ireland many of those who had been jailed after the Rising had been released and shortly after her departure the others had been allowed to return home. The principal reason for this was that the United States had entered the war and pressure was being put upon the British to take some action with regard to Ireland's troubled situation. One of the released prisoners, in fact the only senior officer of the Rising who had not been executed, had returned home to be elected a member of Parliament for East Clare. This was the American-born Eamon de Valera, who before the Rising had simply been a mathematics teacher and unknown nationally. A tall, thin man, with sallow complexion and somber look, de Valera was to play an important part in Hanna's life as well as in the life of the country.

Ireland had never been so united against conscription. Even the Roman Catholic hierarchy were supporting the anticonscription efforts.

Some months before Hanna's return, Lloyd George had, with his Military Service Bill, given the government the power to impose conscription on Ireland whenever the need was felt. At this move, the Irish members had walked out of Westminster, returned to Dublin, and united with other anticonscription forces from every part of the country except Ulster. A conference was then held at the Mansion House at which a pledge (drawn up by de Valera) to resist conscription by any available and effective means received unanimous approval. A National Defence Fund was set up; committees were formed in each parish to coordinate activities; plans were made to set the facts before the president of the United States; and a twenty-four-hour strike, which paralyzed most of the country, was called by the Irish Trades Union Congress.

Naturally, the government, sensing what amounted to a full-scale rebellion in progress, retaliated. Lord French, a military man, was appointed as lord lieutenant, and by the time Hanna reached Dublin practically the entire leadership of Sinn Fein and of the Volunteers had been jailed, meetings of those organizations and of the Gaelic League had been declared illegal, and no public gatherings were permitted without police protection. These moves, the *Manchester Guardian* felt, would result in an Ireland "more ungovernable except by main force, more exasperated in feeling, more alienated than any with which this country has had to deal since the Rebellion of 1798."[31]

Despite all obstacles, however, the Irish Women's Franchise League and the *Irish Citizen* had not slackened in their efforts to obtain the vote, nor had they lessened their pressure upon the government to better conditions for women in every area. At last, in January 1918, there was a genuine breakthrough: the British government granted the vote to women over thirty—Irishwomen included—who were householders, wives of householders, occupiers of property of five pounds or more annual value, or university graduates. There had been a great deal of controversy over even this limited privilege. The question had been raised, with bitter humor, as to whether it was expected that when women reached thirty they would be ashamed to admit their age, or were married and, therefore, harmless. Meg Connery, speaking for the Irish Women's Franchise League, found the limited vote "neither just nor generous nor democratic" and felt there was no need to be grateful for it.[32] Yet Hanna and those colleagues who were eligible were looking forward eagerly to voting at last.

A December 1918 editorial in the *Irish Citizen*, by then once more under Hanna's editorship, stated triumphantly: "The enthusiasm for the votes of women voters continues unabated; all political parties humbly sue for women's favour and the brief memories of politicians are quite touching. Sir Edward Carson leads the way—we remember how two Dublin women who had the temerity to ask Sir Edward questions about votes in 1913 were treated—but times have changed." All along the line, the change in attitude was remarkable. "Had it been earlier, it had been kind," said the editor. [33]

Prison and Platform

ARLY IN JULY 1918, Hanna arrived in Liverpool, looking and feeling stronger than ever. British authorities in New York City had granted her a passport and had even agreed, after receiving a signed pledge that she had nothing objectionable in her possession, to allow her to take with her Owen's school books as well as novels for shipboard reading.[1] As it turned out, Liverpool was as far as she and her son would get for, upon landing, she was informed that she could not go on to Dublin. Taking up residence with Owen at the Bee Hotel in Liverpool, Hanna arranged for her sister Kathleen to come and take Owen back to Dublin, since the detention order did not apply to him. She then wrote to John Dillon, M.P., asking him to intervene on her behalf.[2]

Dillon's reply offered no solace and did nothing to moderate her fury. The Defence of the Realm Act, he pointed out, allowed the government to do as it pleased. Even if he were successful in securing permission for her to return to Ireland, she would, in his opinion, be unable to engage in antiwar activities or assume the editorship of the *Irish Citizen* without instant deportation. In reply to her request that he put the matter before the House of Commons, he argued that covert pressure should be applied first. "If that failed," he wrote, "it might then be some satisfaction to expose your treatment in the House, but I have not the slightest doubt that a question in the House would be met by an emphatic refusal such as would tie the hands of the Government against any further representations.[3] Other Irish members of Parliament did not agree with Dillon's position. Shortly after this letter was written, two members introduced questions asking the chief secretary to the lord lieutenant of Ireland whether it had been by his order that Hanna had been prohibited from returning to Ireland and whether he would now allow her and her nine-year-old son to return home.[4]

As arranged, Kathleen came to Liverpool to take Owen home, freeing his mother to make her own plans. Hanna was back in Dublin by the beginning of August, though the government detention order had not been rescinded. Her return was met with a great deal of publicity because it was "mysterious and passportless and baffled the Castle and the secret service." "They naturally hate to be fooled," she said.[5]

The Dublin Hanna came back to, unlike Liverpool, was undamaged by the war and food was in good supply. Though sugar cards were needed, rationing was not strict; and if one knew the proper channels, almost anything—eggs, butter, meat—could be obtained, though the bread was coarse and jam was hard to find and of inferior quality.

Politically, there had been a definite shift in public opinion in the city and the country as a whole in favor of Sinn Fein. Nationalist Ireland had united behind the organization earlier when the British War Cabinet had decided that conscription should be extended to Ireland.

Upon her arrival in Dublin, Hanna contacted Michael Collins, Director of Organisation for the Volunteers, a group that believed in the use of physical force to win freedom for Ireland. She had been instructed by Sinn Fein to turn funds over to him that she had been holding in an American bank: presumably these had been raised for Sinn Fein in the States. Collins, then a bit beyond his mid-twenties, was a tall, well-built man, with brown hair, deep-set gray eyes, a ready smile, and a dynamic manner. He moved gracefully and was all-in-all quite handsome. Hanna, by her own account, had not known him previously. Since both were prominent Sinn Feiners, this is difficult to comprehend. The explanation may lie in the fact that she was in the United States from 1916 to 1918, that letters were both disguised and censored, and that publications were often withheld.

Hanna, upon meeting Collins, had misgivings. She found his knowledge of the situation in the United States impressive and liked his ability to laugh at himself, but detected in him a lust for power as well as "a touch of the dictator." As for his vision of the future of an Irish republic, she thought it little more than "a middle-class replica of an English state (certainly not an ancient Gaelic Ireland)." His crude, barrack-room humor she found distasteful; his attitude toward women even more so. "He rather liked to shock," she noted, "and had the usual soldier's contempt for civilians, particularly for women, though these after risked their lives to help him."[6] What Hanna did not know was that Collins was extremely well-read, devoting part of each day to this activity, and that he had a good knowledge of, among other things, both French and Irish history. During the next four years, she would see and hear a great deal more of Michael Collins before he was surprised by Irregulars during the civil war and, for his pro-Treaty stand, shot in the back of the head.

It may be that Hanna gave no thought to how the funds were to be used. Robert Kee, the historian, points out that even moderate Sinn Feiners were taking a tolerant attitude toward the Volunteers. Sinn Fein had made remarkable gains in the elections but, as Kee says, the majority of those who voted in its candidates did not want to "win sovereign independence by force of arms or a campaign of terrorism" and only a minority — volunteer activists — "saw violence rather than democratic politics as the final arbiter."[7] Collins was certainly one of that minority, whether Hanna realized it or not. What she must have known was that Sinn Fein at that time was determined to resist conscription at all costs. But what exactly "all costs" meant to Hanna remains unclear.

For the first few days at home, Hanna was not troubled by the British authorities, but scarcely a week later, on her way to the Irish Women's Franchise League office in mid-afternoon, she was taken into custody as she stepped from a tram and sent to Bridewell prison in Dublin. She remained there awaiting sentence for two nights, and, though friends protested, began her hunger strike immediately. She had made no secret of the fact that, if arrested again, she would do just this and continue until released.[8]

Bridewell at that time was used as temporary housing for derelicts of both sexes and as a place where drunks might sober up. During Hanna's first night in jail someone in the next cell attempted suicide. The prison was filthy, the windows dirty and so high up that the effect was of a basement. The stone floor was unwashed and smelled of vomit. The bed was a slab fastened to the wall and the toilet could only be flushed from the outside. A grill in the door made it possible for the male police, patrolling at night, to inspect the cell. Though there was a police matron, she was not in charge, having little more than the status of charwoman.[9]

On her second day, Hanna was served with a deportation order committing her to Holloway Prison in England for the duration of the war under the provisions of the Defence of the Realm Act (DORA). She had not been allowed to tell her family of the deportation order — "secrecy of this stupid kind is the marrow of officialdom," she remarked — but she did manage to slip the order itself to a suffrage friend who had been posted at a Kingstown pier in anticipation of such a move. As the coastline faded from view, Hanna, despondent and weak from her fast, wondered how long it would be this time before she would see Ireland again.[10]

At Holloway, Hanna received a warm welcome. Constance Markievicz, Maud Gonne MacBride, and Kathleen Clarke had been there since May when, with many other Sinn Fein and labor leaders, they had been sent to the English jail for the duration of the war. Kathleen Clarke was the widow of Thomas J. Clarke, one of the first to be executed after the Rising. At that time, and increasingly thereafter, many of the leading women activists were wives, sisters, or mothers of the Easter Rising martyrs. It is significant that Hanna, though she did fit into the category of survivor, was not after a comparatively brief period ordinarily viewed in that role, probably because she had been so important during her husband's lifetime.

The three women had already won political-prisoner status when Hanna joined them and were living well. They had a wing to themselves, hospital beds in their cells, books, sewing materials, papers to a limited extent, and were permitted to have meals together. They were not, however, allowed visitors or mail and, consequently, were especially happy to see Hanna, who brought news of the outside world as well as all the details of her United States tour. Hours were spent discussing the volatile conditions in Ireland, the war, and other world affairs. Hanna, still refusing food, did not join her friends for meals and no amount of persuasion could sway her. She was determined to see her battle through although the smell of food was tantalizing.[11]

The morning after her arrival, Hanna went with her friends Markievicz and Gonne—both converts to Catholicism—to services in the prison chapel. After listening to a patriotic sermon and a glowing assessment of how well the war was going for the British, Hanna was immediately summoned to the governor's office. She was sure that she was to be forcibly fed but instead she was examined by a doctor, informed she was to be given a fortnight to regain her strength, and released under the Cat and Mouse Act.[12]

Though not permitted to say goodbye to her friends, she was allowed to choose where she would like to stay during her recuperative period. She decided on the Gower Hotel, off Euston Road in London, where she had stayed once some years earlier, and, accompanied by a wardress, she was taken to her hotel. Now well versed in the regimen to follow after a hunger strike, she began her diet of fruit juices and milk as

soon as she occupied her room at the Gower. Almost at once she was inun-
dated with mail from friends and relatives offering assistance and congrat-
ulating her on again having bested the government.[13]

The reason for Hanna's immediate release from Holloway was obvious. A Hanna Sheehy-Skeffington on hunger strike and growing weaker
by the day was not something the government could face. "A second
Sheehy-Skeffington tragedy would be too much," as the *Freeman's Journal* pointed out. "Not only would it set Ireland ablaze," but the fury of
American reaction would "startle the Chief Secretary" and "stagger his
masters."[14]

As the days passed and the time drew near for Hanna to return to
prison, she made up her mind to "skip." Two friends from Scotland came
to visit her and plans were made and all details worked out.[15] But it never
came to that for Hanna's friends and relatives were busy at home. Even
the Dublin press seemed to be on her side, and the lord mayor of Dublin
wrote assuring her that he would intercede with the authorities to allow
her to return to Ireland.[16]

Hanna's sisters were, as always, among her strongest supporters.
Margaret was taking good care of Owen. Kathleen was busy "circulariz-
ing" the Labour Party, giving its members the facts of the case and urging
their support in having her sister's sentence commuted. She also wrote
C. P. Scott of the *Manchester Guardian* and Robert Lynd of the *Daily News*
asking for their cooperation. A letter to Hanna, catching her up on details,
showed that she realized how wearing the hunger strike must have been
and that she sympathized. It showed her pride in Hanna as well. "You are
a tough proposition . . . ," she wrote. "I think Cruise [O'Brien] was right
in the main when he suggested that you could settle the world's affairs if
you were only let."[17] Mary Kettle, also busy on Hanna's behalf, had approached the chief secretary for Ireland, Edward Shortt, at the Castle, as
had Hanna's friend Charlotte Despard (Lord French's sister and a passionate suffragette and ardent pacifist). Shortt assured both women that everything possible was being done for Hanna. She would not be forcibly fed,
he said, but so far as her return to Dublin was concerned, she was making things difficult by refusing to promise to refrain from any Sinn Fein
activity.[18]

It took Mr. Shortt a fortnight to come to a decision. With one last effort to save face, he said that she could return if she would live with Mary
Kettle and see no Sinn Feiners. When that was refused, he finally, and

most reluctantly, gave her permission to return to Dublin unconditionally. Her passport was signed by Philip Snowden, "an old friend of Labour days," and she left the Gower.[19]

It was wonderful to be back in Dublin, and the number of letters she received assuring her that she was sorely needed added to Hanna's joy. T. M. (Tim) Healy expressed the reaction of most of her admirers when he congratulated her on victory over the government, "entirely due," he said, "to your pluck and tenacity." At the same time he invited her to visit and bring Owen which, according to his *Letters and Leaders of My Day*, she did in September. Her account of her stay in the United States was most interesting, he recalled. She had said the Irish in America were "as solid as ever for us," adding that they were all "Sinn Feiners, including the priests."[20] It is to be hoped that Tim Healy understood Hanna's proclivity for exaggeration on partisan issues.

One letter received shortly after her return displeased her. It was not only the chief secretary who warned Hanna not to resume her activities. Marking his letter "confidential," John Dillon, M.P., whose predictions thus far had proved accurate, wrote her to offer advice, though he was not sure it would do any good. He urged her, at least for a time, to avoid politics. "I have little or no influence with the people in power here now—and if you are imprisoned again it may very well be your last adventure," he wrote.[21] Hanna's quick-tempered response was characteristic:

> Yours marked "confidential" received—you are, of course, aware that all my letters are read before reaching me & nothing of mine can be "confidential" to the government.
>
> I was surprised & rather amused at your advice to "avoid politics" until some safer time, because next time Mr. Shortt will let me die if I fall into his hands! Had I meant to give up public activities I would have given the guarantee Mr. Shortt first desired & so saved all concerned a good deal of trouble. It is not likely, having wrung the right to live in my own country so dearly, that I shall give up the right to do what I think fit in public matters unconditionally. . . .
>
> I wonder what you would have thought in the old days, when prison was still an "adventure" to you, if a friend suggested that you retire into private life to save Britain the trouble of assassinating you. You must remember, my dear Mr. Dillon, that I am over forty years of age and convictions of a life time are dearer to me than life. Even if my arrest, as you suggest, leads to my death at the government's hands, I do not on that account intend to give up any of my activities

& after all my last adventure might also be the last adventure of my assassins. If our militarists think they can dispose of me by letting me die in prison, it only shows how stupid they are. Life is not such an exhilirating adventure that I would not gladly relinquish it if called upon—as others before me.

Of course, I read in your letter the implication that "next time" you wash your hands of me & of course will not attempt to hold Mr. Shortt's hands. In that case I can only assure you that your future neutrality will not wipe out my former indebtedness. I have explained to my sister & my friends that you are not to be disturbed should I fall into the government's hands again.

Meanwhile, believe me, Sincerely yours,

Hanna Sheehy Skeffington[22]

John Dillon's reply offered an apology for offending her but maintained that she had completely misunderstood him. He assured her that he would never again "commit the offense" of giving her advice.[23]

Hanna did indeed take offense too quickly and react too heatedly, often with little cause. There had been many occasions when she had displayed these tendencies in her relationship with her husband. There had also been instances in the States, judging by her correspondence, when she had been harsh and hasty in dealing with those who arranged her tour and those who published her writings. She was not, however, malicious—except, understandably, toward British officialdom—and she could see reason, though a bit late at times. As a consequence, there seem to have been no lasting animosities among those who knew her well and with whom she worked closely.

Immediately upon her return to Dublin, Hanna resumed editorship of the *Irish Citizen*. An appeal went out to those whose subscriptions had lapsed, asking them to renew, and a circular was sent to news agents as well announcing her return to duty and offering a special rate to those who would take a specific number of copies each month. Both solicitations stressed the importance of the paper "for feminism, for antimilitarism, for labour, & for the right of Ireland to Independence."[24]

When Hanna had left for the States, Louie Bennett and Miss Bourke-Dowling had taken on joint editorship of the *Irish Citizen*. By the time she returned, Bennett had given this up because of the pressure of union work, and a committee had been getting out the paper. They were delighted to have Hanna back and ready to give her any possible assistance. Maurice Wilkins, a member of the committee, wrote from his home in Sandymount that he would help with proofing and other chores and that he would endeavor to prepare an article she had requested. As for the assistance he had given thus far, he felt that the time spent had been sacred to him for "Frank's sake."[25] With cooperation and dedication such as this, by the end of the year Hanna had brought a shrunken *Irish Citizen* back to its original size. Since 1912 it had served as the voice of the disenfranchised woman and its continuation was vital.

What few spare moments Hanna had were spent at the Irish Women's Franchise League headquarters. She had resumed the presidency of the league and late in September she and Owen were given a formal welcome home, cheered lustily by an overflowing audience, and presented with flowers and gifts. Hanna talked at length about the situation in the United States and the "bitter anti-Irish propaganda movement" that had arisen. She felt that the presence there of some twenty million people of Irish birth or descent would, nevertheless, influence the government to assist Ireland in its fight for freedom. Much on Hanna's mind were her three friends in Holloway and she introduced a resolution calling for their release, for their return to Ireland, and for Irish public bodies to be called upon to support these demands.[26]

In order to win public support for the resolution, which had passed, Hanna, Helena Molony, and Madeleine ffrench-Mullen held a protest meeting a few days later in Foster Place. Some three to four hundred people assembled around the jaunting car from which the women were to speak but, before they could begin, the police forced their way through the crowd and arrested Molony and ffrench-Mullen. Following along behind her friends to the police station, Hanna was arrested as well, probably to her delight. All were released, however, "pending further instructions."[27] Arrests were becoming commonplace and were being made often with little pretense of legality. Hanna's papers contain a rough draft of an open letter to be circulated to the press in which she called attention to the danger that this presented, from the point of view of women especially. Women could be arrested by men calling themselves detectives but who wore "no number, badge, or even uniform," she wrote. The police could also, without producing any identification, enter a dwelling ostensibly to search for weapons or documents.

Just as it had when Francis Sheehy-Skeffington was alive, the name Sheehy-Skeffington was appearing in the papers in connection with protests on a variety of fronts. Hanna was writing for the *Labour Leader*, the official organ of the Independent Labour Party based in Manchester; for the *Ploughshare*, a Quaker organ of social reconstruction produced in London; and in publications like the *Christian Commonwealth*, also produced in London.

Her articles were, of course, also appearing in the *Irish Citizen*. One in October 1918, "How the Pickets Won the Vote," caused consternation in United States suffrage circles. Calling the women "constitutional suffragists," Hanna claimed that when the United States entered the war in 1917, the leaders of the American suffrage movement did exactly what Emmaline and Christabel Pankhurst had done in 1914: they turned away from their fight for the vote. She accused Anna Howard Shaw, Carrie Chapman Catt, and other American leaders of telling their followers that it was unpatriotic to ask for the vote—and possibly pro-German. They had "rolled up their banner and handed it over 'for the duration of the war' and it was hoped that no more would be heard of the Federal Amendment till Europe was 'safe for democracy.' "[28]

What had saved the day in the United States, according to Hanna, was the National Woman's Party, a group of militants led by a Quaker, Alice Paul, and an Irishwoman, Lucy Burns. *Suffrage Now* was its motto and its tactic picketing the White House and strategic targets in the various states. Though its members were arrested, brutally beaten, and forcibly fed when they went on hunger strike, they persisted, Hanna said, until prominent Americans protested in horror. It was their pressure, she felt, that caused President Wilson, early in January of 1918, to drop his opposition to a federal suffrage amendment and to urge its passage.[29]

Lengthy protests to Hanna's article reached the *Citizen* office from New York City and from London. Ida Husted Harper, editorial chairman of the National Suffrage Bureau in New York, pointed out that, unlike the action of the Pankhursts, headquarters had not been closed nor suffrage activities suspended. The National Union of Women's Suffrage Societies in the States, though wholeheartedly supporting the war effort, had continued to press for the vote. Only one small organization, the National Woman's Party, had refused to take any part in war work until the vote was won for women and had picketed the White House for months in order to force President Wilson, already committed to women's suffrage, to declare himself in favor of the Federal Suffrage Amendment. As far as public opinion was concerned, the actions of this group, Mrs. Harper wrote, had done more damage to the suffrage movement than had the actions of any previous opponents of the cause. She was not too surprised, she said, at "the glaring untruthfulness" of some of Hanna's statements since "during Mrs. Skeffington's sojourn in the United States she declared in speeches and interviews that the 'Representation of the People Bill,' at that time pending in the House of Commons, did not apply to Irish women and they would not be enfranchised if it became law." Her organization had repeatedly corrected this statement in the press, she explained.[30] The bill referred to, which gave the vote to women over thirty, had indeed passed late in January 1918, and had taken effect in Ireland in February.

Hanna's criticism of the leadership of the American suffrage movement was no doubt strongly colored by her own passionate opposition to the war effort and, particularly, to the participation of women in that effort. Harper was right to point to the distortion present in Hanna's article and she was also right to question the truthfulness of Hanna's statements denying that the Representation of the People Bill would enfranchise Irishwomen. Hanna must have known the truth. In fact, examples of distortion or misrepresentation are not hard to find at this time, particularly in her comments about those who supported the war or about the British. As far as she was concerned, every incident, major or minor, was a result of a British plot. In her pamphlet, *Impressions of Sinn Fein in America*, published in 1919 but compiled much earlier, she lists one occasion after another where British agents interfered with her life and work in the States. Her reporting, however biased, was at least consistently witty. One paragraph from the pamphlet illustrates the point. Great Britain, she wrote, had bombarded the United States with lecturers instructed not only to present the British case for the war to the American people "but to villify, wherever possible, those nations that did not agree with her in her Imperialistic ambitions." She went on:

> There was, for instance, Major Ian Beith Hay, notorious for his book on 'The Oppressed English,' a jovial soldierly type camouflaged to represent the bluff, military man who takes 'no interest in politics.' . . . He told delighted audiences: 'How jolly it was to be in the trenches, don't you know.' and explained how we Irish were paid emissaries of the Kaiser. . . . Some of these lecturers, however, worked unconsciously on behalf of Ireland. Mr. Balfour, Lord Northcliffe, Sir F. E. Smith, did us a world of good by showing the American people what we Irish have to suffer.

A Washington journalist had told her, she said, that listening to Sir F. E. Smith had made him a Sinn Feiner.[31]

Early in September Hanna became a member of the MacDonagh

Sinn Fein Club. By November Sinn Fein had chosen her unanimously "to contest the Harbour Division Parliamentary Election" and soon she was named a member of the Executive Committee. Here again, as with the turning over of funds to Michael Collins, the question arises as to whether Hanna's close connection with this movement indicates that she had abandoned her pacifism. Ernie O'Malley in his *Army Without Banners* states that it was the Volunteers who, after the Rising, advocated force, whose leaders believed that "the only way to speak to the English was down the barrel of a rifle" and who looked down on members of the Gaelic League and of Sinn Fein who did not agree.[32] This last organization, on the other hand, had as its principal aim an appeal to the peace conference that was to be held at the end of the war and that would, it believed, guarantee the rights of small nations, Ireland among them. With this objective, a pacifist could not quarrel.

It was an exciting period for Sinn Feiners. As the *Freeman's Journal* explained, the meaning of the December 1918 general election was quite clear: "more than two-thirds of the electors throughout national Ireland have endorsed the Sinn Fein programme."[33] On 21 January 1919 the first session of the Assembly of Ireland, Dail Eireann, was held. Since unionists and members of the Parliamentary Party who had survived the election refused to attend, the assembly was made up entirely of Sinn Feiners. Many of those were in jail—one of them Constance Markievicz for whom Hanna had campaigned; consequently only twenty-seven were present.

Irish women activists had reason to rejoice during this period as well. Women over thirty were now eligible to vote and, in the December 1918 general election, they exercised that prerogative triumphantly: at the second meeting of the Dail, held at the beginning of April, Constance Markievicz, in jail, was elected labour minister. (De Valera, now out of jail, became prime minister.)[34]

Hanna, able to fill any hall and move virtually any audience, was more in demand as a speaker than ever. The subjects of her lectures were surprisingly diversified. She spoke on the role of the United States in the fight for Irish freedom, on conditions in Ireland in general, and, often, for release of political prisoners—especially her friend Constance Markievicz. Before the Dublin Literary Society she spoke on literary and historical subjects and, occasionally, on German literature. Like many of her friends and colleagues, particularly those in the socialist movement, she was interested in and sympathetic toward the newly born Soviet Union, and she spoke on that subject as well.

She had become extremely active in the City of Dublin Municipal

Teachers Association, fighting hard for higher pay and for compensation for time lost during the influenza epidemic; moreover, she had been instrumental in the formation of a Part-Time Teachers Association. Dublin Castle considered her such a menace, indeed, that, when she was scheduled to speak on technical education before the Central Technical Institute in Clonmel, the institute was informed by the police authorities that "no meeting addressed by Mrs. Sheehy Skeffington can be permitted," and it was warned that, should it persist, steps would be taken to prevent the meeting from being held at all.[35] Similarly, when the Trades Union Congress and Labour Party attempted to get a passport for her and two other delegates to attend a labor conference in Lausanne, they were told by the passport office that the requests for Thomas MacPartlin and James J. Hughes would be honored but that, regretfully, Hanna could not be issued one.[36]

Shortly after the war ended, Hanna once more brought Ireland's case to the attention of the Americans. An undated pamphlet written by Hanna, *Ireland: Present and Future*, gave a vivid picture of postwar Ireland and spared the British not at all. "Ireland still remains the chief difficulty of British statesmanship—the little island which Great Britain will not willingly disgorge and cannot after seven hundred years assimilate," she began. Official figures had set the size of the army of occupation in Ireland at 58,300, but Hanna said that a more accurate estimate would have been three times that number. "One-third of the 'whole truth' is about as much as a British minister can be trusted to give," she wrote.[37] Hanna went on to point out the irony of the people of Ireland supporting their occupiers by their taxes: supplying them, in effect, with food, clothing, and equipment. Although the war was over, the Defence of the Realm Act was still in place and an attempt was being made to make this emergency war measure permanent. "Trial by court-martial has superseded trial by jury," Hanna wrote. Everywhere raids were being made in a search for arms and subversive literature; restrictions were being placed upon meetings, dances, and even funerals; and the police force was going about, Hanna said, "armed to the teeth and in a state of mind bordering on hysteria." It seemed clear to her that the country could not be "governed permanently by the bayonet and the handcuffs." British statesmanship having failed, Ireland's case must now, she argued, be brought before an international tribunal and she called on leaders in the United States to act or be considered "accomplices in Britain's crime."[38] Clearly, if the authorities were under the impression that restrictions upon Hanna's freedom would silence her voice or stay her pen, they were misreading her completely.

Hanna Sheehy-Skeffington and suffragist friends. A "Votes for Women" banner is prominently displayed. (Courtesy of Andrée Sheehy-Skeffington)

Hanna Sheehy-Skeffington addressing a meeting protesting the "Cat and Mouse" Act and held outside Mountjoy Prison, Dublin, in 1914. Through the megaphone she read a message of protest to the prisoner. (Courtesy of Andrée Sheehy-Skeffington)

Constance Markievicz. The portrait of the nationalist leader was done
by Anna Nordgren. (Courtesy of National Gallery of Ireland)

Charlotte Despard. Even in old age she was still very active on behalf of socialist and feminist causes. (Courtesy of Andrée Sheehy-Skeffington)

Sean O'Casey. The drawing of the dramatist was done by the well-known Irish artist Harry Kernoff. (Courtesy of National Gallery of Ireland)

Maud Gonne and her son, Sean MacBride, in Roebuck House. It was here that Hanna spent many hours with the MacBrides. (Courtesy of Imogen Stuart)

Inaugural meeting of the Technical Students' Literary and Debating Society. This November 1940 photograph shows Hanna Sheehy-Skeffington, third from left, seated; Sean MacBride at her left; and Maud Gonne, second from right, seated. (Courtesy of Seamus Scully)

Hanna Sheehy-Skeffington. The photograph was taken only a few years before her death in 1946. (Courtesy of Andrée Sheehy-Skeffington)

In an Ireland at War

NE OF THE STREETS periodically raided and searched by the British was Belgrave Road in Rathmines, an area inhabited mainly by middle- and upper-class professionals and considered a hotbed of Republican activity. It was to this street of two-story, semi-detached houses with varicolored doors and tiny front gardens that Hanna moved on 26 November 1918, and here at No. 7, she would live for the rest of her life.

On the ground floor of her house, in addition to the kitchen, there was a large "breakfast" room. It held a spacious table seating some twelve people and, as one person recalls, a large portrait of Lenin ornamented the wall; it was here that family dinners were always held. On the floor above, and to the left of the front door, was the drawing room, high-ceilinged and dominated by a crammed bookcase. The rest of the furniture, much of it brought from the family home at 2 Belvedere Place, was characterized by at least one family member as "shabby genteel." Behind this room was another having a fine view of the garden and used by Hanna as both bedroom and study. The top floor of the house, she felt, could be turned into a rentable flat.[1] "We have a home at last," she wrote a friend, with obvious satisfaction and with some relief.[2]

The early decades of the century were remarkable for the zeal and idealism of their educated women, and Belgrave Road seemed to house an unusual number of such individuals. Next door, in No. 9, lived the feminists Dr. Kathleen Lynn and Madeleine ffrench-Mullen; another feminist, Helena Molony, lived nearby. All were old friends.

Perhaps the most notable of these neighbors was Dr. Lynn, who had started her private practice at No. 9 and who was not only Hanna's friend but also the Sheehy-Skeffington family physician. Owen recalled his small-boy impression of a crowded waiting room and his mother's astonishment at the smallness of the doctor's fees.[3] Committed from girlhood to women's rights, Dr. Lynn had become convinced through her association with those in the suffrage movement that a free Ireland was essential if women were to become truly emancipated. Her greatest achievement—a project in which Hanna took an active interest—was the founding of St. Ultan's Hospital.

St. Ultan's was initially planned to treat adults since, at the time, the World War I flu epidemic was raging. Acutely aware, however, of the abnormally high infant mortality rate in Dublin (164 out of every 1,000 children dying before the age of one year, mainly from preventable causes), Dr. Lynn and Miss ffrench-Mullen leased an abandoned property in the heart of Dublin and, on Ascension Thursday, 1919, St. Ultan's doors were opened. From the grim, overcrowded tenements near city center, Dr. Lynn and ffrench-Mullen took in malnourished and tuberculosis-ridden infants under one year (other hospitals would not take them without their mothers) and gave them care. In a profession dominated by men, Dr. Lynn, who had known discrimination during her student days and throughout her internship, insisted that, from its inception, St. Ultan's be administered and staffed exclusively by women.

How the idealistic Dr. Lynn managed financially often perplexed Hanna. How Hanna managed must have been equally puzzling to Dr. Lynn and many others. As it had been when Francis was alive, Hanna's financial situation was always uncertain and sometimes precarious. Nonetheless, she managed to live rather comfortably, to employ a maid, and to send Owen to a boarding school.[4] She had a small income from part-time teaching, from writing articles, and from lecturing, for which her traveling expenses were always paid at the very least.

It is possible that J. B. Skeffington contributed toward the upkeep of Hanna's household as he had done while her husband was alive, but there is no concrete evidence that he did and, from the available documents, it is difficult to determine how closely Hanna kept in touch with him after her husband's death. Certainly J. B. had never approved of her way of life and it is equally certain that she condemned him for having her husband's body exhumed and reburied without her knowledge and for his willingness to accept compensation from the British for her husband's murder. But, since J. B. was devoted to his grandchild, it is unlikely that the break was complete.

On 19 August 1919, less than a year after Hanna moved to her Belgrave Road home, J. B. Skeffington died in Belfast, leaving some 2,500 pounds which, she was informed, was substantially reduced by taxes and funeral expenses.[5] Following his death, Hanna continued to correspond with Francis's Belfast relatives, who were genuinely fond of her and of Owen. They, unlike J. B., never seemed to criticize her political involvement, an involvement that—in response to the needs of the turbulent, often bloody months of 1918 and 1919—was greater than ever before.

Though this was a time of suppression by the Castle and every attempt by the nationalists to achieve Home Rule without partition was being fought and sabotaged, it was a period of hope for women. This was reflected in the pages of the *Irish Citizen*, which noted editorially that resolutions were being put forward by legislators for school meals, higher pay for teachers, and aid for widows so that they would be able to remain at home and look after their children. Obviously, the paper pointed out, legislators were becoming interested in the problems facing women and they were urged to extend "family endowments" to include, in addition to widows, the wives of men who were ill, unemployed, on strike, or in prison. Another indication of the changing climate was the response of organized primary teachers to word that they had been granted a war bonus: instead of merely accepting the money, they demanded that male and female teachers be given equal amounts. And in London, a motion before the House of Commons had been passed declaring women eligible to become members of Parliament. Those opposed, commented the *Irish Citizen*, held "the fort of male prejudice to the bitter end" but to no avail. The Parliamentary Party, happily, had supported the reform. In addition, the Sinn Fein convention, meeting in Dublin somewhat earlier, had passed by acclamation a proposition declaring Irishwomen eligible as parliamentary candidates and as members of the National Council. To the Irish Labour Party went the honor of being the first Irish party to choose a woman candidate, Louie Bennett. She had declined but it was hoped that a precedent had been set. "What was revolution five years ago is 'sanity' today," said the *Irish Citizen*.[6]

The women's greatest triumph was celebrated in mid-December 1918, when Anna Haslam led an exuberant victory procession to St. Stephen's Green so that she might cast her first vote in a general election. This she did "amid cheers." At the head of the procession were leaders of many of the women's organizations, Hanna, of course, among them. "All shades of politics were represented . . . ," the *Irish Times* reported.[7] The joy of the group was not unalloyed, however, for women between twenty-one and thirty remained without the vote.

Riding this swell of optimism, the Irishwomen's International League was busily gathering support—and funds—for an international congress of women that would meet early in 1919 to frame a program "having for its object the promotion of a civilisation dominated by justice, liberty and co-operation." It was hoped that the congress might have some small effect upon the Paris Peace Conference to be held later in the year. Though the league realized that its influence would not be great, at least it would assemble women from some twenty-five countries who might, in the future, continue to work together.[8] The conference was finally arranged for May, in Zurich, and four delegates were chosen to go from Ireland: Louie Bennett, Miss Rowlette, Miss Wills, and Hanna Sheehy-Skeffington. By mid-May three of them were on their way to Switzerland for the Women's International Peace Conference. But Hanna was not among them. She had been denied a passport.[9]

While deeply disturbed by the efforts of British authorities to restrain her, Hanna was acutely aware that the injustices being done her were nothing compared to the outrages being committed throughout the country by the Black and Tans and the Auxiliaries. Drawn from among ex-convicts and other unsavory elements of British society, the Black and Tans, with their makeshift uniforms of black tunics and khaki trousers, or the reverse, and their western-style holsters, would have seemed merely absurd had they not been brutal. The Auxiliaries, many of whom were ex-officers, were only one cut above and, as Frank O'Connor put it, "were paid double the salary of the ordinary Black and Tan for an accent savouring more of the public school and a greater savagery and recklessness."[10]

Overlooking Liberty Hall was a machine-gun post and wherever Hanna turned she saw helmeted soldiers with rifles at the ready and bayonets fixed. The Dublin quays resembled the port of an expeditionary force with tanks, armored cars, military lorries, and troops numbering in the thousands. The British had no intention of allowing the one thing that the newly formed government in Dublin wanted—a united and independent Irish republic. By mid-1919 they were maintaining an army of occupation in Ireland at a cost of more than ten million pounds a year.[11] By September the British executive, tightening its grip, labeled the Dail Eireann a dangerous body and suppressed it.[12]

As British pressure increased in severity, the tone of Hanna's speeches increased in fervor. In July, at a meeting to raise funds to save the financially troubled St. Enda's College, she said that the country would no longer settle for Home Rule—the issue was "as dead as Queen Anne." To the accompaniment of loud cheers, she declared that the country was returning to the tradition of Wolfe Tone, of Robert Emmet, of the Manchester Martyrs, and of the leaders of the Easter Rising—all of whom had fought and died for that tradition.[13] As a result of another such address in Co. Westmeath, Hanna was, according to the *Irish Citizen*, "struck and stunned by the butt-end of a police carbine," leaving her "incapacitated."[14] On the whole, however, her ceaseless activity seemed to have a therapeutic effect, for Sir Francis Vane, visiting with her and Mary Kettle, and their children Owen and Betty, found her looking exceptionally well.

Shortly before Christmas, 1919, Hanna was proposed as a candidate for the Dublin Corporation. She had previously been told that she would be disqualified because she was teaching part-time, but apparently that obstacle was overcome for in January Hanna, her sister Mary Kettle, Kathleen Lynn, and Madeleine ffrench-Mullen were elected. "Nearly all the respectable women in Dublin seem to have got in," her friend Rosamund Jacob wrote, and she continued: "I hope you'll get some support now in the corporation for sensible doings, though I suppose most of the Sinn Fein men will be just as hopeless about doing anything for the benefit of women as the old crowd were." Rosamund's brother Tom added: "Rathmines won't know itself with Dr. Lynn & Miss ffrench-Mullen . . . helping to rule its destinies."[15]

Hanna was now Councillor Mrs. Sheehy-Skeffington. One of her first actions in this capacity was to make a survey of the manner in which women were appointed to clerkships in various corporations throughout Ireland in order to determine approximately how many were employed in these positions and whether or not they were paid at the same rate as men. She used the information gathered so effectively that before the end of the year she was receiving letters of appreciation. One, signed by three grateful women, indicated that, thanks to her efforts, women were now being employed as clerks in some districts where they had previously been barred.[16]

It was not only in Rathmines that the Republicans had done well; they had won majorities on 172 councils out of 206. The predictable result was that the British government's policy of suppression was intensified. Before the end of January two of the newly elected councilors were arrested and sent to jail in England; others followed within weeks. Alderman Kelly, who proposed Hanna for the corporation and who was elected lord mayor, had been arrested weeks earlier, even before his election. As historian Dorothy Macardle saw it, the government had done an effective job of instilling in the British military in Ireland, the prison jailers, and even, to a certain extent, the people of England, "a savage hatred against Sinn Feiners." The Irish, they had been told, were "a race of congenital murderers, outside the pale of humanity." Consequently, the "rules of civilised warfare could not be applied."[17]

With so many of the Republican leaders in jail, various labor groups, socialist organizations, and branches of Sinn Fein were harassing government officials to grant prisoner-of-war status to the jailed leaders or to have them released. Typical of their tactics was an appeal, issued late in 1919 by a group of women's organizations, calling for an international committee to be set up to investigate the entire prison situation. Among those signing was Hanna Sheehy-Skeffington for the Irish Women's Franchise League.[18]

In Mountjoy Prison at the beginning of April, sixty men went on hunger strike. Sympathy for them was intense and crowds formed outside day and night, praying and singing protest songs. Mothers and fathers were allowed to visit the prisoners in the hope that they might persuade them to give up but instead most parents urged their sons to be strong and refuse food. Hanna, again on behalf of the Irish Women's Franchise League, wired Charlotte Despard in London: "One hundred men [note her customary exaggeration] dying of hunger-strike in Mountjoy. Irishwomen beg your personal intervention with your brother [Lord French] ere too late to prevent terrible tragedy." A telegram went also to the American ambassador in London asking for intervention by the United States.[19]

The most effective action, however, proved to be that taken by the Irish Labour Party and Trades Union Congress. One week after the hunger strike began, these groups called a general strike and three days later the prisoners were released unconditionally. On that day Charlotte Despard replied to Hanna's telegram. After expressing her joy at the outcome, she added: "I did think of protesting personally but I do not believe it would have done any good. The strike, at present, is the only weapon."[20] The *New Statesman* agreed. "In the last resort subject peoples have an argument to which there is no reply; Sinn Feiners have discovered this argument."[21]

The summer of 1920 found Dublin an armed camp, with raids increasing in harshness and casualties mounting among both the Volunteers and the British. The whole scene sickened Hanna. Her response was to speak out against it as often as possible, preferably out of the country. As she said, there was no reason to speak to those already converted. Her abilities as a speaker—her wit and candor—were becoming widely recognized and highly effective. When, in May, the Transport Workers Union struck, refusing to move any train in which Black and Tans were riding or to move munitions, Hanna was able to raise money through her speeches to augment its depleted funds.[22]

In an appearance before a large labor audience in Bermondsey, a borough of London, Hanna was at her most forceful. Labor alone, she told her audience, could solve the Irish question—"bloodlessly in twenty-four hours." If it did not, Ireland would be a desert. She described the Black and Tans as "war-wrecks, men with shattered nerves, . . . drugged with drink," who were "sent to create terror" in Ireland. "Some of their deeds do not bear telling. I shall sum them up," she continued, "by saying that there was no atrocity alleged against the so-called Huns in Belgium, or against the Turks in Armenia, that [has] not been beaten hollow by your army of occupation, sent by your will into Ireland." Urging British labor to take direct action on the Irish question, she said her country was dealing with a "government of lunatics" and went on to warn her audience that a dehumanized military could be easily turned against the British working class if unemployment increased and industrial unrest grew. She also encouraged English labor to fight to have the army of occupation withdrawn from Ireland and to recognize the Irish government already in existence. There were, she argued, only two ways in which the Irish question could be settled—either by the extermination of the Irish people or by a concession to her legitimate demands.[23]

At least two events in the fall of 1920 bore out some of Hanna's fears: the death of Terence MacSwiney and the hanging of Kevin Barry. Terence MacSwiney, poet, dramatist, I.R.A. member, and lord mayor of Cork, had been arrested in August and tried by court-martial for the possession of documents alleged to be seditious. Refusing to recognize the British court, he was sent to Brixton prison in England where he promptly went on hunger strike. Seventy-four days later, never having broken his fast, Terence MacSwiney died. A few hours later another prisoner, Joseph Murray, also on hunger strike, died. At last England seemed to be shocked and a silent crowd lined the streets when MacSwiney's body was taken from the prison to Holyhead for the trip back to Cork for burial.

On 1 November, Kevin Barry, an eighteen-year-old student at University College, Dublin, and a member of the I.R.A., was hanged. His crime was taking part in an ambush during which six British soldiers had been shot, although there was no evidence that he was responsible. A member of the Barry family, describing the incident, said that he had taken cover under a lorry when a sympathetic bystander gave his position away by calling to him that he had better be careful. While he was awaiting execution—a sentence, incidentally, that the Irish people were unable to believe would be carried out—Hanna wrote letters to members of Parliament and others begging for intercession. A moving reply came from Joseph Devlin, Parliamentary Party M.P., marked confidential and dated the day of the execution: a Monday. "I did everything humanly possible for Kevin Barry," he said. "On Thursday I went to the Prime Minister to whom I had not spoken for two years, and I made what I thought was an effective appeal." Subsequently, Devlin and T. P. O'Connor, a fellow M.P., drafted a telegram to King George V, whom they would have seen personally had he not been in Sandringham. The king replied "that he was communicating with the Prime Minister." At this point, Devlin was sure that his efforts would be successful. "I cannot for the life of me make out who it is has been responsible for defeating what I believed would have been a successful endeavour on our part, or what devilish influences are at work," he wrote Hanna. A final paragraph read: "I have just learned as I am writing this letter that the poor young fellow was executed this morning. I regard this latest as one of their greatest crimes."[24] As Hanna had told her audience in Bermondsey, her country seemed to be dealing with a "government of lunatics."

Violence was spreading. As the unrecognized government of Ireland, Dail Eireann, became more effective and therefore more powerful, the measures employed by the military to impose Britain's will became increasingly severe, sometimes vicious. Country people were being burned out of their homes and many were living in stables and barns. Their need for help was obvious and an effort was made by Arthur Griffith, Maud Gonne, and others to form a group in Ireland to raise funds to be distributed to those who were suffering. At the same time de Valera, then in the United States, was urging Irish-Americans to form a similar group for the same purpose. From their concerted efforts came the formation of the White Cross in both Ireland and the United States, with Hanna a member of the executive committee.[25]

Early in 1921 the lord mayor of Dublin inaugurated the Irish White Cross and distribution of funds began. Contributions were generous—the pope subscribed over five thousand pounds—but there were so many who needed to be helped that each could receive only a bare minimum. Even this help, however, was refused by many because there were others, they said, who might need it more. Their suffering seemed somehow to be lessened by their pride in waging a war against those who were oppressing them. When it became obvious to the British that hunger was not a sufficient weapon and that their campaign was in jeopardy, they began to seize the White Cross collection boxes, to raid the homes of White Cross volunteers, and to break into the White Cross offices. Dorothy Macardle feels that it was only "American vigilance" that kept them from suppressing the White Cross fund altogether.[26]

Dublin, though not under martial law, was living under warlike conditions. Volunteer ambushes provoked retaliatory raids by the military and the police. A curfew was in effect from 8:00 P.M. until daylight and on occasion police would move into the home of a suspect and stay there for days. When, during March 1921, six Republicans were scheduled to be hanged at Mountjoy prison, the day was designated a day of mourning and all businesses closed their doors at 11:00 A.M. More than 20,000 people gathered outside of the prison before dawn and when at 6:00 A.M., and again at 7:00 and 8:00, the bells tolled—each time for two executions—people knelt and prayed. The statistics listing those killed and wounded on both sides were appalling. In the first two months of 1921 alone, 174 of the Crown forces were killed and 288 wounded; among the Irish Volunteers and civilians 317 were killed and 285 wounded.[27]

During those same two months the offices of the Irish Women's Franchise League were raided, and books and documents confiscated. It was only after a series of letters to the Castle that the organization was informed that the confiscated property would be returned.[28]

The reign of terror in Ireland was given as wide publicity as possible by Hanna. Since she was unable to get to England to speak as often as she would have liked, she prepared documents listing the atrocities and distributed them among prominent people such as the archbishop of Canterbury and her British friends in the suffrage movement. Their effectiveness—like that of her speeches—was readily apparent. Emmeline Pethick-Lawrence was so disturbed by the accounts of conditions in the country that she felt she had to come to Ireland and see for herself.[29] Taking a room in a Dublin hotel, she interviewed people "who had nothing more to lose" and who, consequently, were willing to give her sworn statements. In this effort, she was assisted by Hanna as well as by officials of the Irish Trades and General Workers Union. A signed article by Pethick-Lawrence, which appeared in the 27 April 1921 London *Daily News*, created a sensation and distressed Dublin Castle sufficiently to demand that she furnish it with the names and addresses of all those referred to in the piece as well as the precise dates upon which she interviewed them. This she refused to do. Instead she presented the facts in two specific cases and insisted that the Castle investigate. There was no reply.[30]

The ugly situation in Ireland was rapidly approaching a climax. By mid-1921 thousands of Republicans were in internment camps, some of them women. Under the pretext that a state of war existed, the British government was making no attempt to keep them from being shot or hanged. On the other side, there were bloody reprisals by the Volunteers. But at the end of June Prime Minister Lloyd George wrote to President de Valera proposing that a peace conference be held. In reply, de Valera insisted on a truce as a preliminary to the conference and on 11 July the truce took effect. There was jubilation on the part of the general public. As the occupying soldiers withdrew from the streets to their barracks, crowds watched and when the gates of the barracks opened to receive them there were cheers and boos. At last the people felt they could leave their homes without fear and that evening, without thought of curfew, they walked about Dublin, in a holiday mood.[31] In his communiques, de Valera urged restraint and warned against over-optimism in the conference's results. His uneasiness was shared by a friend of Hanna's in London, who wrote that one probably could not "expect the leopard to change its spots."[32]

During this period Hanna was director of organisation for Sinn Fein. In that capacity, she attempted to carry out de Valera's wish that "a campaign of intensive organisation" be conducted while the truce was in effect, in order "to put Sinn Fein Clubs everywhere once more upon a properly working basis." She realized that it had been impossible for them to function during recent months with organizers in prison, local clubs left without leaders and their activities banned, and with their membership "marked." Sinn Fein, she wrote, was the political backbone of the movement; it had to be reorganized without delay. Already some twenty men and women had been appointed as organizers and were communicating with branch secretaries. It was hoped that their efforts would be fully supported and that membership would be increased through the revival of old branches and the establishment of new ones. Hanna called upon the membership to keep the machinery of Sinn Fein working, to assist the work of its courts, and to see to it that "the civil side of the organisation be as perfect and thorough as the military side."[33]

During the uneasy truce, correspondence between London and Dublin continued. In the fall a five-man delegation, representing foreign affairs, finance, and economic affairs, left for London to negotiate with a British delegation appointed by Lloyd George. They were instructed to sign no treaty without ratification by the Dail. The salient points at issue were the unity of Ireland and acceptance of allegiance to the king. What they brought back to the Dail in December was a treaty, made up of eighteen Articles of Agreement, under which the Irish Free State would be born, with dominion status and with a parliament and an executive swearing allegiance to the king. The powers of this government would not apply to northern Ireland for one month. If it were decided during this period that these counties wished to be excluded from the Irish Free State, a boundary commission would be set up to determine what, from that time on, would constitute Northern Ireland.[34]

For the rest of 1921 and into the early days of 1922 debate raged in the Dail as to whether or not the Treaty should be accepted. The six women deputies—Margaret Pearse, Kathleen Clarke, Mary MacSwiney, Kate O'Callaghan, Dr. Ada English, and Constance Markievicz—were solidly behind rejection; this was de Valera's stand as well. Each of the women spoke eloquently and out of deep sorrow. Mary MacSwiney, whose brother had died on hunger strike, said: "If [England] exterminates the men, the women will take their places . . . and if she exterminates the men, women and children of this generation, the blades of grass, dyed with their blood, will rise, like the dragon's teeth of old, into armed men and the fight will begin in the next generation." Her speech against the Treaty lasted more than four hours.[35]

The press, the clergy, and the weariness of the people made the result inevitable. In January 1922, the Treaty was approved by Dail Eireann. The vote was a close one, however, 64 to 57, and de Valera immediately began to organize the anti-Treaty forces. The next step would be presentation of the matter to the people at the June elections. Women's organizations like the Irish Women's Franchise League continued to speak out against the agreement and Cumann na mBan, early in February, rejected a motion to support it by a huge majority. Late that month Hanna wrote to Alice Park in California: "We are all pretty disillusioned just now. I strongly dislike the treaty but I think it will be accepted at the elections. There is a regular stampede for it of all the moderates, and the 'safe' people with stakes in the country, of the press, and the clerics. Women in the main are against it, and as a result, there is great bitterness against us all just now and a decree to extend the franchise was beaten at the Dail the other day. The fight for this absorbed all my energies, and it seemed like old suffragette times again." So far Hanna told her friend, they had only been promised that the new constitution would provide women with full suffrage rights—"Jam tomorrow, but never jam today," she said. On the whole, she felt the Treaty was "a bad compromise" and feared that the country was "in for some decades of reaction under a temporary false prosperity, reinforced by our native militarism!"[36] It was impossible for Hanna to support an agreement that accepted, even temporarily, the partition that both she and her husband had deplored; that had as one of its provisions the swearing of allegiance to the king; and that preserved the bonds with England more fully than she thought acceptable. She feared that under such a treaty the fate of women would be little different from before.

There was, however, one major advance for women following the signing of the agreement. The question of the vote for women between twenty-one and thirty had been raised in the Dail, and placed in the form of a motion. It was defeated nearly two to one, ostensibly because it would require a revision of the voting registers and there was not time before the next election. But by September the Free State Assembly had agreed to prepare such a new electoral register and to allow women to vote under the same rules as men in the next general election.

Actually there could be no complaint about the constitutional status of women in the Free State in 1922. Their voting privileges were equal to those of men and "there were cast-iron guarantees" written into the constitution that they could not be prohibited from holding any public office. What they would be allowed to do with these rights was another matter. Old attitudes and ideas die hard and the attitude toward women in politics would prove to be no exception in this time of general conservatism.[37]

Toward the end of June a general election was held, the results of which gave the leaders of the Free State a clear mandate to create a government designed to preserve the peace. Opposition to the Free Staters and to the election had, all along, been strongest in the ranks of the army; in fact, many of the I.R.A. men had been urging that a military dictatorship be set up. An army convention in April decided, among other things, that the Four Courts, then in the hands of the pro-Treaty forces, should be taken over by force, and this was carried out.

Four days after the election the newly chosen government shelled the Republican-held Four Courts, a fine Georgian building previously used to house legal records, and it was then that Hanna interceded. With Louie Bennett, Maud Gonne MacBride, and Charlotte Despard, she visited the Free State leaders—W. T. Cosgrave, Arthur Griffith, and Michael Collins—and found them willing to talk with the leaders of the Republican forces. Now it was necessary to persuade the men in the Four Courts. Crossing town in an ambulance loaned to them by the lord mayor of Dublin, the women went to the headquarters of the I.R.A., located in what had been a "tram parcels office." There a high-ranking officer talked with Hanna at considerable length but, in the end, remained unconvinced: they would not negotiate on any terms; they had gone this far, he told Hanna, and there was no turning back.[38]

The women had done their best but their efforts and those of all others toward bringing about a settlement between the pro-Treaty and anti-Treaty forces had failed. To those who had lived through the Rising, it must have seemed like 1916 all over again. The attack on the Four Courts signaled the beginning of a year of civil war in Ireland that would tear the country apart. The British ministers were jubilant: the demoralization that they had been unable to bring about would be brought about by the Irish themselves.

Even the Sheehy family was split between anti-Treaty and pro-Treaty adherents. Eugene, Hanna's brother, enthusiastically supported the government and was, in fact, a judge advocate-general for the Free State during the civil war period. Hanna, on the other hand, "belonged," Conor Cruise O'Brien said, "to the most uncompromising faction of the Republicans." He maintained that, although she felt she was carrying on her husband's role as a pacifist as well as a feminist and socialist, "in practice, as a result of Frank's murder, she had been drawn into close association with violent revolutionaries." He added that from Eugene's point of view his sister was a "criminally irresponsible firebrand."[39]

O'Brien was, of course, correct when he said that Hanna staunchly opposed the Free State government and also that she associated with "violent revolutionaries." Yet his estimate of her brother Eugene's opinion of her may have been unduly harsh. In his memoirs, published long after the passions of civil war had cooled, Eugene draws a kindly picture of her, tinged with amusement at times but always with admiration. One of his anecdotes mentioned a visit to her when she was a prisoner in Armagh jail in the north of Ireland in 1933. During that visit, he talked with the governor of the jail, who seemed surprised that Hanna had a brother who was a respected member of the judiciary; Eugene mentioned to him that their father had served many prison terms "in his fight for fair play for the tenant farmers of Ireland." So politics went, he said, and he offered no apologies for Hanna. Instead he pointed out that it was not beyond the realm of possibility that the governor might, before too long, see Hanna "sitting as Minister for Justice in an Irish Republic," instead of sitting in jail.[40] In Hanna's own speeches and in her writings during the early months of 1922, she gave every indication of being sickened by the violence on both sides.

There is further confusing and contradictory testimony by J. F. Byrne, who stated that, at the time Hanna came to New York in the fall of 1922, the civil war in Ireland was at its height and families were "divided in allegiance, separated one from another by chasms of hatred." He talked with her "for hours," he said, and told her he had not realized how bad conditions were, adding: "I can sense an actual exudation of hatred for certain people from every pore in your body." She admitted readily, he recalled, that his impression was correct.

It seemed to Byrne that steps needed to be taken to "pour a few drops of oil on the troubled waters." Hanna agreed and, in fact, encouraged him to draw up an appeal to all Irishmen "to stop their demoralizing fratricidal struggle." This Byrne proceeded to do, getting an impressive list of prominent Irishmen to sign the document. On 29 October 1922, it appeared as a two-column article on the first page of the *New York American*. In a preamble, Byrne called for a truce and a conference between Free State and Republican leaders to take place immediately. He also made clear that, in his opinion, "there was no more reason for refusing the Free State treaty than there would be for refusing a lift to Los Angeles because the car wasn't going to the Golden Gate." Conditions in Ireland, he wrote, would not be improved by "recrimination and abuse," especially from the Irish-Americans. He then asked that the appeal receive "countrywide endorsement." Compared to this preamble, the appeal itself was mild, merely calling for a laying down of arms and an immediate conference.[41] According to Byrne, Hanna wrote "disparagingly" about the appeal, indicating in no way that she had approved of the idea. "However, I don't now, nor did I then, blame her for her inconsistent disparagement—the good lady was distraught," he wrote.[42] It seems likely, though, that Hanna was objecting less to the appeal than to the preamble, about which she may not have been told earlier.

Hanna would have been furious had she known that Byrne considered her attitude merely that of a distraught widow. She would have been equally upset by O'Brien's belief that her desire for peace in Ireland and in the world was less strong after her husband's murder. Her actions, mirrored in the visit to the Four Courts, for example, were those of a person desiring the end to the fighting of brother against brother in Ireland. The strength of her beliefs (if not always of her actions) can be seen in the organizations she joined, in the antimilitarism and antiwar statements she made, and even in her attitude toward her husband's murderer. She did not want his life to be taken, but only to have the truth revealed so that the world might see the damage caused by the military and by war hysteria. It would be nearer the truth to say that Hanna was beset by the intellectual conflicts that beset many pacifists.

The Treaty and After

T HERE WAS, in the four years after Hanna returned to Dublin, a definite shift in her priorities. Nationalist concerns now took precedence over feminist. It was an inevitable shift, given the political and social climate during the years of the Black and Tan war and the civil war. Like everyone else, women were caught up in the crosscurrents of nationalist politics and their demands for equality paled in significance amid the bloodshed.

One result of the change in emphasis—and a major loss for Hanna, for the Irish Women's Franchise League, and, in the light of its importance to the women's movement since 1912, for Irishwomen as a whole — was the demise of the *Irish Citizen*. Throughout 1919 , the paper experienced serious difficulties. There was very little money with which to operate and finding people who had time to devote to it was trying at best and sometimes impossible. So pressing were the problems that early in 1920 Louie Bennett proposed taking over the publication completely and transforming it into an organ of the women's trade union movement. This effort failed, however, primarily because of friction between Hanna and Bennett over various issues, including the acceptability of carrying tobacco ads—something Hanna opposed. During the first half of 1920 the paper came out only sporadically and finally, in September 1920, it closed its doors.

In the final issue of the *Irish Citizen*, Hanna explained that without a strong feminist movement and "without earnest and serious minded women readers and thinkers," there could be no women's paper. She regretted that the number of such individuals had "dwindled perceptibly of late," to some degree, she thought, because "the national struggle overshadows all else" but also because the vote had become an actuality for at least some women.[1]

Free of the demands of the *Irish Citizen*, Hanna was able to devote even more time than previously to obtaining the release of political prisoners and to the well-being of their families. It was largely on their behalf that she was soon back in the United States on lecture tour. Speaking in twenty-five states and in Canada during several months of 1922 and 1923, she and women from various Irish societies succeeded in raising more than $120,000, much of which went to the Prisoners' Dependents' Committee.[2] Like the newly formed Women's Prisoners' Defence League, this organization assisted political prisoners and their families in any way possible. The service it provided was badly needed, for by the end of the first quarter of 1923, some three hundred girls and women, many of them Hanna's friends, were in Dublin prisons.

The Women's Prisoners' Defence League had been formed in Roebuck House, the home of Maud Gonne, in 1922 and it was there that the organization was headquartered. She was its secretary and Charlotte Despard its president. With a membership consisting primarily of the mothers, wives, and sisters of political prisoners, its primary functions were to collect food and clothing for the imprisoned, to look after the needs of their families, and to arrange for visits by their relatives. Its efforts to elicit support were carefully planned and executed. Elaborate processions of children paraded to church to pray for the release of their fathers, mothers, brothers, and sisters, and much publicity was released on prison conditions throughout Ireland.[3]

This organization, to which Hanna had devoted a large share of her time in 1925, was meeting with considerable success. According to a report by Maud Gonne in her regular column in *An Phoblacht* (The Republic), prisoners were now allowed to have pencil and paper, to study Irish, and to use needle and thread; the prison board had even hired two wardens who spoke Gaelic. Protest marches were being held regularly and were even occasionally viewed with "sympathetic interest" by prominent citizens, who sometimes walked and talked with the protestors. The success was deserved, for the triad of Gonne, Despard, and Sheehy-Skeffington worked tirelessly and at some personal risk. They could be seen on the streets of Dublin collecting for imprisoned Irish Republicans and they, as well as others working for the cause, were often threatened and on occasion attacked. At one point, Maud Gonne reported, "Mrs. Sheehy-Skeffington was threatened by a gentleman motorist sporting a Union Jack, who brandished an iron spanner over her head."[4]

On the broader political front, terrorist tactics were continuing on

both sides and de Valera and others were growing weary of the whole battle. Hanna was back from the States when, in May 1923, the Republican
forces agreed to a truce. In a very emotional message to the "Soldiers of
the Republic," de Valera said that further sacrifice of life would be contrary to national interest. Though the fighting ceased as far as the Republicans were concerned, the Free Staters did not consider it over. A letter
from Hanna to the adjutant general's office reported that during a raid on
her residence a typewriter, among other things, was "removed." Just a
few months later her house was raided once more; this time the cutlery
was taken.⁵

The Republicans continued to function clandestinely as a government under de Valera's guidance and to consider themselves the true government of all Ireland. Hanna's position in that organization was an important one. It had been learned that W. T. Cosgrave, head of the Irish
Free State government, was to attend the League of Nations meeting in
Paris with the purpose of asking that body to accept the candidature of his
government on behalf of the nation. Since, as the Republicans declared,
he did not represent all of Ireland but only twenty-six counties of the
thirty-two, he had no right to do so. Hanna, accordingly, was assigned by
the acting minister for foreign affairs of Dail Eireann to go to Paris to
"counter this move." While in the city, her instructions read, she was to
meet with L. H. Kerney, diplomatic and consular representative of the
Irish Republic in France, who would give her the necessary introductions
and credentials and she was to "carry out the mission under his supervi-
sion." A sum sufficient to cover expenses would be placed at her dis-
posal.⁶

Hanna carried out her assignment as directed for, in September,
Mr. Kerney sent a dispatch to Austin Ford of the *Irish World* reporting
that she had "lodged protest with League of Nations Geneva on behalf
Irish Republic against proposed admission of portion of Irish Nation
falsely described as free state, for whose debts and obligations republican
government of all Ireland declines responsibility."⁷ The Irish Free State,
despite the protest, was admitted to membership in the League of Nations, though its status was not spelled out and though Britain protested
its acceptance as an entity separate from the British Commonwealth.

The continued Free State agitation against the Republicans had at
least one positive result: as distaste for its tactics grew, public apathy subsided. By 1924 Sinn Fein, whose numbers had been steadily declining,
was once again attracting members. There were resignations from the

Free State Dail and those Republicans who had been elected to that body refused to take their seats. Some said that if the oath were abolished they would do so; others claimed that they would not even under those conditions, since they would not support a parliament that accepted partition.

Hanna's position was never in doubt. She was firmly against both the oath and partition. As principal speaker at a Republican rally in Manchester, sponsored by the Cathal Brugha Branch of Sinn Fein, she called for the support of all men and women who were for "Freedom, Justice and an Undivided Ireland."[8] At a protest meeting against the continued internment of political prisoners in Northern Ireland, she said that "as an unrepentant and convinced Republican" she "recognized no boundary in Ireland" and, like other Republicans, was "not worried by any Boundary Commission." She saw "the whole thing as a humbug and a fraud."[9]

For Hanna, this was a year taken up as usual with a heavy speaking schedule, writing, and on the lighter side, plays and family gatherings. At the latter, Bessie and Father Eugene were deeply missed, as was Hanna's brother Richard, who had died in October 1923. Though he had been teaching in Galway and therefore seldom saw the family, his death nonetheless left a void. A family story, attested to by Richard's daughter, Pan Collins, maintains that his wife, Catherine, refused to speak with her sister-in-law for many years after the funeral because Hanna, instead of attending, had addressed a meeting. The account may well be true, for Hanna would have found it hard to see how her being there could do Richard any good; consequently, her time would be better spent doing good for someone or something. It certainly was not because of lack of love for her brother since they had always been extremely fond of each other.[10] Also missing at the family gatherings was Margaret, who had remarried in 1921 and was living in Canada.

Hanna at this time was giving serious thought to writing a life of her husband and in 1925 Alice Park suggested it also. "Of course you are busy with present problems," she wrote, "but you prolonged his life by your lectures and can prolong it further by a printed volume."[11] Hanna, however, was much too involved with her numerous causes, each urgent, to devote the necessary time to such a venture. It was probably just as well. A wife—especially one as devoted and as involved with her husband's life as Hanna had been—would have found drawing a balanced portrait difficult and perhaps impossible. In later years, she thought of writing her memoirs and this certainly would have been an invaluable contribution to the social history of the period. But again, nothing came of the project.

As though Hanna were not involved in enough controversies, Gretta Cousins wrote urging her to take up the battle against drink, that "awful curse of Ireland." The problem had been brought home to her, she said, at a performance of O'Casey's *Juno and the Paycock* "when that packed Abbey audience turned the whole tragedy into farce by its laughter at every drink episode, oblivious to its satire on the country."[12] Hanna really needed no urging, for Ireland's "curse" was something both she and her husband had long been aware of.

There is no way of knowing how Hanna felt about O'Casey's *Juno* but her reaction to *The Plough and the Stars* is another matter. For her, *The Plough* was more than just a play: it was a desecration of the memory of the men who fought in the Rising.

There are many accounts of the controversy over the play, and from them these details emerge. On opening night, 8 February 1926, the house was sold out. W. B. Yeats had invited some members of the executive council of the Irish Free State—among them the vice-president, the finance minister and the lord chief justice—to be his guests for the performance and dinner. Gabriel Fallon, O'Casey's close friend, suggested that Yeats, then a Free State senator, might have been hoping that the play would "score over his Republican enemies."[13] On the second night, there were some audience objections when the Republican flag was brought into the pub in Act II and on the third night these protests were even more pronounced and seemed to be directed toward the young prostitute.[14]

All accounts agree that on Thursday night, disapproval climaxed in a Republican demonstration; all seem to agree that Hanna led it, although accounts of later events differ. According to one, during the second act she arose and shouted that the play was "traducing the men of 1916." From that point on nobody could hear the dialogue on stage and minor battles were breaking out in various parts of the theater. Through it all, Hanna continued to orate.[15] Before the fourth act began, Yeats brought in the police and the hall was cleared of protestors. Hanna, leaving the theater under police escort, made one last dramatic speech. "I am one of the widows of Easter Week," she said. "It is no wonder that you do not remember the men of Easter Week, because none of you fought on either side. The play is going to London soon to be advertised there because it belies Ireland. . . . All you need do now is sing *God Save the King*."[16]

Fallon, at the theater on Thursday night, saw the protestors as divided into two groups: those, like Hanna, who objected on nationalistic grounds and others who found the play morally offensive. Of the latter group, he wrote, "Poor Rosie Redmond became the target. . . . I can still hear the Joxer-Daly-like accents of that fruity Dublin voice that wanted 'that wumman taken offa th'stay-age.'"[17]

A week or so after the opening of the play, a lengthy and heated interchange began between O'Casey and Hanna in the pages of the *Irish Independent*. Hanna began by insisting that the demonstration against *The Plough* was purely "on national grounds" and indicated a "passionate indignation" against a national theater staging a play that mocked the men of Easter Week.[18] In his reply, O'Casey spoke to both the nationalists and the moralists. "The National tocsin of alarm was sounded because some of the tinsel of sham was shaken from the body of truth," he said. As for those women who objected to Volunteers and Irish Citizen Army men visiting a public house, did they think "all Ireland's battles [were] fought by Confraternity men?" As for Hanna, her talk about "the Ireland that remembers with tear-dimmed eyes all that Easter Week stands for" made him sick. "Is the Ireland that is pouring to the picture houses, to the dance halls, to the football matches remembering with tear-dimmed eyes all that Easter Week stands for?" Mrs. Skeffington, he added, should not be taken seriously as a drama critic: "she is singing here on a high note wildly beyond the range of her political voice, and can be given only the charity of our silence."[19]

And on they went, with Hanna matching O'Casey in hyperbole. Any play, she wrote, "in which every character connected with the Citizen Army is a coward, a slacker, or worse, that omits no detail of squalid slumdom, the looting, the squabbling, the disease and degeneracy, yet omits any revelation of the glory and the inspiration of Easter Week, is a 'Hamlet' shown without the Prince of Denmark." She found Nora Clitheroe "no more 'typical of Irish womanhood' than her futile, snivelling husband" was of Irish men. She continued:

> The women of Easter Week, as we know them, are typified rather in the mother of Padraic Pearse, that valiant woman who gave both her sons for freedom. Such breathe the spirit of Volumnia, of the Mother of the Gracchi. That Mr. O'Casey is blind to it does not necessarily prove that it is non-existent, but merely that his vision is defective. That the ideals for which these men died have not been achieved does not lessen their glory nor make their sacrifices vain. "For they shall be remembered for ever" by the people if not by the Abbey directorate.[20]

Quoting from Yeats's nationalistic *Cathleen ni Houlihan* was a superb touch.

The exchange of insults finally culminated in a debate between the antagonists on 1 March, under the auspices of the Universities' Republican Club, an organization made up of both students and graduates of Republican sympathies. Owen Sheehy-Skeffington, who was well aware that his mother's objection to the play "was not a silly moralistic one about having a prostitute appear on an Irish stage," recalled that the audience was almost entirely sympathetic to her from the beginning.[21] "She was a very good speaker and debater, witty and factual, and she was given first chance." When O'Casey's turn came, he had to face an already hostile audience. His vision was bad, his glasses blurred, and he had great difficulty deciphering his notes. After struggling for some five minutes, he said that he could not go on and sat down. Hanna sympathized, sensing that, had he been an experienced public speaker like herself, he would have "had a lot more to say."[22]

At the time of the controversy, Owen had argued with his mother. He felt then (and nearly forty years later still felt) that the play was not primarily concerned with the rebellion but with drawing a vivid picture of how the "lumpen proletariat," conditioned by the life allotted to them by society, behaved in time of war and revolution. His mother's reply was that since this "was the first attempt by an Irish dramatist of great ability to write a play involving 1916, he had no right to treat it as merely incidental, and to suggest by implication that there was no other side to the Rebellion than this tawdry aspect." With the event still in the near-past, O'Casey should not have forgotten that men had given their lives for their ideals, she said, adding that had those ideals been carried out, "the slumdom conditions which produced the poltroons with whom O'Casey is so exclusively concerned in this play" would have been eliminated.[23]

Why Hanna gave so much of her valuable time to *The Plough and Stars* controversy is puzzling unless, as has been suggested, the Republicans were using this issue in their struggle against the Free Staters.[24] Possibly they were but, in Hanna's case, it seems more likely that her lack of objectivity and restraint was due to her temperament and to the comparatively short time that had elapsed since the Rising and the murder of her husband.

That same year, 1926, Hanna was appointed to the executive of a new party, Fianna Fail, formed by de Valera when he broke with Sinn

Fein. Her career with the new party was short-lived, however, for a year later, when de Valera found what was for him a satisfactory way of getting around the oath of allegiance and took his seat in the Dail, she broke with him and with his party.

Hanna was unable to accept his reasoning. It was merely quibbling, she thought, for de Valera and his followers to say that, since the Bible was not used, signing the oath of allegiance was "an empty formula" and that they swore no allegiance to anyone other than the people of Ireland. She saw signing the oath of allegiance as "a lapse from Republican principles & traditions" by the Free State and its British advisers, and even as poor tactics. Opposition to the oath from that time on, she felt, would be more difficult than ever and she closed the door firmly between herself and Fianna Fail. But she ended the association on a hopeful note: the repressive measures of the Free State government would, before too long, bring about its downfall.[25]

Amid the political turmoil, Hanna was deeply saddened by the death of an old friend, Constance Markievicz, on 15 July 1927. Hanna was one of those at her bedside when Markievicz died in a hospital ward "among the poor where she wanted to be,"[26] and to Hanna fell the task of administering her friend's estate. It was more than a year before the innumerable details connected with the executorship were resolved.

There was another death in 1927 which shocked the entire Sheehy family. On Christmas Day, Cruise O'Brien, Kathleen's husband, died suddenly, leaving her with her son Conor, then ten years old. Coincidentally, each of the three Sheehy girls, now widowed, had been left with one child. Mary Kettle had Betty and, of course, Hanna had her son Owen.

Now seventeen years old, Owen had been taking entrance examinations for Trinity College with great success. A letter to Hanna from her cousin in New York City, Margaret Blue, put it this way: "Kindly convey to Owen my Congratulations on the winning of University Prize. I am not surprised as you are a Family of Scholars. When I was in Dublin I remember you won Highest Honors in all Ireland."[27]

With a university scholarship achieved, Owen went to Amiens for the summer to study. There had been a connection between the Sheehy family and a family in France for many years. In 1903 Mary Sheehy had attended the Ecole Primaire Supérieure in Amiens and had become friendly with Germaine Fontaine, a fellow student. It was a lasting friendship and one that extended to the entire family, for Germaine came to Dublin in 1906 to teach for a year, staying at 2 Belvedere Place, while

Kathleen spent that year in Amiens.[28] Now, in 1928, Germaine Fontaine was Madame Denis and the mother of three children, all of them close in age to Owen. It was with them that he was going to be staying in France. Though Hanna would miss him very much, she had her own life to lead and she knew the importance of freedom for a maturing youngster.

That Owen should have a scholarship to Trinity College was important as far as family finances were concerned. Hanna was managing as she had all her married life—in a carefree fashion. A little money was coming in from her reports to the *Irish World*; a little from her numerous speaking engagements; a little from part-time teaching; and a little from what she called "pot-boilers"—articles that she was writing for various small publications, such as travel and nature magazines. Two titles are self-explanatory: "Michael Davitt: Father of the Land League, 1846–1906" and "Irish Women Writers of Today." Another piece called "That Little Flat: How Not to Make Ends Meet" was the story of two young people, just beginning their life together, with not much more than "hope and love," who decide to add to their income by renting out part of their home. Written in an amusing fashion it ends with the admonition: "So my dear young people, try taking in washing, paint Christmas cards and calendars and sell them to your friends, breed rabbits and sell their fur, run a chicken farm, peddle books—try anything and everything but letting a flat."[29] There is a touch of the autobiographical in the piece, for Hanna had indeed converted the top floor of her house into a flat from which she derived a little income. For many years her friend Rosamund Jacob occupied it.

Writing for the *Irish World* must have been a safety valve for her, as well as a fine antidote to the popular essays. When, in 1928, Asquith died, an article by her appeared, headed "Asquith, the Butcher of MacDermott and Connolly—The Inside Story of the Treachery and Cold-Blooded Murder, Lust of England's Late Premier—How Irish Patriots, Weak and Wounded, Were Shot Like Dogs."[30] The adage that one should not speak ill of the dead had never appealed to Hanna.

With Owen happy in France, Hanna and Rosamund Jacob decided on a Kilkee holiday, one that Hanna seemed to feel she could manage financially. While there they saw a performance of a play called *Felons of Our Land* which both recognized as an adaptation of Francis Sheehy-Skeffington's novel, *In Dark and Evil Days*. Hanna called it "cribbed" and thought it a badly garbled version but "good propaganda," with the gallery cheering madly at every English death and the reserved seats stiffening and muttering, "I wonder when will the shooting end?" What they really meant, Hanna said, was, "When will a rebel be shot?" She had been introduced to the audience and, when she was leaving, was cheered. "I couldn't forbear seizing the moment for an 'Up the Republic!' which was cheered to the echo!" she said. "I really can't say whether I enjoyed the piece or not—my feelings were too mixed to be weighed up definitely! I fear it was really the propaganda that pleased me best!"[31] This was undoubtedly true of her reaction to other plays but Hanna deserves full marks for at last recognizing it.

Back in Dublin after her vacation, Hanna, refreshed, resumed her duties with the Dublin County Council and her speaking schedule. She had been asked by Sinn Fein to talk at one of its meetings on behalf of political prisoners and had agreed. "They want me to return to their fold," she said, "but I'm not having any."[32] While making an effort to cut down on committee work, she was accepting any assignment that would supplement the family finances. When, for example, a superintendent was unable to fulfill an assignment to supervise university exams in Athlone, she was pleased to be asked to take his place. As she wrote Owen, "It's a soft thing & about £10 or so for week—'jolly good' as y'd say!"[33]

The correspondence between Hanna and Owen that summer was a lively one. Roger McHugh, in an interview, mentioned Owen's keen sense of humor—though he added that it was not as good as his mother's—and Owen's letters reveal his wit. Early in their correspondence Hanna twitted him about not giving her details and sent a numbered questionnaire. In answer to a question concerning the ages of the Denis children, he wrote: "I heard that Jacques is 15 ½ the other day. It must be remembered that by the time this reaches you they will all be a bit older. The system of aging is very similar to our own." The same letter ended with, "That, I think, concludes this evening's entertainment. Ladies and gentlemen, The King!"[34] Earlier, Owen had informed his mother that the oldest of the three Denis children was Andrée, about eighteen, he thought.[35] Hanna would hear much more of her for this was the girl Owen was to marry.

Prague, Moscow, Dublin

FTER ANOTHER YEAR of wearying activity Hanna, as the summer of 1929 approached, eagerly looked forward to going to Prague in August as a delegate to a conference of the Women's International League for Peace and Freedom. Plans were shaping up well: Owen would once again be going to France and to Amiens and the Denis family; expenses for Hanna's trip would be paid in part by the league; and in addition she had been commissioned to do articles on the conference for the *Irish Independent*. To her delight, Rosamund Jacob was to be a fellow delegate.

Composed mainly of feminists, the league had come into being during the war, at a time when many of the leading figures in the feminist movement were turning their backs on their goals—temporarily, they felt, of course—in order to help win the war. Hanna chose to describe it as turning from "Internationalism to Nationalistic Jingoism." At the time of the organization's first conference in 1915 at The Hague, feelings were running so high over this shift in direction that women's groups in many countries had refused to send delegates. Now, more than a decade later, the league, headquartered in Geneva, had branches in all major countries; Jane Addams was its president, as she had been from its inception. At this conference, thirty countries would be represented, though the Soviet Union and Italy declined to send delegates. Hanna, sympathetic to the Soviet Union, did not seem troubled by its abstention, sensing a growing conservatism in the organization as it grew older, which was not to her taste either.[1]

Before the Prague conference, she had ten relaxing days in Vienna and stayed at a friend's house with a glorious view of the Alps. She had always had a special fondness for Germany and, on this visit, Austria pleased her equally. Cautioning Owen not to breathe a word of it, she said she liked it better than France.[2]

Ten days of inactivity were sufficient for Hanna, however, and she left happily for Prague and the excitement of the conference, where she proceeded to renew old friendships and establish new ones. Sessions started at nine in the morning—Sundays no exception—and the delegates were busy until almost midnight, with time out for meals on the premises. Afterwards, though, Hanna could relax in a comfortable drawing room she shared with Rosamund Jacob. It was all "very charming and stimulating," she said, noting that she was busily spreading the word about how far Ireland was from real freedom.[3]

Since revival of Gaelic was an ongoing issue in Ireland, Hanna took special interest in the Czechoslovakian success in restoring—after a three-hundred-year eclipse—its own language, culture, literature, and traditions. Long an advocate of Irish instruction in the schools, she wished fervently that all Irishmen could be exposed to the Czech accomplishment.[4] To attempt to draw an exact parallel, however, might have been an error. Michael Tierney, a professor at University College, Dublin, presented a cogent argument about this time against just such a comparison. The Czechs, he contended, were "restoring" their language "to cultivated use," while in Ireland an attempt was being made to revive an already dead one. To revive a language, when no neighboring people spoke even a vaguely similar dialect and when the English language was there "to contend against," had, according to Tierney, never been accomplished. But despite the formidable obstacles, a program was established in 1922 by which all teaching in the National Schools would be in Irish for the first two grades. By 1928, more than a thousand schools were following this program, while some three and a half thousand employed both Irish and English. Fewer than four hundred used English alone in these grades.[5]

The Prague conference and travel before and after it seemed to have great restorative powers for Hanna. She had a "natural roving propensity," she said, which this trip enabled her to indulge to the full.[6] Nothing delighted her more than visiting new places and experiencing every moment fully. That was the way Hanna wanted to live.[7]

It was on this trip, also, that she visited Paris and James Joyce. As an old Dublin friend, she was given a cordial reception by the family and had dinner in Joyce's favorite restaurant. Hanna thought he was acquiring a definite French look but noted with interest that he spoke Italian with both his children, Georgio and Lucia. There was, though, the same "sudden hearty laugh" of old and he seemed eager to talk about Dublin. "I'm like that English Queen," he said, "on whose heart Calais was written. Dublin will be written on mine."[8]

Returning home at the end of the summer, Hanna was much in demand to speak about her travels and the work of the Women's International League for Peace and Freedom, of which she was now a vice president. She was also becoming active in the Friends of Soviet Russia, an organization attempting to establish a climate in Ireland that would ensure worker resistance to any aggression against the Soviet Union—a constant fear of that government—and to improve relations between the Irish and Russian peoples. These were aims to which Hanna, the internationalist, socialist, and follower of James Connolly, could subscribe, since she saw in the Soviet Union a state where production would be controlled, where better conditions and a better education would be available to the workers, and where there would be a more equitable distribution of wealth. As she told a reporter for the *Daily Express*, she was a "believer in Soviet Russia," as, she maintained, "left wing Irish Republicans" were.[9] This love affair was destined to break many a heart.

In August 1930 the Friends of Soviet Russia sent a delegation to study the Soviet system of government and to attend a conference being held in Moscow. Hanna was one of the delegates as were, among others, Maud Gonne, Charlotte Despard, and Harry Kernoff, a well-known Dublin artist. The first stop was Leningrad but they wasted no time on the way over. As they sailed across the North Sea, all-day conferences were held during which the delegates learned a few words of Russian and a great deal of history. Hanna had a "lovely" breakfast each morning in her cabin—caviar with lemon, cold meat, white bread and rolls, butter, and coffee served in glasses. She loved the boat and the food but also noted the "strict discipline"—a bit "like a monastery," she thought.[10]

On 11 August the delegates reached Leningrad. Breakfast was at noon, dinner at six and supper at eleven, and there were speeches during both breakfast and dinner. Several days later they went on to Moscow. On the train trip Hanna took particular note of the women conductors and of a countryside resembling, she thought, that of parts of the United States. Moscow she found crowded with technical experts as well as with assorted exiles and rebels.[11] As at most conferences, the delegates were kept busy from morning until night. During the several days spent in the city, the group toured "factories, craft schools, and rehabilitation centers for prostitutes and minor criminals," and Hanna was pleased to see that the institutions were administered by elected committees and that women were in responsible positions on an absolutely equal footing with men. She was distressed, however, that not once in the many speeches was Ireland mentioned and she was upset when she came across a man lying "dead drunk" in a Moscow street.[12]

On the whole, the delegates were happy with what they saw. They had come there predisposed to see the future and, so far as they could tell, the future worked. Charlotte Despard was especially excited about the joyful and outgoing children, and she was gratified to find that the discipline was mild. There was hesitation to respond, however, when she asked about serious crime in the Soviet Union and the form punishment took. The answer she was finally given was that every attempt was made to rehabilitate inmates. This failing, a person might be sent to an island penal settlement. There, prisoners were permitted considerable latitude in governing themselves and in the manner in which they lived—but they could not leave the island.[13] This was the idyllic picture painted of the Gulag. Stalin's purges, massive and savage, were only a few years away.

After three days in Moscow, the group traveled to Baku, on the west coast of the Caspian Sea (cameras banned, Hanna noted), and then back again to Moscow. From there they returned to Leningrad and, early in September, set out for home by way of London.

Hanna's experiences in the Soviet Union had done nothing to weaken her belief in its experiment, but according to a family member she never joined the Communist party, although she did attend meetings from time to time. Her relationship to the party was one of sympathy, not allegiance.

Hanna, always a better leader than follower, was never one to subordinate independence of thought to political discipline. This was quite evident in her break with Fianna Fail over the issue of the oath. While she understood the difficult position of that party—and said so—she refused to accept its decision, because it ran counter to her principles. "We will have to wait now for the emergence of a new party," she explained.[14]

She may have meant a women's party, for dissatisfaction with the antifeminism of the Free Staters was growing and the need for greater involvement on the part of the feminists in politics was becoming clear. At a Women's Freedom League meeting in London, Hanna, to illustrate the attitude of the Free State leadership, pointed out that where once there had been seven women in the Dail there was now only one. On the same platform with her was Louie Bennett. Speaking as secretary of the Irish Wom-

en's Workers Union, the only trade union for women in Ireland, she dis-
closed that her union was indeed soon to vote on the question of forming a
women's political party. She felt that such an organization was inevitable
if existing parties failed to respond to the needs of women. "Some one
must lead the way," she said. Bennett, however, was not as categorical as
Hanna—few people ever were—in her charge against the established parties. They were not, she felt, "absolutely and definitely anti-feminist." It
was more a matter of indifference to the interests and point of view of
women, despite the "real and urgent need" for them in the political
field.[15]

Louie Bennett was essentially right. To blame the Free State politicians completely for the lack of women in the Dail, for instance, was quite
unfair. Understandably, Sean Lemass, prominent at that time in Fianna
Fail, denied the charge that his party was discriminating against women
and did make one telling point: women were included in the list of candidates at the general elections and this practice would continue. "If they are
not supported by their own sex, it is difficult to see what we can do."[16]

There were reasons, social rather than political, that explained why
so many Irishwomen were reluctant to support those who were working
on their behalf. In the rural areas in the 1930s, as Professor Terence
Brown of Trinity College has observed, women were married to small
farmers who made all major decisions in the household. The wife did the
household chores, raised the children, and took care of the poultry, the
milking, and the production of dairy products. Sons were the mother's responsibility only until they made their first communion at the age of
seven. From then on they answered to the father or to their older brothers.
The daughters worked with the mother until they were married, at which
time they simply shifted their work schedule to their own homes. Often
these women moved to the city but they took with them patterns and values established over the years in their homes and in the Catholic church, a
church whose clergy came from backgrounds similar to their own and
were the product of a fairly unintellectual and culturally stagnant semi-
nary training.[17]

Following World War I, there was a period of conservatism and repression in many countries but, as Brown points out, "extreme" repression was disastrous in a country like Ireland, which, thanks to "protracted
colonial mismanagement," was badly in need of both cultural and social
development.[18] This was the situation that faced such feminists as Hanna
and Louie Bennett: the women they were attempting to influence and as-

sist were accustomed to following blindly the orders of the church and of the men in their families. The less open-minded feminists could not seem to see that this posed a problem for the Free Staters as well.

The impression should not be given that the apathy of so many women caused the feminists to despair. Pressure of work was probably the chief reason that they did not become discouraged. There wasn't time. Inevitably, action, successful or not, produced a sense that something important was being accomplished. For Hanna there was—in addition to her popular articles, her speaking engagements, and her teaching—her work with *An Phoblacht*, a publication founded in 1925 by de Valera. The first issue of the paper had contained an article by her and she had been a frequent contributor ever since. Its editor, Frank Ryan, a prominent left-wing Sinn Feiner, was in and out of jail and Hanna had assumed a great many of the paper's editorial chores, was writing much of its copy, and eventually became assistant editor.

One of *An Phoblacht*'s first editors, Peader O'Donnell, remembered it as a paper that attempted to consider a world outside of Ireland and to cover art, literary criticism, and the theater. It also carried on a full-scale war against the government and, as a result, led a precarious existence, with those who worked on the paper hunted and harried.[19]

The period when Hanna was assistant editor was one of feverish activity and confusion at the St. Andrew Street office of the paper. There was a constant stream of visitors coming up the "creaky stairs: visiting pressmen on the prowl, Republicans from different parts, I.R.A., Cumann na mBan with reports, ex-prisoners and prisoners-about-to-be." Adding to the confusion was the need to shout at Frank Ryan, who was very hard of hearing. One of Hanna's duties was to visit the Fodla Printing Works on the day the paper went to press. These were no ordinary visits: detectives were generally about and there was a constant threat of raids and seizures. The printer, understandably nervous, had to be humored and cajoled. At the end of these long days—there was no such thing as office hours for the dedicated staff—Hanna would be exhilarated but exhausted, and also hoarse from shouting at Frank.[20]

By the end of 1931, *An Phoblacht*, the *Irish Worker*, and the *Workers' Voice* had all been confiscated and suppressed at one time or another. In order to circumvent this drying up of news of interest to Republicans, *An Phoblacht* was replaced by the *Republican File*, which resembled Arthur Griffith's famous *Scissors and Paste*. Hanna described it as consisting of "quotations neatly compiled and often deadly." An early editorial stated piously that the paper would express no opinion but simply present the news to its readers and allow them to form their own conclusions.[21]

What the *Republican File* was replacing must have been obvious to everyone, since Frank Ryan was its editor and Hanna Sheehy-Skeffington his assistant. Its contents were uniformly antigovernment; its items, carefully selected from newspapers whose political orthodoxy could not be challenged, appeared under headings artfully designed to circumvent suppression. A piece in one of its early editions, for example, was from the *Evening Mail* and reported that Sheila Humphreys, the "first woman before Military Tribunal" had spoken in Irish and then said in English, "I refuse to recognise the authority of this Court. You are a self-appointed clique of members of the British Army of Occupation, making what I hope will be the final effort to hold this country for England." At the conclusion of her evidence, when asked if she had anything else to say, she replied, caustically, that she had "plenty to say about a lot of things," and then went on to declare: "I am charged with being a member of Cumann na mBan and I admit it. You are very foolish to try and suppress that organisation for we thrive on suppression." The message was obvious.[22]

Item after item in the paper listed Hanna as either a member of a deputation or a speaker at a rally. She was speaking out again and again on the subject of Free State censorship and its effect on women in Ireland, as she had been even before the Censorship of Publications Act of 1929 had passed. Before one group she had called the then-proposed legislation "ridiculous," adding "The Minister for Justice apparently is to decide for us what is good and what is bad." This legislation was to be imposed upon women by "the other sex," by a group of "prudish" men who felt women should not be allowed to serve on juries because it wasn't "nice" and who had women stenographers banned from court work for the same reason. Actually, she said, it was fear of the women's superior skill that motivated them. To underline the threat of this type of censorship, she pointed out that the books and ads banned by the bill might include parts of the Bible and a play like *Romeo and Juliet* since these, as well as ads dealing with birth control and venereal disease in such respected publications as the *Observer* and the *Spectator*, might come under the heading of "literature which would excite sexual passions."[23]

It was a sexually enlightened Hanna Sheehy-Skeffington who was confronting issues of the day. In *The Vote* she reviewed Vera Brittain's *Halcyon, or The Future of Monogamy*, a book whose author, Hanna commented, had condemned conventional marriage as responsible for much present-day suffering and confusion. Only through the breaking down of "Victorian and Georgian pruderies, taboos, inhibitions" could monogamy triumph, Brittain maintained, and Hanna made it clear that she agreed. The controversial topics upon which Brittain touched were sex education for the young, companionate marriage, and the ban upon married women working at their chosen professions which, Hanna wrote, Brittain correctly condemned as tending to discredit marriage. Of all these, it was perhaps sex education for the young that most concerned Hanna, since she had spent many unhappy hours herself as a result of the lack of such education. But she believed the other issues important too and supported the author's liberal position on them, urging all feminists to become familiar with Brittain's work.[24]

An inevitable result of the repressive measures introduced by the government in Ireland was an exodus of men and women in the arts. In a 1930 *Irish Independent* article, Hanna pointed with pride to the number of Irish writers, dramatists, and journalists in London. If you took away the Irish, she wrote, London's literary life would suffer seriously. Three theaters were running Shaw plays; a St. John Ervine play was drawing record crowds; and O'Casey's first sound film, *Juno and the Paycock*, was showing in one of the movie houses. Among novelists, poets, and critics, she said, could be found the names of James Stephens, Liam O'Flaherty, Con O'Leary, Robert Lynch, W. P. Ryan, Eimar O'Duffy, and Austin Clarke. As for women, there were actress Sara Allgood, critic Sylvia Lynch, and writer Rebecca West, to name only a few. Since this was one of Hanna's lighter pieces, she gave no reason why these people preferred London to Dublin.[25] Perhaps she should have echoed the words of the Anglo-Irish Dublin architect, P. L. Dickinson: "To those who, like myself, have had to leave their native country owing to the acts of their fellow-countrymen, a perfectly dispassionate judgement of the situation must be a little difficult. I love Ireland; few people know it better." But, he said, like thousands of other Irishmen who shared his views, there was no room for him in the present Ireland.[26]

Repression, however, was by no means the only problem from which the country was suffering in the early thirties. Economically, agrarian Ireland had not felt the depression of the period as deeply as other nations. Nonetheless, because of the terrible economic conditions in other countries, the international market for Irish farm products was curtailed drastically, as was the price that could be obtained for them within Ireland. By the eve of the 1932 election, incomes were declining steadily.

Thanks to the darkening economic picture and the increase in repressive measures, the Cosgrave administration was unseated in the elections and in February 1932 Eamon de Valera, intransigent advocate of complete Irish independence, became prime minister of the Irish Free State. He immediately abolished the oath of allegiance to the British Crown. Also, pending independent arbitration, he intended to annul certain provisions of the 1921 peace treaty that provided for the payment of land annuities to the United Kingdom exchequer. It was only then that Hanna made her uneasy, and in the end impermanent, peace with him. Maud Gonne, however, accepted him without reservation. At a meeting of the Women's Republican Prisoners' Defence League in October she thanked God for him and said that within a year, through the government's efforts, there would not be an unemployed man in the state.[27]

It was around this time, for reasons not completely clear from available material, that Hanna refused to sit on the Sinn Fein executive. Perhaps she agreed with Maud Gonne, who thought the members lived "in too rarefied an atmosphere for poor mortals" and who objected particularly to their lack of imagination and also to their unwillingness to boycott English manufactured goods in an organized fashion, to help political prisoners, and to work in "mixed" company—that is, along with Protestants. But the heavy demands on Hanna's time also offer a quite reasonable explanation for her refusal.[28]

Though Hanna was giving fewer lectures, she was doing more writing and she had been promised radio work as well. She had severed her connection with the *Irish World* but was doing popular articles for the *Irish Press*, the *Independent*, and publications like the *Distributive Worker*. Her pieces covered a great variety of topics and showed a light, witty style; moreover, they often made telling points. In "Wives of Great Men—Their Side of the Story," for instance, she makes a good case for the argument that although many wives were talented, their literary or artistic efforts were generally treated impatiently or condescendingly—and so were they. "True," Hanna wrote, "Wordsworth wrote lyrics about [his wife]" but they had "a kitchen flavour." As for Rossetti, he had been so shattered by his wife's death that he had had a manuscript buried with her, but later, after a change of mind or heart, he had her exhumed so that he could get it back and have it published. Summarizing, Hanna wrote: "Addison married for money; Byron made a disastrous husband; Thackeray's wife became insane; Dickens and Ruskin were unhappily married—yet in none of these cases was the tragedy due to their wives, but to circumstances and to their own nature." From this one might conclude, Hanna thought, that men and women of genius make difficult mates and need "patience and self-control enough for two."[29]

Hanna's reviews—and she was doing a great many at this time—revealed an analytical flair but at times were embarrassingly biased. About *Young China and New Japan* by Mrs. Cecil Chesterton, she stated, unconvincingly, that here, once again, was proof of how suited women were to writing travel books and "infusing into them a freshness of outlook and a personality" that men usually seemed ill-equipped to give them.[30]

Both her personal and her professional life was going well in 1932. Hanna was needed almost full time on the *Republican File* and enjoyed the excitement. Owen had been home all summer and, thanks to delightful weather, they had taken long walks and an occasional trip. But at year's end—17 December—her father died, leaving, as she said, "a great gap."[31]

Though David had been failing for some time, his death came quite suddenly. He and Bessie had been living with Margaret when Bessie died in 1918, and he had continued to live with Margaret until she left Dublin in the early twenties. He had then moved in with Mary. Since family had always meant a great deal to him, he was grateful when his son Eugene, after his marriage in 1923, had continued the tradition of bringing the family together for holidays. Pan Collins, David's granddaughter, recalled one of these occasions in 1929 when she saw tears of happiness streaming down David's face at the sight of the whole family gathered there.[32]

His grandson, Conor Cruise O'Brien, fifteen when David died, remembered him as an absent-minded old man whom daughter Mary was "inclined to bully" and who went off "to Mass six times a day, once for each of his six children."[33] How David saw his family, on the other hand, is uncertain but he must have realized early on that he had not spawned an average brood. His son Richard, who died some ten years before him, had begun a promising career as a law professor. Eugene was a circuit court judge. As for his daughters, they seemed to be proving Bessie's contention that they could accomplish anything they set out to do. Kathleen was teaching in the Rathmines Technical School, Mary was deep in political activity and a member of the Dublin Corporation, and Hanna was a driving force in political, labor, and feminist circles. That she no longer practiced Catholicism did not seem to alter his regard for her.

Since Margaret was not in Dublin, David could probably maintain a certain amount of objectivity toward her rather bizarre way of life. At the age of forty-two, some five years after the death of her husband, Margaret Culhane, the mother of four, had fallen madly in love with a twenty-one-year-old poet named Michael Thomas Casey. In 1921 she became pregnant out of wedlock and, as her oldest child, Garry Culhane, told the story, this was too much even for the liberal Sheehys and Margaret thought it best to "get the hell out of the country." She married Casey and they went to live in Canada, taking Garry with them. The Culhane family took in the three younger children. In mid-August 1922 in Montreal, Margaret gave birth to another son, Ronan. Letters to Hanna requesting money indicate that they were very poor, but also that she was ecstatically happy. Garry Culhane remembered that his mother was always the center of an "intellectual" and theatrical group in Montreal.[34] David would have had to admit that the Sheehy girls were a remarkable, if sometimes unpredictable, lot.

The next upheaval in Hanna's life came scarcely a month after her father's death. The government of Northern Ireland had forbidden her to enter the six counties because of her political record. Refusing to obey this order, she crossed the border, was taken into custody, and was detained for ten days while awaiting trial. From the Armagh jail, she wrote her sister Mary a cheerful note, urging her not to worry and adding: "I needn't tell you I'm not doing so!"[35]

Once more Hanna saw her arrest as an opportunity to express her views. Notes that she made during or just prior to her trial and that apparently outline her testimony read, in part: "The authorities, de facto not de jure, are making themselves *ridiculous* & obnoxious by such arbitrary procedure. . . . As an *Irish Republican* I stand for an unpartitioned, independent Ireland—of 32 counties. . . . My arrest or rather kidnapping only serves to emphasize the scandal of Partition. . . . I would shame my race & my murdered husband's name if I submitted to a decree that makes an alien of me—in Ulster."[36] She was sentenced to one month in Armagh jail.

The governor of the jail would remember Hanna for reasons other than her having received a visit from her brother Eugene, a prominent judge, as witness the letter she sent the governor the day before her release. "I do not know whether you were joking merely when you spoke of a *police escort*, not to border, but to my own home!" she wrote. If he was indeed serious, she planned to "take strong exception." It did not matter to her whether the police were in uniform or not, because they had no right outside their own territory. She wanted it clearly understood that once she crossed the six-county border, she was on her own.[37]

An enthusiastic group welcomed Hanna home—some accounts mentioned as many as five thousand—and somewhat later the Irish Women's Franchise League gave a supper party to celebrate her release.[38] The speeches made up in hyperbole for what they lacked in accuracy. "Mrs. Skeffington has started a fire which will end the hated partition of Ireland, doubly hateful because it is on a sectarian basis," said Meg Connery. And Maud Gonne said Hanna had done more than anyone else to end partition and presented her with a medal on behalf of the Women's Prisoners' Defence League for helping to end Cosgrave's Coercion Acts.[39]

This latest prison episode behind her, Hanna firmly resolved to drop all of her committees and spend more time on her personal affairs. A split in the Republican movement strengthened her resolution. One group was now primarily concerned with establishing a republic; the other called for complete socialization of the country. Hanna had very little sympathy with the former group, which was led, very badly she thought, by Sean MacBride. But she was not completely happy with the latter group either, perhaps because of its impracticality and fanaticism.[40]

In reality, there was very little chance at that time of socializing Ireland. Economic conditions were bad, leading to a general restiveness and a search for scapegoats. Communism and Communists seemed a logical target and the Catholic church was helping to sharpen the sights. The bishops' lenten pastorals consisted of strong attacks not only on communism as a theory but also on its practice in the Soviet Union. The propaganda barrage was effective and soon gangs of youths began to disrupt left-wing meetings. A bitter attack was made on Connolly House, the headquarters of the Irish Revolutionary Workers' Party which later became the Irish Communist Party. During the rioting, Hanna, openly sympathetic not only to the Republican cause but to the Soviet Union, was assaulted by angry citizens shouting "Up the Pope!" and "Down with Russia!" and singing "Faith of Our Fathers."[41] A blow to her left eye was severe enough to cause a hemorrhage. "For faith & fatherland," Hanna noted acidly.[42]

Charlotte Despard was another who felt the barbs of anti-left hysteria. She had left Roebuck House to move into a house in Eccles Street. She had intended to use the house both as the headquarters of the Friends of Soviet Russia and as the home of the Irish Workers' College, expressly set up for I.R.A. members. At the time of the Connolly House riot, an attempt was made to burn down the Eccles Street house and Despard, almost ninety, decided to flee the country. Accordingly, she gave that house to the Friends of Soviet Russia, Roebuck House to Maud Gonne, named Hanna her trustee and, with others, her executor, and left for Belfast, where, Hanna told her, conditions were suitable for left-wing agitation.[43]

One of the attempts made to fight the rising tide of conservatism was the formation of the Irish Secular Society in late 1933. This group, with Owen Sheehy-Skeffington as its vice-chairman, sought to establish in Ireland "complete freedom of thought, speech and publication, liberty of the mind in the widest toleration compatible with orderly progress and rational conduct." Its program called for an end to clerical management of schools and the introduction of secular education, the lifting of the rates and taxes exemption for churches, removal of the ban on divorce, repeal of the censorship of publications act, and promotion of sectarian interests by combating clerical influence in public and business life.[44]

So bitter was the feeling against any organization professing to be antichurch that the Irish Secular Society had difficulty in renting a meeting place. The Contemporary Club, to which some of the I.S.S. members belonged (Owen was a member as his father had been before him), offered to rent them a room but rescinded the offer under pressure from publications such as the *Irish Catholic* and the *Irish Press*. Finally the society was forced to meet in private homes.[45]

It was becoming apparent that Owen planned to lead as active a life as his mother was leading and as his father had led. He had actually sparked the formation of the Irish Secular Society and Hanna was proud that his liberalism paralleled her own. She was happy, too, that he had obtained a three-year contract from Trinity College to teach French and that he was unofficially engaged to Andrée Denis (the eldest child of the family in Amiens with whom he had spent several summers), for Hanna liked her. She had come to know her well when Andrée, then teaching in Scotland, had come over in 1929 to spend Christmas with the Sheehy family and had stayed with Hanna at 7 Belgrave Road.[46]

There was no sign, however, that Hanna was ready to turn over the reins. In addition to such dramatic adventures as being jailed and beaten in the Connolly House riot, she had been lecturing, had been appointed second drama critic for the *Irish Press* and had, as always it seems, prospects for new literary ventures. She was also involved in preparing a series of radio broadcasts. As part of the series, she planned to devote three segments to Constance Markievicz and she hoped to do two each on James Connolly, Padraic Pearse, Thomas MacDonagh, Tom Clarke, and Roger Casement. As she visualized the talks, they were to be merely personal impressions, in a popular style and quite uncontroversial.[47]

Apparently the radio was a good medium for Hanna, for even decades later there were still those who remembered her broadcasts discussing the art of film. Some recalled also that she debated the question of the appointment of women to the police force, at that time a controversial issue. An undated transcript of one such discussion shows her facility. The questioner expressed surprise that Hanna, who had so little use for the police, "male or female, foreign or domestic," should want to see women engaged in that ignoble profession. Hanna explained, probably not patiently, that since we did not live in an ideal world where police would be unnecessary, law enforcement, as well as all other fields, should not exclude women. As she saw it, women could perform a variety of important duties: take depositions from women and children, escort women prisoners to and from court, search women prisoners, administer women's sections in prisons, find shelter for women and children stranded in cities, inspect places of amusement like dance halls, act as school attendance officers, inspect lodging houses for women, check on cases of neglect or cruelty to children and to animals, and deal with prostitutes in the streets. One can be sure Hanna made it quite clear that women could carry out these duties far better than men.[48]

Continuing the Struggle

ANNA BEGAN 1934 by adding another confrontation to her already long list. She instituted suit against the New Catholic Press of Manchester, publishers of the *Irish Catholic Herald*, when that paper carried an item claiming that she had accepted a pension from the British government. In her opinion, the article made her out a hypocrite who, as editor of *An Phoblacht*, denounced the British government and anyone willing to come to terms with it while at the same time accepting from it a pension and provision for the education of her son. "I deny that I have ever accepted a pension from the British Government for the death of my husband," Hanna countered; she denied also that she had allowed that government or anyone acting in its behalf to give her money toward her son's education. Her sole income came from her work as lecturer and journalist; consequently, the libel of the *Irish Catholic Herald* report would, she argued, interfere with her ability to sell her writings to Irish Catholic publications.[1]

Her case was listed at the end of May, in early June it went to court, and by the end of the year she had won the libel suit and been awarded £750 in damages. Unfortunately, the New Catholic Press went bankrupt and she never received the money. But the verdict gave Hanna one of her brighter moments.[2]

This matter settled, she once again resolved to cut back on her crowded schedule and, once again, failed. It was fortunate that her work as drama critic for the *Irish Press* also provided one of her favorite forms of relaxation, for she was required to attend plays and movies, both of which she loved. Early in the year, during a fortnight's visit to London, she saw five plays and an equal number of films. One of the plays—*The Double Door*, with Sybil Thorndike—she thought admirably suited for the Gate Theatre: the "Grand Guignol type," she called it. Of the films, she felt only *The Late Christopher Bean* and *Catherine the Great* were worth mentioning. She particularly admired the first and hoped that it would escape the censor's scissors if it came to Dublin, convinced that cuts in sound films were intolerable and that the practice should be stopped. She was also giving thought to the need for an academy in Dublin where foreign films could be shown.[3]

Despite the depressed economy and the tremendous amount of unemployment in London, Hanna noted that both plays and movies were very well attended even though, by Dublin standards at least, they were expensive: a seat in the pit was four shillings, one in the upper circle between five and eight shillings, and a program sixpence.[4]

While in London, Hanna attempted to get a position as a correspondent for the *Christian Science Monitor* but without success. It was probably just as well. A certain amount of her time was now being spent preparing for her radio broadcasts and she was also making up a French examination for the Civil Service Commission, an assignment that would involve correcting four hundred papers in July.

Though she had wanted the previous year to get to the United States and Canada to lecture—it was always a trip she enjoyed—that plan had been dropped. Now she was again attempting to complete arrangements and before the end of 1934 she succeeded. The subjects of her talks were "Dublin Memories Grave and Gay," "Irish Writers of Today," "The New Ireland," "Women in Public Life," and "From Leningrad to Baku"[5]—all general enough to allow her to cover a variety of issues and, above all, to underline the position of women in and out of Ireland.

For the most part, Hanna's lectures took a positive view. In the Irish Free State, she told her audiences, women were being elected to all commissions and trade boards—for example, she had been elected to the Dublin City Council as well as to the Dublin County Council—and women were proving especially effective in work for libraries, education, and child welfare, since they were the "practical sex." Feminists, Hanna made clear, had no desire to usurp the position of men; they wanted merely to work side by side with them in "abolishing war, cut throat capitalistic competition," and other evils. Feminism, she said, was an enduring movement that would grow in strength regardless of current difficulties. She took no hard-and-fast stand on whether or not women should work after marriage, believing that this had to be decided on an individual basis. It seemed a pity to her, though, for a woman to abandon a profession or a career upon marriage and it was surely unjust that women should be denied employment simply because they were married. In most cases, after all, they were working because their money was needed to support their homes.[6]

The rise of fascism was, of course, a subject on the minds of many in her audiences and she did not ignore it. In the light of the appalling events to come in Nazi Germany, however, Hanna's remarks to a Canadian audience seem startlingly narrow and unprophetic. Hitler, she told them, was "one of the worst opponents of feminism" but he and his "whole Fascist scheme" were only temporary. "The women are very strongly in rebellion against Hitler and I think they will have the last word," she said.[7]

Hanna's tour included a period in New York City in mid-December, and she found the city changed dramatically. Wherever she turned there was another new skyscraper, "remote, inhuman, rather terrifying" in its effect. The dark years of the depression had left their mark as well. On the streets she saw men and women peddling matches, laces, dying flowers; old men and women shivering in the sharp December wind; garbage cans being searched for bits of food, for firewood, or for empty bottles that could be redeemed for a few pennies. Homeless men and women were being housed in armories. But despite the depression, Fifth Avenue was as resplendent as ever, the beauty of the shop windows excelling any she had seen in Paris, Berlin, London, or Vienna.[8]

How well Hanna did financially on this trip is unclear but it did give her a chance for a long visit with her sister Margaret in Montreal and did provide material for a number of talks she delivered in Ireland upon her return in mid-winter. Before the Dublin Literary Society she spoke on "The Books They Read and the Plays They See in the U.S.A." To the Women's Freedom League, an organization formed by Charlotte Despard as a break-away group from the Women's Social and Political Union, Hanna offered her conclusion that the position of women was no better in the United States than in most other countries. Their wages were considerably lower than men's for the same work, and married women workers were generally faced with dismissal. But, Hanna said, women were aware of all these difficulties and this was the important thing. She did note, however, that five women had been elected to Congress, more than a hundred were serving in "State parliaments," child labor had been virtually abolished "through the efforts of women," and women doctors were working in "new relief schemes."[9] Clearly the outlook was not altogether bleak.

Hanna's devotion to the feminist cause has never been open to question but this was not true of her pacifism. Over and over the question has been raised as to whether, after her husband's murder, her convictions continued to be as strong as his—in fact whether she continued to be a pacifist at all. Unfortunately, a conclusive case cannot be made for either view. In a 1935 collection of essays by prominent pacifists, edited by Julian Bell, Hanna wrote of her husband's efforts on behalf of pacifism and described graphically the manner in which he met his death. Could she, when she wrote the following lines, have no longer believed them? "When the war clouds gathering over Europe at last burst in 1914," she said, "Francis Sheehy Skeffington at once ranged himself against the militarists. His logical brain grasped the falsity and hypocrisy of the war slogans—'For the Freedom of Small Nations'—and his pen . . . was at once in the service of war's debunkers."[10] Further, a cable to Jane Addams, undated, reads: "Believe World Peace only securable by scrapping capitalism & Imperialism & outlawing armament-makers. Consider League of Nations merely a shield for the victors."[11]

Hanna's daughter-in-law, Andrée Sheehy-Skeffington, saw her as something less than a "total pacifist," however: in international affairs, she could be considered one but she saw the conflict between Ireland and England in a different light. Andrée stated further that Owen Sheehy-Skeffington, a pure adherent to the doctrine, often disagreed with his mother on this matter. But both he and Andrée, whom he married in 1935, felt that any deviation after her husband's death was understandable.[12]

The truth probably is that Hanna retained her attachment to pacifism in the abstract but, at the same time, tacitly accepted force (perhaps reluctantly) when it was in the cause of Irish freedom. While she never advocated violence against the British, she never—so far as present evidence indicates—condemned those, like Michael Collins, who employed it in the name of a free and united Ireland.

At any rate, she constantly used every propaganda tool available to further the causes of feminism and peace. She had always felt that her husband's novel, *In Dark and Evil Days*, was a strong testament to both ideals and she made every effort to have it reprinted. In 1936 her efforts succeeded. She also petitioned to have it selected as a school text but here she failed. In her opinion, it was passed over by the authorities because of certain uncomplimentary references to the Irish.[13]

It is possible she was right in her assessment of the motives behind the decision, for the climate under the Free State government in 1936 seemed nearly as repressive as it had been in the twenties. In its strenuous attempt to return to the values of the past—which were idealized and usually provincial—the government imposed harsh restrictions on art, drama, and music. As Terence Brown put it: "An attitude of xenophobic suspicion often greeted any manifestation of what appeared to reflect cosmopolitan standards. An almost Stalinist antagonism to modernism, to surrealism, free verse, symbolism and the modern cinema was combined with prudery . . . and a deep reverence for the Irish past." There was even opposition to paintings of nudes hanging in the National Gallery of Art in Dublin.[14]

"What a time we live in!" Hanna noted scornfully, adding that Ireland was "rapidly becoming a Catholic statelet under Rome's grip," with censorship, provincialism, and smugness. While she thought de Valera better than his predecessor, she had no faith in him, convinced that he was "essentially conservative & church-bound" as well as antiwomen. Like the professorial President Wilson, he seemed to revel in abstract phrases and ideas.[15]

Certainly as far as women workers were concerned there were no radical changes under the de Valera government. Most women worked in agricultural occupations, or in personal service as domestics and as workers in hotels, restaurants, public houses, and hairdressing salons. A substantially smaller number worked as factory and workshop laborers in such industries as textiles, food, tobacco, paper, and printing; and about as many more were professionals—primarily nuns, nurses, and teachers. As for types of work, then, there seemed to be none open to women that had not been available previously. Aside from agricultural occupations, women were employed mostly in personal service and it is interesting, and revealing, to compare the number of women in that field—109,500, with the figure for men in the same category—18,000.[16]

Early in 1937, there were some attempts to counteract the government's lack of interest in the status of women. The *Irish Times*, in a supplement, carried a story that began: "Despite the new Constitution, which appears to suggest that the activities of women should be confined to the home circle, the modern Irishwoman appears to have taken a very prominent part in many departments of public life during the past year." The article, headed "Irishwomen's Place in the National Life—Their Contributions to the Arts," went on to list an impressive array of female writers, artists, scientists, and politicians.[17]

Hanna added her voice several months later when she spoke before a capacity audience at a meeting of the Women's Freedom League in London. Limiting herself to current Irish female writers, she presented a lengthy list of poets, novelists, dramatists, scholars, and historians, noting approvingly that some ot the poets, such as Eva Gore-Booth, Alice Milligan, and Lady Augusta Gregory, were also "propagandists and rebels of the first order." Kate O'Brien, the novelist who chaired the meeting, Hanna called the Irish Galsworthy, mentioning that O'Brien had had the honor of having one of her books banned in Ireland. Dorothy Macardle's *The Irish Republic*, upon which the author had worked for eight years, had just come out and Hanna predicted, accurately, that it would be "epoch-making."[18]

Greatly concerned about the lack of recognition of women, the National University Women Graduates' Association sponsored the formation of the Women's Social and Progressive League late in 1937. At its first formal meeting, a provisional committee of twelve was appointed to act for the first six months, with Hanna as one of the honorary secretaries. The aims of the association as set forth at this meeting were ambitious: to ensure and advance the rights of Irishwomen; to organize women voters so that they might better work for equal opportunity, and equal pay for equal work for men and women; to promote women candidates for the Dail, for various public boards, and for all commissions set up by the government; and to be constantly alert to and to take action on "all matters affecting the interests of women."[19] It was an organization for which Hanna had high hopes.

Busy as she was, Hanna still found time to remember the birthdays of her nieces and nephews and to take a keen interest in all of them. Conor Cruise O'Brien was a frequent visitor. Another nephew, David Sheehy, a judge like his father, remembered visiting her when he was a teenager, having tea with her, and being taken into town to the stores. Of all his aunts, he said, she was the one he admired most. This is not surprising, since all accounts indicate that Hanna was vitally interested in the ideas of the young, and was always ready to listen with an open mind.[20] She once told a friend that she hoped she would "never grow elderly-minded" and added, "one needn't."[21]

She was always active in family gatherings as well. Eugene, David's father, did not marry until he was thirty-nine, but when he did, he assumed the role formerly played by his parents. Christmas Day, for example, was celebrated at his home and David recalled Hanna, Mary, Kathleen, and Owen ransacking the house for charade costumes. Hanna he remembered as having "a tough face redeemed by a beautiful smile."

There was, however, except for the Cruise O'Brien branch, a certain amount of disapproval within the family of her ideas, as well as of those of her son. They were, the family thought, too radical and, of course, the matter of religion entered into it as well. David says, regretfully, that for this reason he did not get to know Owen well.[22]

In the fall of 1937, when Hanna was once more planning to go to Canada and the United States to lecture, Owen became acutely ill and was sent to a sanatorium in Switzerland. His wife Andrée, admirably suited to instruct his French students, took over his classes at Trinity College and moved in with Hanna. Their mutual concern strengthened the bond between them and it was during this period that Andrée began to see more clearly than ever that behind a sometimes stern demeanor, there was a warm, romantic, and even sentimental woman. The thought of Owen alone in Switzerland troubled his mother greatly for she had a vivid memory of the period when her brother Richard, also ill, spent nine lonely months in the West Indies. Since arrangements were nearly complete for her to leave for the States in December, she decided to go to Switzerland first to visit her son, convinced that this would be the last time she would ever see him. But Owen, with his mother's determination and remarkable recuperative powers, was back in Dublin less than a year later.

Hanna's fourth United States tour began in December. She went first to Montreal to spend Christmas with Margaret and to do some speaking. From there she went to Chicago and, without a break, to California where she spoke in Carmel and in San Francisco. Under the lead "Fascism and Nazism Hit by Speaker," the *Carmel Herald* reported that she had addressed "one of the largest audiences ever to attend a session of the Carmel Forum." What the reporter saw was a quiet woman whose "gentle voice and charming diction" masked a crusading zeal. She told her audience that she believed the "destruction of capitalism would go a long way toward ending war in Europe" and that Soviet Russia was the only country in the world where women were considered absolutely equal with men. But, she added, she did not mean to say that she thought the Soviet Union had the ideal government—that honor she reserved for Denmark. She felt that Great Britain, by no means a democracy in her view, was merely playing its "balance of power" role as usual. What she wanted to see was a United States of Europe. Instead, as she traveled about these countries, she saw militarism, imperialism, and fascism all driving the Continent inexorably toward another war and threatening all democratic forms of government.[23]

A reporter interviewing Hanna for the *San Francisco Chronicle* was surprised to find that this noted rebel from the "most rebel of all places, Ireland," was a small, trim woman, her gray hair worn in a coil, who seemed just as willing to talk about Clark Gable as to discuss the situation at home. In Ireland, she told him, there was "a deal on." Britain will agree to "a plebiscite of Ulster by counties for joining Eire if de Valera will guarantee either Irish neutrality or non-action in the event of another world war."[24]

After San Francisco, Hanna returned to New York City for a series of meetings at which she spoke on "Lights and Shadows in Europe Today" and "What Hope for Peace in Europe?" Actually, she saw very little hope if countries continued to arm and to increase the size of their armies and navies. Sooner or later, she felt, the "powers" would "use the quickest way—war—as the solution of world problems."[25] Publicity for a lecture at the First Unitarian Church in New York City billed Hanna as "Foremost Feminist Leader of Europe, Author and Lecturer."[26] If she winced at this, she would also have excused it on the grounds that it was typically American.

Before sailing for home, Hanna visited Margaret in Montreal once more. She needed badly to talk with her sister since, in Hanna's absence, tragedy had struck the Sheehy family: Kathleen, Mrs. Cruise O'Brien, had died in February. There would be only two Sheehy girls in Dublin now but, as fate would have it, Margaret would be joining them within months. At the end of August a cable reached Hanna in Ireland: "Michael passed away on Sunday while on holiday in USA. Sudden heart attack. He received last sacraments. Funeral on Wednesday."[27] Incredibly, Margaret's young husband had predeceased her. Incredibly also, since she must have known Hanna's views on religion, Margaret felt it necessary to assure her sister that Michael had received the last rites. There was very little to keep Margaret in Montreal now. Michael had left her with nothing but his poetry and their son Ronan, with whom she was soon on her way back to Dublin.

Hanna reached home in May—her fourth and what proved her final trip to the United States behind her. Her first, December 1916 to June 1918, had served as therapy following her husband's tragic death and had resulted in financial gain for herself and Sinn Fein; her second, 1922–23, during the civil war, had helped to raise money for Republican prisoners; her third, 1934–35, had served, as had the others, to publicize conditions in Ireland; her latest had given her an opportunity to speak out for peace at a time when the threat of war was growing.

By the time Margaret came home, life for Hanna was fairly normal once more. Every Sunday the family—her sisters and the children— gathered for dinner and it was good to have Margaret and Ronan as part of the group. Owen was back in Dublin now, feeling well, and had returned to his teaching position at Trinity. Often he and Andrée would join the circle. This period of relative normality was not to last, however, for the crises leading to war were mounting. Though Ireland maintained its neutrality, some fifty thousand Irishmen volunteered for service in the British armed forces soon after the war began in September 1939.[28] As usual, the war hysteria was having its effect on the feminist movement. Much to Hanna's distress, women were flocking to air-raid precaution meetings and, in Britain, were being lured into something called the Women's Land Army to train for all forms of agricultural work.[29]

During the 1930s, censorship and the general reactionary climate had severely limited Hanna's Irish markets but she had been able to place her articles abroad. Now these markets, too, were closing because of the unwillingness of British journals and publishers to accept material from neutral Ireland and because of the paper shortage. Publications such as the *New Republic* and the *Saturday Review* in the United States were still serving as outlets and her light, amusing style seemed to assure her a ready market for articles on her prison experiences and on her stint in the Dublin Corporation in publications like the *Distributive Worker* and newspapers like the *Irish Press*, but more and more she was feeling the "press boycott."[30]

Hanna had, when she returned from the United States, received an appointment to teach German part-time at the Technical Institute. She was also, as usual, in considerable demand as a speaker before various progressive groups, but these engagements gave her little more than traveling expenses and a small honorarium. Financially, she was having an even more difficult time than previously and her creditors were growing impatient.

Though Hanna periodically resolved to cut down on her organizational work, there is very little evidence that she ever succeeded. In fact, to the already lengthy list of organizations to which she was giving her time, she added several more late in the thirties. One, formed in 1938, was the Married Women's Association, which concerned itself primarily with the status of the housewife. Originally established in Britain, the Irish branch was part of its attempt to expand. Two of its aims are still unrealized: legal monetary recognition for wives' services and national health insurance for wives. Although Hanna did not formally join, she did devote considerable energy to it. Another thirties organization was the Women's Aid Committee of the Irish Friends of the Spanish Republic and Hanna, a staunch supporter of the Loyalist cause, was an active member. Ryan, her colleague at *An Phoblacht*, and others had gone to Spain to join the International Brigade in the fight against Franco. Some, including Ryan himself, had been captured by Mussolini's fascist volunteers and it was to assist these prisoners and to obtain their release that the women's committee was set up.

Hanna's oft-repeated resolution to get her papers in order and to work on her memoirs had been broken year after year but finally, in 1940, she was making a real effort to sort them out and prepare at least a rough inventory. Very possibly Dr. Lynn's pronouncement that Hanna's blood pressure was slightly high and her admonition that Hanna avoid red meat and salt may have been contributing factors, but also Hanna was considering selling some of the papers to the Hoover Institution on War, Revolution, and Peace at Stanford University in California. Her American friend Alice Park, who was selling her papers to the Hoover, had suggested that Hanna do so as well, since Park thought this library "the best depository for historic, pacifist files in all the world."[31] The task, however, was not completed, partly at least because Hanna was not feeling well. As a friend wrote, "The passing of the years—alas—is a thing we cannot prevent."[32]

With a little more time on her hands as a result of the shrunken market for her writings, Hanna was attending meetings of the Irish Film Society regularly and getting to the theater as often as possible, though she had no requests for play reviews. She was able also to participate more often in hiking trips with members of the Field Club, an activity she had always enjoyed. But ranged side by side in her diary with items such as the purchase of a new dress and hat, tea with the lord mayor, and "dinner chez Mary," were soberer items such as "War goes on," "France collapses," and "A. [Andrée] cut off from [her] people from May." She recorded as well that censorship was tightening and that the government was growing increasingly antilabor.[33]

As the war continued, commodities were growing scarcer in Ireland and some were vanishing altogether. After 1942, bread was rationed and before that tea and sugar. Coal, gas, and petrol were also in short supply.

For Hanna, however, there was a "slight betterment" in her finances, thanks to a full teaching schedule. The Technical Institute had chosen not to extend her provisional part-time employment as a German teacher, but she was given an Irish history class and was fairly regularly appointed as an examiner in French. In this position, she not only set the questions but also marked the candidates' completed papers, a task that she had always found onerous.

Even with a lighter schedule (she was giving very few radio talks— only two in 1941 as a matter of fact), Hanna's health continued to deteriorate. She tired easily and, though she made light of it, an increasing hearing loss in one ear troubled her. "I hear enough," she reassured herself. But her enjoyment of controversy seemed not to be diminishing in the slightest. She and Rosamund Jacob had been attempting for some time to get an increased pension for the mother of Liam Mellows, executed for his anti-Free State activities in 1923. Hanna had written to Judge Wyse-Power, the son of her colleague Nancy Wyse-Power, asking him to intervene on Mrs. Mellows' behalf. His lengthy reply stated that the gratuity she had been awarded was the best that could be obtained and gave the reasons.[34] Hanna's equally lengthy reply informed him that she remained "entirely unconvinced and unsatisfied," and accused him of failing to appreciate Liam Mellows since he, Judge Wyse-Power, had supported the 1922 Treaty. She took the occasion to attack de Valera also. As far back as 1934 he had promised Mrs. Mellows that she would be remembered and he had not kept his promise.[35]

A fine touch on Hanna's part was a quote from Goethe, in the original German, followed by the suggestion that Judge Wyse-Power's sister might translate it for him if he asked her. His reply assured her that he was perfectly able to read and understand it without assistance, and testily reminded her that he had not been the one to draft the Pensions Act, that he had not been the one to send Mrs. Mellows a check without an explanation, and that he had not done any of the things for which her letter seemed to hold him responsible. The poor man then concluded with "it will be a very long time before I again interfere in anything on behalf of anyone."[36]

Death and the Legacy

NDORSED by the Women's Social and Progressive League, of which she was a founding member and, that year, the chairman, Hanna, at age sixty-six, stood for the Dail in the general election of 1943 as an Independent candidate for the Dublin South City District—an area she had represented for seven years, 1918 to 1925, in the Dublin Corporation. In a note to Sighle O'Donoghue, long prominent in the Republican movement, Hanna made the point that, since a declaration of allegiance to the Crown was no longer required, Republicans should make every effort to enter the Dail in opposition to the Free State government and "leaven the mass" just as they had done at the local level.[1]

The time was right to press such feminist issues as "equal pay for equal work, equal opportunities for women, the removal of the marriage ban on teachers, doctors, and other skilled women, the restoration of jury rights, the abolition of the Means Test, proper pensions for the aged, widows and the blind." It was time to demand proper meals and free books for schoolchildren, to see that the milk supply was clean, and to obtain better treatment for the unemployed: "civilised treatment," Hanna called it. "If elected, I shall be a representative not tied to, nor gagged by, any party, but free to vote on progressive lines on all issues requiring independence," she told her constituents. She had not, she said, been a member of any political party since 1927, when she had resigned from Fianna Fail.[2]

From the start of the campaign, Hanna's positions were clearly defined and unequivocal. Nationally, she stood for the end of partition and for an independent Ireland. As a feminist and a socialist, she stood by James Connolly's doctrine that "the worker is the slave of capitalist society: the female worker is the slave of that slave. In Ireland that female worker has hitherto exhibited in her martyrdom an almost damnable patience." It was time to be patient no longer. As she saw it, though the 1916 Proclamation had promised equal citizenship, equal rights, and equal opportunities to women, subsequent constitutions had made those assurances simply empty phrases. Young Irishwomen were being forced to emigrate in large numbers and Ireland had the lowest marriage rate in Europe. If elected, she promised, she would give active support to all progressive legislation, and she emphasized the desperate need of the country for the expertise and the assistance of its women.[3]

Four women's organizations, in addition to the Women's Social and Progressive League, endorsed Hanna's candidacy: the Women Graduates' Association, the Irish Countrywomen's Association, the Irish Housewives' Committee, and the Women Citizens' Association. Despite their hard work, the active support of her son Owen, and the strong advocacy of more women in national government by such publications as the *Bell* and *Dublin Opinion*, Hanna lost.

Altogether, four women ran in the general election as Independents, pledging themselves to a program addressed primarily, though not entirely, to women. Two of them—both active members of the Irish Countrywomen's Association—were experienced in local politics and conducted a vigorous joint campaign. A third stood for Galway, where she had been chairman of the council and had proved herself an able administrator. The fourth was Hanna. For the first time in Irish politics, women Independents from both urban and rural districts had campaigned for the Dail and, though all were defeated, Hanna felt a possible nucleus for a woman's party had, finally, been established.[4]

She saw several possible reasons for their defeat: voter aversion to Independents; powerful, male-dominated party organizations antagonistic to both women and nonaligned candidates; soaring campaign costs (where three hundred pounds would formerly have sufficed, now more than three times that was required); and fear of altering the existing system at a time when it appeared that the de Valera government would keep the country out of the war in Europe. Women voters themselves, however, were not without blame, as Hanna was quick to acknowledge. There were those who declared smugly that they had no interest in politics. There were others who were politically ignorant and reluctant to vote for women, largely, Hanna believed, because of a press boycott and the disregard of women by the various political machines.[5]

The outcome of the election, though disappointing, had its positive side. The established parties had been challenged and the women, by their campaigns, had stirred public debate on issues critical to them. At least for a little while, Hanna noted, the sign "Bisurated Magnesia" on Dublin's billboards had been replaced by "Equal Pay" and "A Square Deal for Women."[6]

As a matter of fact, the defeats were a continuation of the generally distressing record of women in Irish politics. The 1916 Proclamation assured them equal freedom and opportunity. Two years later, the war over, women thirty and over were allowed access to the ballot for the first time; and, in another five years, the franchise was extended to those twenty-one and over. They were off to "a good flying start," Anna Kelly wrote in the *Irish Times*. Now, some two decades later, only 3 women were in an Irish parliament of nearly 140, half the number elected to the first Dail. This could hardly be judged progress. Nor was it heartening, as Hanna Sheehy-Skeffington had said, that the three women who had been returned to the Dail were all widows of former members, uninterested in feminist issues and so obedient to party orders that they were known as "the Silent Sisters."[7]

Why this lack of success? Anna Kelly offered three reasons, which are not mutually exclusive and which, taken together, go a considerable distance toward a convincing explanation. She pointed out, first, that twenty-five years is a short time and that Irishmen, after all, had not really secured their "right to the ordinary decencies of life after 728 years." Perhaps she should have stressed how short a quarter century is in a country where cultural inertia meant the perpetuation of an especially rigid form of male dominance, supported by church and custom. Her second point, on the face of it, seems especially persuasive in the light of the revolutionary fervor that marked much of the period. For a quarter of a century, she observed, Irishwomen had dedicated themselves—their time and their energies—to nationalism. "We sacrificed the claims of our sex to the claims of our country. We voted Party and not Woman." Yet such an explanation obviously does not account for the equally halting progress of women in English politics. Finally, she explained, women had been effectively excluded from the Irish political scene, since they had no power to select party candidates and scarcely any say in either local or national affairs.[8] It was, of course, in an attempt to reverse this last situation that Hanna and the other women Independents had stood for the Dail. Their defeat indicates just how powerful the forces still were—whatever their precise nature—that had restrained women all along.

Throughout the election campaign and immediately following it,

Hanna continued to carry a heavy teaching load at the two technical schools and to attend meetings of the many organizations to which she belonged, serving as chairman of the Women's Social and Progressive League from 1943 to 1944. She had been warned by her doctor that the strain was too much for her health. Owen, too, had pleaded with her to give up at least one of the two schools and to come to live with Andrée and him. Hanna, however, ignored her doctor's advice and Owen's suggestions, only to find that in May 1945 the question of slowing down was taken largely out of her hands when, as she put it, her health was "crushed suddenly."⁹ Writing to Alice Park some six months later, she explained that her heart had simply gone on "strike in May, not weak, but jerky, and overstrained, then liver got out of order & Blood pressure went from low to high." She was taking digitalis, calomel, and coramtine, and dieting rigidly.¹⁰ Nonetheless, because she desperately needed the money, she went on teaching, though on a limited schedule, and she remained at her home, not wanting to burden her son and daughter-in-law, to whom a son of their own had been born in May.

Hanna's debilitating health problems, her disappointment over the slow, often dishearteningly slow, progress of the feminist causes for which she had long fought, and even family disappointments—Owen had been passed over for a full professorship at Trinity College—had combined to produce a recurrence of the melancholy that had afflicted her at various points in her life. The tone of her correspondence late in 1945 reflects her fatigue and her despair. "The horror of the Atomic Bomb," she wrote a friend, "is just ghastly & there's a scramble for it for the next War." Though pleased that a peace group had been formed in the United States and in Britain, she still felt that, whatever those who desired peace did, countries would nonetheless be "swept in." At least the war was over, she said: "It's great to have an end to the carnage." But the note of despair returned when she spoke of the birth of her grandson: "Children are being born in great numbers here, in Great Britain, France. I guess Nature is filling up gaps, but one wonders for what?"¹¹

While her mood was grim at the time, there were events that gave Hanna happiness and satisfaction. The birth of her grandson was one. Another was her selection to be interviewed on the radio in November as part of a Distinguished Irishwomen's series.¹² Still another occurred near the end of the year. With Louie Bennett as the moving force, a group of Hanna's friends, concerned about both her finances and her health, subscribed varying amounts toward a gift to assist her. Such a testimonial, they thought, would be not only fitting but difficult to refuse. The list of subscribers read like a Who's Who in the feminist movement.[13] One unsolicited contributor, Margaret Gavan Duffy, informed Bennett that she did not believe there was "one subject on which Mrs. Sheehy-Skeffington and I would agree," but since she had so very much admiration for "her courage and her character," she wanted to contribute toward the gift.[14] The first installment, one hundred pounds, was given to Hanna at Christmas and the next was to follow at Easter. A note accompanying the gift called it "a small token of our respect and admiration for your long, brave, and self-sacrificing service to the cause of justice and freedom" and instructed her to spend it all on herself. Hanna, sorry that her friends had been troubled, nevertheless felt that the matter had been handled so discreetly that she could not refuse the money.[15]

Meanwhile, her health showed no lasting signs of improvement. She had lost thirty-five pounds by December, found walking difficult, was not permitted to climb stairs, and had been forced to discontinue many of her activities, including attending the theater. She was able, however, to do a certain amount of reading and writing and consequently hoped to be able to finish her memoirs and something on Francis as well as see about the republication of her husband's *Davitt* and her own *British Militarism as I Have Known It*. She mentioned to Alice Park that she would be sixty-nine the following May but that Shaw, after all, was still vigorous at ninety. "I wouldn't mind dying," she said, "but I *would* being a helpless invalid."[16]

On Saturday, 20 April 1946, Hanna Sheehy-Skeffington's long struggle with a failing heart ended. She died as she had wanted to die—a burden to no one, her faculties keen, and her battle lines still drawn. During the several months prior to her death, she was working on her memoirs and friends were writing to urge her on. She was taking a vital interest in the strike for higher wages in which the Irish National Teachers Organisation was engaged and, only days before her death, wrote one of her usual letters to the editor pleading the teachers' cause.[17] She retained to the end a strong interest in feminist activities and in those of the labor movement as well. A confirmed reservation for the period 18 to 27 April shows that she was planning to go to the Seaview House in Wicklow, possibly to recuperate.[18]

Hanna was confined to her bed for scarcely three weeks before her death and Owen was with her during that time. Aware that she was dying, she told her son that she was without fear but nonetheless hoped the end would come quickly. What did worry her was the chance that she would become irrational in the final hours, revert to childhood beliefs, and ask for a priest. She wanted him to know that, should this happen, he was to ignore her request.[19]

Following Hanna's death, Anna Kelly, a friend and colleague, wrote perceptively of her. She remembered a quiet person, without "the dash" of Constance Markievicz but with more intelligence and more understanding; a person who possessed exceptional ability in debate and who hated injustice of any kind—"from the injustice of war to injustice to animals." Kelly also recalled a woman who never lost touch with simple human pleasures—the love of clothes, especially hats, the enjoyment of the flowers in her garden and of the movies and the theater. "She'd go off by herself with her modest shilling, and sit in the back seats of the theatre. She would meet her sisters, Mrs. Kettle and Mrs. Casey, to go to the pictures as happy as larks," Kelly wrote.[20] Very few people, however, knew the side of Hanna that was filled, especially when she was younger, with self-doubt, with a tendency toward snap judgments—often wrong—and with an inability to put small issues behind her, which sometimes led to self-destructive brooding.

Among the other tributes, one that appeared in the *Irish Press* was typical. Calling her "a fighter whose cause was peace; an idealist who never lost sight of her star; a controversialist who neither sought nor gave quarter; a woman to whom every humanitarian cause made instant appeal," the piece went on to note that she had known virtually everyone who had taken part in progressive and democratic movements during the past forty years.[21]

The words of praise for Hanna were deserved. It took strong conviction for this basically shy, naturally retiring woman to lead processions, to fight police, and to face death and imprisonment time after time. She managed also, as Constance Markievicz and Maud Gonne had not, to be a key political figure and at the same time a devoted, understanding wife and mother. But during the three weeks that she lay dying, lucid and well aware that the end was approaching, she must have pondered whether her efforts had been fruitful and if, indeed, she had, in a significant and lasting way, strengthened the feminist, socialist, pacifist, and nationalist movements.

It is impossible to measure precisely the extent to which Irish men and women were affected by her opposition to the 1922 Treaty, her opposition to the signing of the oath of allegiance to the Crown, her work for prison reform, her militant pacifism, and her advocacy of a world community of nations and a socialist Ireland. It is easier to measure what she accomplished for women through the Irish Association of Women Graduates and organizations like the Women's Social and Progressive League. But her lasting contribution toward obtaining the vote for women through the formation of the Irish Women's Franchise League and through the pages of the *Irish Citizen* must go unquestioned. There is ample evidence as well that she did much to form a bridge between members of the women's movement in the United States and England and those in Ireland.

To Hanna, however, the value of her contributions, clear in the light of history, would have seemed inconsequential compared with what might have been done, what there still was to do, and what she wished she had had time to attempt. After her death, Owen wrote to those who had subscribed to the testimonial fund. His mother, he said, had wanted to thank them personally but had not had the strength to do so. In closing his letter he said: "I would like to add my own thanks to you for the deep pleasure which it gave my mother to know that she had so many warmhearted and generous friends, who still remembered her with affection, and with an admiration which always surprised her, but no one else."[22]

Hanna Sheehy-Skeffington may never have believed she was as beloved as she was or that she had achieved what she had for the women of Ireland. Perhaps, however, she came to understand, in time, that her accomplishments—far from being merely the result of her husband's influence and an attempt to fulfill his dreams—were the result of her own energy, the clarity of her own vision, and a singular dedication to her own principles.

Notes

Correspondence, rough drafts of speeches and articles, and diaries cited throughout the notes are among family papers released to the National Library of Ireland by Andrée Sheehy-Skeffington and consulted by special permission before being catalogued. Consequently, catalogue numbers have not been given. Unless otherwise indicated, it should be assumed that such material is from the Hanna and Francis Sheehy-Skeffington Papers, National Library of Ireland, Dublin.

CHAPTER I — THE FASHIONING OF A MILITANT

1. Incomplete, undated transcript of radio interview with Hanna Sheehy-Skeffington.

2. *The Freeman*, 15 December 1887.

3. David Sheehy to Owen Sheehy, 6 February 1888.

4. Andrée D. Sheehy-Skeffington, "The French Connection," *Irish Times*, 26 October 1981.

5. Eugene Sheehy to John Devoy, 14 December 1904, *Devoy's Post Bag, 1871–1928*, ed. William O'Brien and Desmond Ryan (Dublin: C. J. Fallon, 1948), 2:352–53.

6. F. X. Martin, "MacNeill and the Foundation of the Irish Volunteers," in *The Scholar Revolutionary: Eoin MacNeill, 1867–1945, and the Making of the New Ireland*, ed. F. X. Martin and F. J. Byrne (Shannon: Irish University Press, 1973), 159.

7. Eugene Sheehy, *May It Please the Court* (Dublin: C. J. Fallon, 1951), 152.

8. Conor Cruise O'Brien, *States of Ireland* (Frogmore, St. Albans: Panther Books, 1974), 62.

9. Ibid., 81.

10. Hanna Sheehy-Skeffington, "Looking Backward," *The Distributive Worker*, December 1941, 201.

11. Ibid.

12. Notes for speech delivered at Sinn Fein headquarters, 24 October 1932.

13. O'Brien, *States of Ireland*, 63.

14. Grainne O'Flynn, "Some Aspects of the Education of Irish Women through the Years," *The Capuchin Annual* (1977): 177–79.

15. Ibid.

16. Certificate signed by William Delany, S. J., Director, and issued by Congregation of the Children of Mary.

17. Recommendation for Hanna Sheehy by William Magennis, M.A., 12 December 1903.

18. Hanna Sheehy, "Satirical Literature in English," 11 May 1902.

19. Stanislaus Joyce, *My Brother's Keeper*, ed. Richard Ellmann (New York: Viking Press, 1969), 72.

20. Margaret Sheehy Casey to Hanna Sheehy-Skeffington, 9 August 1926. Commenting on a trip that Hanna had made to Paris, Margaret said: "Strange how he [Joyce] remembered Geofrey [Geoffrey] Fortesque [a part he had taken in one of Margaret's plays during college days] after all these years; & of course he was not a bit épis on me—it was Mary. She always appealed to the 'Joyces'! Her little demure Madonna face got them every time—the change from their usual fare I suppose."

21. Stanislaus Joyce, *My Brother's Keeper*, 72.

22. Patricia Hutchins, *James Joyce's Dublin* (London: Grey Walls Press, 1950), 72.

23. James Joyce, *Stephen Hero*, new ed., ed. Theodore Spencer (New York: New Directions, 1963), 46.

24. Ibid., 66.

25. Roger McHugh, "Thomas Kettle and Francis Sheehy-Skeffington," in *The Shaping of Modern Ireland*, ed. Conor Cruise O'Brien (London: Routledge and Kegan Paul, 1960), 126.

26. Hanna Sheehy-Skeffington Diaries, 1907.

27. Ibid., 4 January 1902.

28. Ibid., 7 February 1902.

29. J. [Johanna] Sheehy, "Life's Choosing," *The Weekly Freeman*, 29 June 1901. The piece appeared as "The Story of the Week" and won Hanna a prize of two guineas.

30. Ibid.

31. The questionnaire prepared by the Subcommittee of Women Graduates was issued 4 December 1901. Those appointed to the subcommittee were Annie Woods Haslett, M.A.; Mary Hayden, M.A.; Mary Olivia Kennedy, B.A.; Maud Joynt, M.A.; Annie M'Eldery, M.A.; Agnes O'Farrelly, M.A.; Alice Oldham, B.A.; and Hanna Sheehy, B.A.

32. Ibid.

33. A. W. Haslett and M. O. Kennedy, recruiting letter, 11 April 1902.

34. Anna M. Haslam to Hanna Sheehy, September 1902.

CHAPTER 2 — A UNION OF IDEALS

1. J. B. Skeffington to Francis Sheehy-Skeffington, 2 October 1911.

2. Hanna Sheehy Diaries, 1 January 1903.

3. Francis Sheehy-Skeffington to Very Rev. W. M. Delany, President, University College, Dublin, 1 June 1904.

4. Hanna Sheehy Diaries, 13 January 1903.

5. Hanna Sheehy-Skeffington Diaries, 1905.

6. J. B. Lyons, *The Enigma of Tom Kettle: Irish Patriot, Essayist, Poet, British Soldier, 1880–1916* (Dublin: Glendale Press, 1983), 67.

7. *The Nationist*, 16 November 1905.

8. J. B. Lyons, *Enigma of Tom Kettle*, 78–79.

9. *National Democrat*, May 1907.

10. Ibid., April 1907.

11. Hanna Sheehy-Skeffington, "The Women's Movement—Ireland," *Irish Review*, July 1912, 225.

12. George Dangerfield, *The Strange Death of Liberal England* (New York: Harrison Smith and Robert Haas, 1935), 144, 147.

13. Jesuit Fathers, *A Page of Irish History: Story of University College, Dublin, 1883–1909* (Dublin: Talbot Press, 1930), 472.

14. Hanna Sheehy-Skeffington Diaries, 1905. According to this item, during the previous year Hanna made "roughly £70 by teaching." She added, "but it's not good enough for the trouble."

15. Ibid.

16. Ibid.

17. Ibid.

18. Ibid., 1907.

19. James Joyce to Stanislaus Joyce, 6 November 1906, *Selected Letters of James Joyce*, ed. Richard Ellmann (New York: Viking Press, 1975), 124.

20. Hanna Sheehy-Skeffington to Mary Sheehy, 20 November 1905.

21. Dr. Elizabeth A. Tennant to Francis Sheehy-Skeffington, 13 and 17 July 1908.

22. Hanna Sheehy-Skeffington to Francis Sheehy-Skeffington, 8 July 1908.

23. Ibid., 14 June 1908.

24. Ibid.

25. Ibid., 23 June 1908.

26. Ibid., 5 July 1908.

27. Ibid., 12 June 1908.

28. Ibid., 17 June 1908.

29. Rosemary Owens, "Votes for Women: Irishwomen's Campaign for the Vote, 1876–1915" (M. A. thesis, University College, Dublin, 1977), 33.

30. *Sinn Fein*, 27 March 1909.

31. J. B. Lyons, *Enigma of Tom Kettle*, 61–62.

32. *Irish Nation*, 6, 13, and 20 March 1909.

33. Ibid., 20 March 1909.

34. Gretta Cousins to Francis Sheehy-Skeffington, [1909].

35. Hanna Sheehy Diaries, 6 January 1903.

36. Ibid., n.d.

37. R. Dudley Edwards, personal interview, 1 November 1979.

38. Owen Sheehy-Skeffington, "Francis Sheehy-Skeffington," in *1916: The Easter Rising*, ed. Owen Dudley Edwards and Fergus Pyle (London: MacGibbon and Kee, 1968), 139.

39. R. Dudley Edwards, personal interview, 1 November 1979.

40. Garry Culhane, personal interview, 18 June 1980.

41. Ibid.

42. Owens, "Votes for Women," 9.

43. Francis Sheehy-Skeffington to J. B. Skeffington, 6 October 1909.

44. Francis Sheehy-Skeffington to "Molloy," 26 March 1910.

45. *Irish Nation*, 11 June 1910.

46. Ibid., 28 May 1910.

47. J. Doran O'Reilly, "Mother to a Thousand Children," *Sunday Chronicle*, 31 October 1948.

48. Irish Women's Franchise League to members and friends, 28 April 1911.

49. H. Campbell, Town Clerk, to Hanna Sheehy-Skeffington, 10 May 1911.

50. Andro Linklater, *An Unhusbanded Life: Charlotte Despard, Suffragette, Socialist and Sinn Feiner* (London: Hutchinson, 1980), 143.

51. *Irish Times*, 3 April 1981.

52. Ibid.

53. *The Leader*, 6 April 1912.

54. Hanna Sheehy-Skeffington, "Reminiscences of an Irish Suffragette," in *Votes for Women: Irish Women's Struggle for the Vote*, ed., Andrée Sheehy-Skeffington et al. (Dublin: Andrée D. Sheehy-Skeffington and Rosemary Owens, 1975), 16–17.

55. Francis Sheehy-Skeffington to J. B. Skeffington, 15 November 1909.

CHAPTER 3 — STONES AND GLASS

1. *Weekly Irish Times*, 6 April 1912.

2. *Irish Times*, 3 April 1912.

3. Ibid.

4. Hanna Sheehy-Skeffington to *Evening Telegraph*, 22 April 1912.

5. J. B. Lyons, *Enigma of Tom Kettle*, 209–11.

6. Ibid.

7. Isabella Richardson to Hanna Sheehy-Skeffington, 24 April 1912.

8. Patricia Hooey to Hanna Sheehy-Skeffington, 24 May 1912.

9. *Votes for Women*, 19 April 1912, as quoted in Andrew Rosen, *Rise Up, Women! — The Militant Campaign of the Women's Social and Political Union, 1903–1914* (London and Boston: Routledge and Kegan Paul, 1974), 165–66.

10. Annie Kenney to Hanna Sheehy-Skeffington, 29 May 1912.

11. Ibid.

12. Hanna Sheehy-Skeffington, "An Impression from the Platform," *Irish Citizen*, 8 June 1912.

13. Ibid.

14. *Irish Times*, 14 June 1912, as quoted in Owens, "Votes for Women" (see chap. 2, n. 29), 74.

15. *Irish Citizen*, 22 June 1912.

16. Ibid., Report of Phoenix Park meeting held 15 June 1912.

17. Ibid., 29 June 1912.

18. Ibid.

19. Governor, Mountjoy Prison, to Francis Sheehy-Skeffington, 25 June 1912.

20. Hanna Sheehy-Skeffington, "Reminiscences" (see chap. 2, n. 54), 20–22.

21. Ibid.

22. Hanna Sheehy-Skeffington Notebook, n.d., labeled "Prison."

23. Hanna Sheehy-Skeffington, "Reminiscences," 20–21.

24. Ibid., 21.

25. Hanna Sheehy-Skeffington, "The Women's Movement—Ireland," *Irish Review*, July 1912, 225–27.

26. *Evening Telegraph*, 8 July 1912, as quoted in Owens, "Votes for Women," 79–80.

27. *Irish Citizen*, 27 July 1912.

28. Transcript of interview with Mary Leigh, 1965, as quoted in Owens, "Votes for Women," 81.

29. Hanna Sheehy-Skeffington, "Reminiscences," 22.

30. Marie Johnson to Andrée Sheehy-Skeffington, 24 January 1972, as quoted in Owens, "Votes for Women," 82.

31. T. M. Healy, *Letters and Leaders of My Day* (London: Thornton Butterworth, 1928), 2:507.

32. Owens, "Votes for Women," 81; Hanna Sheehy-Skeffington, "Reminiscences," 22–23.

33. Owens, "Votes for Women," 82–83.

34. *Evening Telegraph*, 19 July 1912; *Irish Independent*, 20 July 1912, as quoted in Owens, "Votes for Women," 83.

35. J. B. Lyons, *Enigma of Tom Kettle*, 212–13; Sidney Gifford Czira, *The Years Flew By* (Dublin: Gifford and Craven, 1974), 57–58.

36. Hanna Sheehy-Skeffington, "Reminiscences," 23.

37. *Irish Citizen*, 16 November 1912.

38. Rough draft of "Statement for Press re Rathmines School of Commerce," n.d.

39. Hanna Sheehy-Skeffington, "Irish Secondary Teachers," *Irish Review*, October 1912, 393–98.

40. Ibid.

41. Ibid.

42. Ibid.

43. *Irish Review*, September 1912, 388–89.

44. Joseph Holloway, Journal, 11 April 1912, in *Joseph Holloway's Abbey Theatre*, ed. Robert Hogan and Michael J. O'Neill (Carbondale, Ill.: Southern Illinois University Press, 1967), 153.

45. Hanna Sheehy-Skeffington, "The Women's Vote in Western America: A Factor in the Presidential Election," *Irish Citizen*, 12 October 1912.

46. Dangerfield, *Strange Death of Liberal England*, 181.

47. *Irish Citizen*, 4 January 1913.

48. Ibid., 11 January 1913.

49. Francis Sheehy-Skeffington to Mrs. George Bernard Shaw, 14 December 1914.

50. Francis Sheehy-Sheffington to Maurice Wilkins, 25 October 1914.

51. *Irish Citizen*, 22 March 1913.

CHAPTER 4—A HARROWING GAME

1. *Dublin Evening Mail*, 4 April 1913; *Irish Independent*, 12 May 1913.

2. *Evening Herald*, 13 May 1913; *Evening Telegraph*, 14 May 1913.

3. Midge Mackenzie, *Shoulder to Shoulder: A Documentary* (New York: Alfred A. Knopf, 1975), 226.

4. *Evening Telegraph*, 14 May 1913; *Irish Citizen*, 17 May 1913.

5. *Irish Citizen*, 5 July 1913.

6. Ibid.

7. Ibid.

8. Ibid., 5 July 1913 and 10 January 1914.

9. Ibid., 15 November 1913.

10. Ibid., 3 January 1914.

11. Ibid.

12. Ibid.

13. Hanna Sheehy-Skeffington, "Reminiscences," 24.

14. *Irish Citizen*, 10 January 1914.

15. Ibid.

16. Dangerfield, *Strange Death of Liberal England*, 182. There was little doubt of Mrs. Pankhurst's dislike of men in general. According to Dangerfield, she had written a pamphlet around that time called *The Great Scourge* in which she "discussed venereal disease and the sex excesses of men. Seventy-five to eighty percent of them, she declared, were afflicted with gonorrhea and twenty-five per cent with syphilis." Presumably some had both. Having revealed the dissolute nature of virtually the entire male population, she went on to claim that most women's "minor ailments" were due to their husbands' venereal disease and that many childless couples were without children for this reason. "She made it pretty clear that the very act of sexual intercourse with a man was highly injurious to female susceptibilities. . . . The Vote, it appeared, was something between a prophylactic and a call to the higher life," Dangerfield observes (pp. 182–84).

17. Christabel Pankhurst to Hanna Sheehy-Skeffington, 26 September 1913.

18. *Irish Citizen*, 30 May 1914.

19. Mackenzie, *Shoulder to Shoulder*, 311.

20. *Irish Citizen*, 22 August 1914.

21. Emmeline Pankhurst, "A Procession and Deputation to Mr. Lloyd George on Saturday afternoon, July 17th, 1915," communication of Women's War Service, 9 July 1915.

22. *Irish Citizen*, 24 July 1915.

23. Ibid., 3 October 1914.

24. Ibid.

25. Ibid.

26. Ibid., 15 August 1914.

27. Ibid.

28. Alice Park to Hanna Sheehy-Skeffington, *Irish Citizen*, 3 October 1914.

29. Hanna Sheehy-Skeffington, "Irish Militants and the War," *Jus Suffragii*, April 1915, as reprinted in *Irish Citizen*, 1 May 1915.

30. *Irish Citizen*, 10 April 1915.

31. Ibid., 8 May 1915.

32. Louie Bennett to Hanna Sheehy-Skeffington, 12 May 1915.

33. Louie Bennett, "Concerning the Protest Meeting," *Irish Citizen*, 22 May 1915.

34. Francis Sheehy-Skeffington, *Speech from the Dock: With Letter from George Bernard Shaw* (Dublin: Irish Workers' Cooperative Society, n.d.).

35. Father Eugene Sheehy to Hanna Sheehy-Skeffington, 10 June 1915; David Sheehy to Hanna Sheehy-Skeffington, n.d.

36. George Bernard Shaw to Hanna Sheehy-Skeffington, 14 June 1915.

37. *Irish Citizen*, 19 June 1915. Resolution passed 14 June 1915 by the Irish Women's Franchise League.

38. J. B. Skeffington to Hanna Sheehy-Skeffington, 5 and 10 June 1915.

39. J. B. Skeffington to Hanna Sheehy-Skeffington, 12 June 1915; Dr. A. P. Mac-Mahon to J. B. Skeffington, 16 June 1915.

40. Owen Sheehy-Skeffington, "Francis Sheehy-Skeffington," 143.

41. *New Ireland*, 26 June 1915.

42. J. B. Skeffington to Hanna Sheehy-Skeffington, 19 June 1915.

43. Testimonial to Hanna Sheehy-Skeffington from Charles Hubert Oldham, professor of commerce at University College, Dublin, and formerly principal of Rathmines School of Commerce, 28 August 1915. In his recommendation, Professor Oldham defines Hanna's technique—the "Direct Method"—as one that "trains students to *Think in the Language They Are Studying*, and not merely to translate into it. It, therefore, works through the ear, listening to the speaking voice, rather than through the eye, using a dictionary. This Method requires that the Teacher shall speak the language as fluently and correctly as a native speaker." It was his feeling that "an English or Irish person, who has acquired that command of the foreign tongue, can better foresee the difficulties, phonetical and idiomatic, of our students than one to whom the tongue came without conscious effort in its acquirement."

CHAPTER 5 — DARKNESS AT EASTER

1. J. B. Skeffington to Hanna Sheehy-Skeffington, 26 November 1915.

2. Francis Sheehy-Skeffington to Hanna Sheehy-Skeffington, 15 October 1915. A note on this letter indicates that it is the twenty-second sent to her from the United States; the first twenty-one are missing and believed to have been confiscated when the couple's home was raided after Francis Sheehy-Skeffington's murder.

3. Hanna Sheehy-Skeffington to Meg Connery, n.d.

4. Editorial, "No Vote, No Register," *Irish Citizen*, 14 August 1915; "What Is a Popular Franchise?" *Irish Citizen*, 28 August 1915.

5. *Irish Citizen*, 11 September 1915.

6. Ibid.

7. Francis Sheehy-Skeffington to Hanna Sheehy-Skeffington, 23 October 1915.

8. Ibid., 16 October 1915.

9. Ibid., 23 October 1915.

10. Ibid., 16 October 1915.

11. Ibid., 30 November 1915.

12. *Nationality*, 4 and 18 September 1915.

13. *Workers' Republic*, 1 and 8 January 1916.

14. *Irish Citizen*, Mid-February 1916.

15. I.W.F.L. form letter, January 1916. The letter was signed by Hanna Sheehy-Skeffington and is in the Alice Park Collection, Hoover Institution on War, Revolution, and Peace, Stanford University.

16. *Irish Citizen*, April 1916.

17. Ibid., April 1916 and May 1916.

18. Ibid., May 1916.

19. Hanna Sheehy-Skeffington to Owen Sheehy-Skeffington, 19 August 1928.

20. Dorothy Macardle, *The Irish Republic* (New York: Farrar, Straus and Giroux, 1965), 157.

21. *Irish Times* Summary, "The Events of Easter Week," in *Dublin 1916*, ed. Roger McHugh (New York: Hawthorn Books, 1966), 51.

22. Leah Levenson, *With Wooden Sword: A Portrait of Francis Sheehy-Skeffington, Militant Pacifist* (Boston: Northeastern University Press, 1983), 215.

23. Ibid., 216–17.

24. Ibid.

25. Hanna Sheehy-Skeffington to Joseph McEvoy, 28 February 1933. This letter is in the possession of Seamus Scully, Dublin.

26. Earl of Longford and Thomas P. O'Neill, *Eamon de Valera* (New York: Houghton Mifflin, 1970), 38, as quoted in "Cumann na mBan at Easter Week," undated communication in Maire Comerford's Papers, Dublin.

27. "Cumann na mBan at Easter Week," Maire Comerford's Papers.

28. Macardle, *Irish Republic*, 183–84.

29. Hannah [*sic*] Sheehy-Skeffington, "A Pacifist Dies," in *Dublin 1916*, ed. Roger McHugh (New York: Hawthorn Books, 1966), 276.

30. Ibid., 282.

31. *Irish Independent*, 26 August 1916.

32. Hanna Sheehy-Skeffington, "A Pacifist Dies," 282.

33. *Irish Independent*, 26 August 1916; "John Dillon's Speech in the House of Commons on 11 May 1916," in *1916: The Easter Rising*, 76–77.

34. F. S. L. Lyons, *Ireland Since the Famine* (London: Collins/Fontana, 1973), 377–78.

35. Hanna Sheehy-Skeffington to Editor, *Irish Press*, 9 May 1932.

36. "John Dillon's Speech," 77.

37. Ibid.

38. Hanna Sheehy-Skeffington, "A Pacifist Dies," 285.

39. Monk Gibbon, "Murder in Portobello Barracks," *The Dublin Magazine* (Spring 1966), 12–13.

40. Ibid.

41. Sir Francis Fletcher Vane, *Agin the Governments: Memories and Adventures* (London: Sampson Low, 1929), 262–69.

42. Ibid.

43. Ibid.

44. Anna Vane to Hanna Sheehy-Skeffington, 29 May 1916.

CHAPTER 6 — AFTERMATH OF A MURDER

1. J. B. Lyons, *Enigma of Tom Kettle*, 298.

2. Maurice Wilkins to Hanna Sheehy-Skeffington, 7 September 1916.

3. Gretta Cousins to Hanna Sheehy-Skeffington, 17 August 1916. So great had been Gretta's affection and respect for Hanna that, when she sailed from England to Madras in 1915, she drew up a will appointing Hanna executrix.

4. Ibid.

5. Ibid., 12 October 1916.

6. Two letters purported to have been written by Francis Sheehy-Skeffington through Gretta Cousins, one dated 1 May 1917, the other undated.

7. Francis Sheehy-Skeffington to Edward Martyn, 28 March 1913.

8. Deborah Webb to Hanna Sheehy-Skeffington, 28 June 1916.

9. Transcript of conversation at seance held 8 August 1916.

10. Leslie Pielon to Hanna Sheehy-Skeffington, 20 November 1916.

11. R. M. Fox, *Louie Bennett: Her Life and Times* (Dublin: Talbot Press, 1958), 59–62.

12. Ibid.

13. Healy, *Letters and Leaders*, 2:562–63.

14. "Courts-Martial at Richmond Barracks," in *Sinn Fein Rebellion Handbook, Easter 1916* (Dublin: *Weekly Irish Times*, 1916), 85–86.

15. Undated clipping; newspaper unidentified.

16. "Courts-Martial," 88.

17. Ibid., 90.

18. Monk Gibbon, personal interview, 18 December 1976.

19. "Report of the Royal Commission," in *Democracy in Ireland Since 1913*, ed. Hanna Sheehy-Skeffington (New York: Donnelly Press, [1917]), 49. This is the John Simon report of the inquiry into the Skeffington murder.

20. "Courts-Martial," 89–90.

21. W. D. Henry, "The Case of Captain Colthurst," *The Practitioner*, 1981, 418–20. Clipping is in the possession of Andrée Sheehy-Skeffington.

22. Ibid.

23. Philip Snowden to Hanna Sheehy-Skeffington, 21 June 1916; W. C. Anderson to Hanna Sheehy-Skeffington, 23 June 1916.

24. *New Ireland*, 1 July 1916.

25. Hanna Sheehy-Skeffington, "A Pacifist Dies," 286.

26. J. B. Skeffington to Hanna Sheehy-Skeffington, 30 August 1916.

27. *Labour Leader*, 27 July 1916.

28. Kathleen Sheehy O'Brien to Hanna Sheehy-Skeffington, 15 August 1916.

29. Robert Lynd, *If the Germans Conquered England and Other Essays* (Dublin: Maunsel, 1917), 142.

30. Healy, *Letters and Leaders*, 2:575.

31. St. John Ervine to Hanna Sheehy-Skeffington, 9 August 1916; St. John Ervine to Owen Sheehy-Skeffington, 18 November 1955. The letter to Owen is in the possession of Andrée Sheehy-Skeffington.

32. *Cork Constitution*, 29 August 1916.

33. Owen Sheehy-Skeffington, "Francis Sheehy-Skeffington," 147–48. In 1940, Hanna marked a passage in a leaflet concerning the execution of two I.R.A. members that read: "Consigned to quicklime graves in a prison yard, in the vain hope that such barbarous treatment would cause the people of Ireland to regard them as criminals."

34. *Irish Independent*, 26 August 1916.

35. "Report of the Royal Commission," 54.

36. Maude L. Deuchar, *The Sheehy Skeffington Case* (Manchester: National Labour Press, 1916), 13.

37. Sir Francis Vane to Hanna Sheehy-Skeffington, 17 October 1916.

38. Healy, *Letters and Leaders*, 2:575.

39. Hannah [*sic*] Sheehy-Skeffington, *British Militarism as I Have Known It*, in *Democ-*

racy in Ireland Since 1913, ed. Hanna Sheehy-Skeffington (New York: Donnelly Press, [1917]), 86.

40. Hanna Sheehy-Skeffington, "Soldiers and Skeffington Property," *The Herald*, 5 August 1916; Pan Collins, personal interview, 20 July 1981.

41. Testimony of Alice Schmitz, Hanna Sheehy-Skeffington's landlady, 27 October 1916.

42. Ibid.

43. Question No. 53, put by T. P. O'Connor, M.P., before the House of Commons, Thursday, 26 October 1916, H. Doc. 99, 3094.

44. Secretary to Chief Commissioner of Police, Dublin Castle, to Hanna Sheehy-Skeffington, 23 October 1916 and 2 November 1916.

45. N. Bonham Carter to Hanna Sheehy-Skeffington, 7 November 1916 and 21 November 1916.

46. Hugh C. Love to Henry Lemass, 3 November 1916; Henry Lemass to Hugh C. Love, 4 November 1916.

47. Henry Lemass to The Right Hon. H. H. Asquith, 20 September 1916.

CHAPTER 7 — A JOURNEY ALONE

1. J. F. Byrne to Hanna Sheehy-Skeffington, 19 October 1916.

2. *New York Times*, 20 December 1916.

3. *Daily Express*, 3 May 1930.

4. *Gaelic American*, 5 January 1917.

5. *Freeman's Journal*. Undated clipping, probably 8 January 1917.

6. *Boston Herald*, 28 December 1916.

7. *Boston Advertiser*, 15 January 1917. Report of meeting on 14 January 1917 in Faneuil Hall.

8. *New York Sun*, 21 December 1916.

9. *Boston Sunday Globe*, 14 January 1917.

10. *Buffalo Express*, 5 March 1917.

11. Lydia Avery Coonley Ward to Hanna Sheehy-Skeffington, 23 March 1917.

12. Owen Sheehy-Skeffington to Hanna Sheehy-Skeffington, 20 March 1917.

13. Mollie Price Cook to Hanna Sheehy-Skeffington, 25 November 1917.

14. William J. Moroney to Hanna Sheehy-Skeffington, 10 September 1917.

15. Ibid., 27 September 1917.

16. Principal, Marlborough School, to Hanna Sheehy-Skeffington, 27 August 1917.

17. Oswald Garrison Villard to Hanna Sheehy-Skeffington, 31 March 1917.

18. Donnelly Press, New York, brought out a second edition of *Democracy in Ireland Since 1913* in 1918; a third edition appeared the same year, published by James H. Barry Co., Portland, Oregon. A fourth edition came out in 1936 with a foreword by Hanna Sheehy-Skeffington stating that she had let the text stand as it was "with the exception of a few minor alterations." One alteration is significant. In the original version, speaking of her mission in life, Hanna wrote: "I want to continue my husband's work so that when I meet him some day in the Great Beyond, he will be pleased with my stewardship" (p. 33). This sentence does not appear in the fourth edition.

19. *Evening Mail*, 11 October 1917. The letter appeared originally in the *Irish Times*, 4 October 1917.

20. *Irish News*, 15 October 1917.

21. Hanna Sheehy-Skeffington to Editor, *London Morning Post*, 2 April 1918, in *Democracy in Ireland*, 61.

22. Cumann na mBan petition, n.d.

23. H. Sheehy-Skeffington to John Devoy, n.d., in *Devoy's Post Bag* (see chap. 1, n. 5), 2:519–20. A possible date is given as January 1917 but contents indicate January 1918.

24. Hanna Sheehy-Skeffington, *Impressions of Sinn Fein in America* (Dublin: Davis Publishing Co., 1919), 29.

25. E. D. Nola to Hanna Sheehy-Skeffington, 17 April 1918.

26. W. C. Moore to Hanna Sheehy-Skeffington, 6 May 1918, in *Evening Call*, 25 May 1918.

27. Hanna Sheehy-Skeffington, "Sinn Fein—What It Stands For," n.d. Rough draft of speech notes.

28. David Sheehy to Hanna Sheehy-Skeffington, 13 September 1917.

29. Kathleen Sheehy O'Brien to Hanna Sheehy-Skeffington, 7 February 1918.

30. Mary Kettle to Hanna Sheehy-Skeffington, [late November 1917].

31. *Manchester Guardian*, 13 May 1918, as quoted in Robert Kee, *The Green Flag: The Turbulent History of the Irish National Movement* (New York: Delacorte Press, 1972), 620.

32. *Irish Citizen*, April 1917.

33. Editorial, "Suitors for Our Favour," *Irish Citizen*, December 1918.

CHAPTER 8 — PRISON AND PLATFORM

1. Major W. G. Thwaite, Military Control Officer, to Hanna Sheehy-Skeffington, 24 June 1918.

2. Hanna Sheehy-Skeffington to John Dillon, 16 July 1918.

3. John Dillon to Hanna Sheehy-Skeffington, 17 July 1918.

4. Questions introduced by Mr. King and Mr. Trevelyan in the House of Commons, 18 July 1918.

5. Hanna Sheehy-Skeffington, "Home Again in 1918," n.d. Notes apparently designed to be used in speeches and articles.

6. Ibid.

7. Kee, *Green Flag*, 624–26.

8. Hanna Sheehy-Skeffington, "Home Again."

9. Ibid.

10. Ibid.

11. Ibid.

12. Ibid.

13. Ibid.

14. *Freeman's Journal*, 10 August 1918, as reprinted in the *Irish Citizen*, August 1918.

15. Hanna Sheehy-Skeffington, "Home Again."

16. Lord Mayor of Dublin to Hanna Sheehy-Skeffington, 13 August 1918.

17. Kathleen Cruise O'Brien to Hanna Sheehy-Skeffington, n.d.

18. Hanna Sheehy-Skeffington, "Home Again."

19. Ibid.

20. T. M. Healy to Hanna Sheehy-Skeffington, 22 August 1918; Healy, *Letters and Leaders*, 2:606. Hanna visited Healy on 5 September 1918.

21. John Dillon to Hanna Sheehy-Skeffington, 21 August 1918.

22. Hanna Sheehy-Skeffington to John Dillon, 24 August 1918.

23. John Dillon to Hanna Sheehy-Skeffington, 27 August 1918.

24. Drafts of letters of solicitation for *Irish Citizen*, n.d.

25. Maurice Wilkins to Hanna Sheehy-Skeffington, 11 September 1918.

26. *Weekly Freeman*, 21 September 1918.

27. *Daily Express*, 23 September 1918.

28. Hanna Sheehy-Skeffington, "How the Pickets Won the Vote," *Irish Citizen*, October 1918.

29. Ibid.

30. Ida Husted Harper to Hanna Sheehy-Skeffington, 15 November 1918.

31. Hanna Sheehy-Skeffington, *Impressions of Sinn Fien*, 13–14.

32. Ernie O'Malley, *Army Without Banners* (London: Four Square Books, 1967), 50. First published in Great Britain by Rich and Cowan under the title *On Another Man's Wound*.

33. *Freeman's Journal*, 30 December 1918, as quoted in Macardle, *Irish Republic*, 267.

34. F. S. L. Lyons, *Ireland Since the Famine*, 400, 405–06.

35. P. J. Reilly, Principal Secretary, Central Technical Institute, Clonmel, to Hanna Sheehy-Skeffington, 8 November 1919.

36. William O'Brien to Hanna Sheehy-Skeffington, 24 January 1919.

37. Hanna Sheehy-Skeffington, *Ireland: Present and Future* (New York: Donnelly Press, n.d.), 3–11. This pamphlet was part of the Progressive Ireland series.

38. Ibid.

CHAPTER 9—IN AN IRELAND AT WAR

1. Pan Collins, personal interview, August, 1984; Andrée Sheehy-Skeffington, personal interview, August 1984.

2. Hanna Sheehy-Skeffington to Alice Park, 23 January 1919, Alice Park Collection.

3. Andrée Sheehy-Skeffington, personal interviews, July 1981.

4. Rosamund Jacob to Hanna Sheehy-Skeffington, 23 July 1920.

5. Thomas Maguire, Solicitor, to Hanna Sheehy-Skeffington, 8 November 1919. £100 was left to Owen (Andrée Sheehy-Skeffington, personal interview, August 1982).

6. Editorial, *Irish Citizen*, November 1918.

7. *Irish Times*, 16 December 1918.

8. Irishwomen's International League form letter, 9 December 1918.

9. *Freeman's Journal*, 12 May 1919.

10. Frank O'Connor, *The Big Fellow: Michael Collins and the Irish Revolution*, rev. ed. (London: Burns and Oates, 1966), 80–81.

11. Macardle, *Irish Republic*, 299–300.

12. Ibid., 308.

13. *Manchester Guardian*, 29 July 1919.

14. *Irish Citizen*, September 1919.

15. Rosamund and Tom Jacob to Hanna Sheehy-Skeffington, 18 January 1920.

16. Una O'Farrell, Ethel O'Kelly, and Annie Browne to Hanna Sheehy-Skeffington, 31 December 1920.

17. Macardle, *Irish Republic*, 327–29.

18. Margaret Ward, *Unmanageable Revolutionaries: Women and Irish Nationalism* (Kerry, Ireland: Brandon Book Publishers, 1983), 147.

19. Drafts of telegrams from Hanna Sheehy-Skeffington to Charlotte Despard and American Ambassador to Ireland, April 1920.

20. Charlotte Despard to Hanna Sheehy-Skeffington, 14 April 1920.

21. *New Statesman*, 17 April 1920, as quoted in Macardle, *Irish Republic*, 345.

22. *Catholic Herald*, 19 June, 3 July, and 18 December 1920.

23. Ibid., 18 December 1920.

24. Joseph Devlin to Hanna Sheehy-Skeffington, 1 November 1920.

25. Macardle, *Irish Republic*, 390; Ward, *Unmanageable Revolutionaries*, 148.

26. Macardle, *Irish Republic*, 435–36.

27. Ibid., 425–29.

28. Irish Women's Franchise League officers to Lt. Colonel R. S. Amin, General Staff, Dublin District, Lower Castle Yard, Dublin. An exchange of correspondence, 8, 17, and 25 February 1921.

29. Emmeline Pethick-Lawrence to Hanna Sheehy-Skeffington, 19 March 1921.

30. Emmeline Pethick-Lawrence, *My Part in a Changing World* (London: Victor Gollancz, 1938), 340–42.

31. O'Connor, *Big Fellow*, 125.

32. Henrietta MacDonnell to Hanna Sheehy-Skeffington, 8 July 1921.

33. Hanna Sheehy-Skeffington, "Report of Organisation," n.d. Rough draft signed Director of Organisation.

34. Macardle, *Irish Republic*, 590.

35. Ward, *Unmanageable Revolutionaries*, 167–68.

36. Hanna Sheehy-Skeffington to Alice Park, 25 February 1922, Alice Park Collection.

37. Maurice Manning, "Women in Irish National and Local Politics 1922–77," in *Women in Irish Society: The Historical Dimension*, ed. Margaret MacCurtain and Donncha O'Corrain (Dublin: Arlen House, 1978), 92.

38. Fox, *Louie Bennett*, 77–78.

39. O'Brien, *States of Ireland*, 102.

40. Eugene Sheehy, *May It Please the Court*, 147.

41. J. F. Byrne, *Silent Years: An Autobiography* (New York: Farrar, Straus and Young, 1953), 139–43.

42. Ibid.

CHAPTER 10—THE TREATY AND AFTER

1. Hanna Sheehy-Skeffington, "Do You Want the *Irish Citizen?*" *Irish Citizen*, September-December 1920, as quoted in Beth McKillen, "Irish Feminism and Nationalist Separatism, 1914–23," *Eire-Ireland* (Winter 1982): 84–85.

2. "Funds Raised in U.S.A." Undated newspaper clipping; paper unidentified.

3. Linklater, *Unhusbanded Life*, 223–24. Though the Free State government banned the league before the end of 1923, the members continued to meet illicitly and finally the authorities tired, feeling that, as Maud Gonne said, "those damned women make more trouble than the meetings are worth" (Samuel Levenson, *Maud Gonne* [New York: Reader's Digest Press, 1976], 346).

4. *An Phoblacht*, 20 November 1925, as quoted in Samuel Levenson, *Maud Gonne*, 351–52.

5. Hanna Sheehy-Skeffington to Office of Adjutant General, General Headquarters, Dublin, 10 October 1923; Adjutant General to Hanna Sheehy-Skeffington, 24 June 1924.

6. Acting Minister for Foreign Affairs, Dail Eireann, to Hanna Sheehy-Skeffington, 20 August 1923.

7. L. H. Kerney to Austin Ford, 5 September 1923. Hanna had, some months earlier, been authorized as a special correspondent and general press representative for Austin Ford's journal in New York City (Austin Ford to Hanna Sheehy-Skeffington, 12 July 1923).

8. Handbill, 25 May 1924. Announcement of public meeting in Manchester.

9. "The Ulster Internees," 29 September 1924. Newspaper clipping; paper unidentified.

10. Pan Collins, personal interview, 20 July 1981.

11. Alice Park to Hanna Sheehy-Skeffington, 20 July 1925.

12. Gretta Cousins to Hanna Sheehy-Skeffington, 23 August 1925.

13. Gabriel Fallon, *Sean O'Casey: The Man I Knew* (Boston: Little, Brown, 1965), 86.

14. Hogan and O'Neill, eds., *Abbey Theatre*, 252–53.

15. Stephen Gwynn, "The Dublin Play Riots," *The Observer*, 14 February 1926, as reprinted in *Sean O'Casey Review*, 2 (Spring 1976) 230.

16. Donal Dorcey, "The Great Occasions," in *The World of Sean O'Casey*, ed. Sean McCann (London: Four Square Books, 1966), 65. McCann comments that one of the players was Arthur Shields, who had fought in the G.P.O. during the Rising. He also says that Hanna Sheehy-Skeffington took no part in the violence.

17. Fallon, *Sean O'Casey: The Man I Knew*, 92.

18. *Irish Independent*, 15 February 1926.

19. Ibid., 20 February 1926. One of those women who participated in the demonstration gives this version. On opening night one of the members of Cumann na mBan had seen the play and been horrified—not at the prostitute but at the unfurling of the flag in the pub. She had reported to the organization's headquarters and its members had then begun to organize a demonstration, scheduled for Thursday night. They had been delighted when Hanna, not a member of Cumann na mBan had agreed to join them (Sighle O'Donoghue, personal interview, 21 August 1984).

20. *Irish Independent*, 23 February 1926.

21. Owen Sheehy-Skeffington to Robert Hogan, 5 August 1962.

22. Ibid.

23. Ibid.

24. C. Desmond Greaves, *Sean O'Casey: Politics and Art* (London: Lawrence and Wishart, 1979), 122.

25. Rough draft of article, written in France and prepared for the *Irish World*, August 1927.

26. Jacqueline Van Voris, *Constance Markievicz: In the Cause of Ireland* (Amherst, Mass.: University of Massachusetts Press, 1967), 347.

27. Margaret Blue to Hanna Sheehy-Skeffington, 6 March 1928.

28. Andrée Sheehy-Skeffington, "The French Connection," *Irish Times*, 26 October 1981.

29. Hanna Sheehy-Skeffington, "That Little Flat: How Not to Make Ends Meet." Rough draft of article.

30. *Irish World*, 10 March 1928.

31. Hanna Sheehy-Skeffington to Owen Sheehy-Skeffington, 19 August 1928.

32. Ibid., 26 July 1928.

33. Ibid., 12 September 1928.

34. Owen Sheehy-Skeffington to Hanna Sheehy-Skeffington, n.d.

35. Ibid., 16 July [no year].

CHAPTER 11 — PRAGUE, MOSCOW, DUBLIN

1. *Irish Times*, 19 October 1929.

2. Hanna Sheehy-Skeffington to Owen Sheehy-Skeffington, 14 August 1929.

3. Ibid., 25 July 1929.

4. *Irish Times*, 19 October and 29 November 1929.

5. Terence Brown, *Ireland: A Social and Cultural History, 1922–79* (Great Britain: Fontana, 1981), 52–53.

6. Hanna Sheehy-Skeffington, "The New Europe: A Trip of Scenes, Sights, and Impressions," *Sunday Independent*, 27 October 1929.

7. Hanna's daughter-in-law, Andrée, said: "Her motto was 'Do everything once, try everything once.'" In 1939, when Aer Lingus established a flight to Shannon from Dublin, Hanna insisted on taking the trip. Her son and daughter-in-law accompanied her, reluctantly, but Hanna enjoyed every minute of the flight (Andrée Sheehy-Skeffington, personal interview, October 1979).

8. Hanna Sheehy-Skeffington, "Irishwoman Rebel's Memories," *Daily Express*, 3 May 1930. Hanna noted that the pamphlet written by her husband and Joyce had sold for 2d. [pence] and was now selling for five to seven pounds. Andrée Sheehy-Skeffington said that, a year after Hanna's visit with Joyce, Owen visited Paris and had an extremely cordial visit with Joyce. At the latter's request, Owen wrote to him upon his return to Dublin to report on "the statues in O'Connell Street," but there was no further contact (Andrée Sheehy-Skeffington, "The Hatter and the Crank," *Irish Times*, 5 February 1982).

9. Hanna Sheehy-Skeffington, "Irishwoman Rebel's Memories," *Daily Express*, 3 May 1930.

10. Hanna Sheehy-Skeffington Diaries, 7–21 August 1930.

11. Ibid.

12. Hanna Sheehy-Skeffington Diaries, 7–21 August 1930; Linklater, *Unhusbanded Life*, 236–37.

13. Linklater, *Unhusbanded Life*, 236–37.

14. *Daily Express*, 3 May 1930.

15. Ibid., 7 May 1930.

16. Ibid.

17. Brown, *Ireland*, 24–26.

18. Ibid., 41.

19. Interview with Peader O'Donnell, Commandant General, Irish Republican Army, in *Survivors*, ed. Uinseann MacEoin (Dublin: Argenta Publications, 1980), 32.

20. Copy of Frank Ryan obituary by Hanna Sheehy-Skeffington, sent to Eilis Ryan. Hanna became assistant editor of *An Phoblacht* in 1931.

21. Ibid.; *Republican File*, 28 November 1931.

22. *Republican File*, 23 January 1932.

23. *Irish Times*, 13 April 1928. The Censorship of Publications Act, when it was finally passed in 1929, not only banned material considered prurient but also contained a section that would ban any publication that advocated birth control. It called as well for the establishment of a Censorship Board responsible for submitting to the Ministers of Justice the names of books they considered indecent with the recommendation that they be banned.

24. *The Vote*, 25 October 1929.

25. Hanna Sheehy-Skeffington, "The Irish in London," *Irish Independent*. Undated clipping.

26. F. L. Dickinson, *The Dublin of Yesterday*, as quoted in Brown, *Ireland*, 117.

27. Samuel Levenson, *Maud Gonne*, 369. The Women's Republican Prisoners' Defence League had replaced the Women's Prisoners' Defence League when the latter was suppressed.

28. Ibid., 370.

29. Hanna Sheehy-Skeffington, "Wives of Great Men—Their Side of the Story," *Distributive Worker*, November 1932.

30. *The Vote*. Clipping dated only 1933. One of three reviews by Hanna of *Young China and New Japan* by Mrs. Cecil Chesterton; *Modern France* by Cecily Hamilton; and *The Revolt of Women* by Hamilton Fyfe. In the review of *The Revolt of Women*, Hanna points out: "The leisure of the married woman of the middle-class, particularly of those who live in cities, is a new phase of civilisation's problems that open [*sic*] up many possibilities; there is a stream of service and devotion here needing to be tapped and directed, lest it become stagnant and a breeder of parasites."

31. Hanna Sheehy-Skeffington Diaries, 1932.

32. Pan Collins, personal interview, 20 July 1981.

33. O'Brien, *States of Ireland*, 104.

34. Garry Culhane, personal interview, 18 June 1980.

35. Hanna Sheehy-Skeffington to Mary Kettle, 15 January 1933. At the time of Hanna's jailing, her sister Kathleen O'Brien wrote a poem about the incident entitled "A Border Ballad." It opens:

> The Police of Six Counties are out in their best
> With tanks, 18-pounders, armed cars and the rest.
> They've spread thro' the Border, they're up at the train,
> She may come by motor, and why not by 'plane?
> Oh, man all the outposts, double-padlock the gates;
> "We'll not let her in!" said the bold Dawson Bates.

The poem ends:

> "Now *we* thought you couldn't, but since you are here
> The paper is wrong, but we're not at all clear,
> Och, how did you come in the face of our fuss?"
> "It's simple," the lady said, "I came by the bus,

I took a return—it's a bit cheaper rate,
    I'll get a refund through your good Dawson Bates."

Well, the long and the short is, they took her to goal,
    And asked her to give them a £50 bail.
"I'll give you no bond but An Phoblacht Abu!
    Who gave you the right to cut Ireland in two?
You couldn't exclude me, now sore are your straits!"
    "Well, we'll not let you out!" said the logical Bates.
        (K. Cruise O'Brien, "A Border Ballad," [1933].)

36. Hanna Sheehy-Skeffington, rough notes, [1933].

37. Hanna Sheehy-Skeffington to A. Lyons, 19 February 1933.

38. The I.W.F.L. supper party was held 21 March 1933; "73 or more" attended, Hanna said, calling it "very jolly" (Hanna Sheehy-Skeffington Diaries, 22 March 1933).

39. *Irish Press*, 22 March 1933.

40. F. S. L. Lyons, *Ireland Since the Famine*, 532; Hanna Sheehy-Skeffington Diaries, 1933.

41. John Swift, "Report of Commission on Vocational Organisation," *Saothar*, May Day 1975, 57–58. *Saothar* was the journal of the Irish Labour History Society.

42. Hanna Sheehy-Skeffington Diaries, 1933.

43. Linklater, *Unhusbanded Life*, 241–42; Hanna Sheehy-Skeffington Diaries, 1933.

44. Swift, "Report of Commission on Vocational Organisation," 58–59.

45. Ibid.

46. In 1933, the year of their unofficial engagement, Andrée was spending a full year at Smith College, Northampton, Massachusetts, and was already a graduate of the Sorbonne. During this period she visited Margaret Sheehy Casey in Montreal, Canada, and was quite taken with the young poet husband (Andrée Sheehy-Skeffington, personal interview, June 1980).

47. Hanna Sheehy-Skeffington to Mr. Clamlillon [?], 7 February 1934.

48. Hanna Sheehy-Skeffington, transcript of radio broadcast, n.d.

CHAPTER 12—CONTINUING THE STRUGGLE

1. *Belfast Telegraph*, 9 February 1934.

2. *Daily News-Chronicle*, 12 June 1934.

3. Hanna Sheehy-Skeffington, "London Theatres and Cinemas," n.d. Draft of article.

4. Ibid.

5. Leaflet of Open Forum Speakers Bureau, n.d.

6. *Irish Press*, 28 November 1934. Report of a lecture to the Montreal City Subdivision of the Catholic Women's League in Montreal, Canada.

7. Ibid.

8. Hanna Sheehy-Skeffington, "The U.S.A.—Ten Years After: Is the Depression Over?" and "A Recent Visit to U.S.A.—New York," n.d. Drafts of either speeches or articles.

9. Dublin Literary Society lecture, 1 March 1935; *Women's Freedom League Bulletin*, 5 April 1935, 4–5. The latter is an account of Hanna Sheehy-Skeffington's lecture at the Minerva Club, London.

10. Hanna Sheehy-Skeffington, "An Irish Pacifist," in *We Did Not Fight*, ed. Julian Bell (London: Cobden-Sanderson, 1935), 339–40.

11. Indications are that the cable was sent between 1932 and 1935.

12. Andrée Sheehy-Skeffington, personal interview, August 1982.

13. Hanna Sheehy-Skeffington Diaries, 30 March 1936.

14. Brown, *Ireland*, 147.

15. Hanna Sheehy-Skeffington Diaries, n.d.

16. "Irish Free State 1936 Census," 1936. Information from census in Hanna Sheehy-Skeffington Papers.

17. "Irishwomen's Place in the National Life—Their Contributions to the Arts," *Irish Times Supplement*, 1 January 1937.

18. *Women's Freedom League Bulletin*, 19 March 1937.

19. *Irish Press*, 27 November 1937; Hanna Sheehy-Skeffington, "Irish Women Writers of Today," n.d., Alice Park Collection. The latter is a draft of her speech.

20. Hanna Sheehy-Skeffington Diaries, 1936; David Sheehy, personal interview, 20 June 1980.

21. Ethel Mannin, *Privileged Spectator* (London: Jarrolds, 1938), 258.

22. David Sheehy, personal interview, 20 June 1980.

23. *Carmel Herald*. Undated clipping.

24. *San Francisco Chronicle*. Undated clipping.

25. Speech given 7 February 1938 under auspices of Manhattan Division of Women's International League for Peace and Freedom.

26. Speech at First Unitarian Church, New York City, 12 April 1938.

27. Margaret Sheehy Casey to Hanna Sheehy-Skeffington, 28 August 1938.

28. F. S. L. Lyons, *Ireland Since the Famine*, 557.

29. *Daily Herald*, 27 May 1939.

30. Hanna Sheehy-Skeffington Diaries, 1940.

31. Alice Park to Hanna Sheehy-Skeffington, 7 February 1940, 19 April 1940, and 12 September 1945.

32. William O'Brien to Hanna Sheehy-Skeffington, 16 August 1945.

33. Hanna Sheehy-Skeffington Diaries, 1940.

34. Charles Wyse-Power to Hanna Sheehy-Skeffington, 21 January 1942.

35. Hanna Sheehy-Skeffington to Charles Wyse-Power, 28 January 1942.

36. Charles Wyse-Power to Hanna Sheehy-Skeffington, 9 February 1942.

CHAPTER 13 — DEATH AND THE LEGACY

1. Hanna Sheehy-Skeffington to Sighle O'Donoghue, 22 February 1943.

2. "General Election 1943: To the Electors of Dublin South City," n.d. This is an election leaflet issued by the Women's Social and Progressive League.

3. Ibid.

4. Hanna Sheehy-Skeffington, "Women in Politics," *The Bell* 7 (November 1943):143–48.

5. Ibid.

6. Ibid.

7. Anna Kelly, "Women Must Fight on!" *Irish Times Pictorial*, 6 February 1943. Anna Fitzsimons Kelly, well-known in Republican circles, had been a Sinn Fein secretary prior to her marriage and subsequently became an editor of the *Irish Press*.

8. Ibid.

9. Hanna Sheehy-Skeffington Diaries, 1945.

10. Hanna Sheehy-Skeffington to Alice Park, 17 December 1945, Alice Park Collection.

11. Ibid., 17 September 1945.

12. Note from broadcasting station to Hanna Sheehy-Skeffington, 6 November 1945. The interview was scheduled for 15 November 1945; the fee paid was four pounds for a twenty-minute appearance. It must have been very difficult for Hanna to keep this engagement for she was ill at the time. When asked by the interviewer about her health, however, she echoed Mark Twain: "The report of my impending death was greatly exaggerated" (transcript of broadcast, n.d.).

13. "Testimonial to Mrs. Sheehy-Skeffington—List of Subscribers," n.d. Among those listed were George Bernard Shaw, Maud Gonne MacBride, and the Pethick-Lawrences.

14. Margaret Gavan Duffy to Louie Bennett, 3 November 1945.

15. Louie Bennett and others to Hanna Sheehy-Skeffington, 12 December 1945; Hanna Sheehy-Skeffington Diaries, 1945.

16. Hanna Sheehy-Skeffington to Alice Park, 17 September 1945, Alice Park Collection.

17. Obituary, *Irish Times*, 22 April 1946.

18. Seaview House to Hanna Sheehy-Skeffington, 19 February 1946.

19. Andrée Sheehy-Skeffington, personal interview, 21 July 1981.

20. *Irish Press*, 27 April 1946.

21. Ibid., "An Appreciation," 22 April 1946.

22. Owen Sheehy-Skeffington to Rosamund Jacob, 20 July 1946.

Bibliography

In addition to the major writings of Hanna Sheehy-Skeffington and the few published sources that deal, at least in part, with her life, we have listed here works that will provide insights into the social, political, and economic conditions that played such a large role in shaping her views and her career.

Beckett, J. C. *The Making of Modern Ireland, 1603–1923*. New York: Alfred A. Knopf, 1977.

Bell, J. Bowyer. *The Secret Army: A History of the I.R.A., 1915–1970*. London: Sphere Books, 1972; *The Secret Army: The IRA, 1916–1979*. Rev. and enl. ed. Dublin: Academy Press, 1979.

Bell, Julian, ed. *We Did Not Fight*. London: Cobden-Sanderson, 1935.

Boyle, J. W., ed. *Leaders and Workers*. Dublin and Cork: Mercier Press, n.d.

Brown, Terence. *Ireland: A Social and Cultural History, 1922–79*. Great Britain: Fontana, 1981.

Burke's Irish Family Records. London: Burke's Peerage, 1976.

Byrne, J. F. *Silent Years: An Autobiography*. New York: Farrar, Straus and Young, 1953.

Carroll, F. M. *American Opinion and the Irish Question, 1910–23: A Study in Opinion and Policy*. Dublin: Gill and Macmillan, 1978.

Caulfield, Max. *The Easter Rebellion*. London: Four Square Books, 1965.

Coffey, Thomas M. *Agony at Easter: The 1916 Irish Uprising*. New York: Macmillan, 1969.

Colum, Mary. *Life and the Dream*. New York: Doubleday, 1947.

Colum, Padraic. "Francis Sheehy-Skeffington." In *The Irish Rebellion of 1916 and Its Martyrs: Erin's Tragic Easter*, edited by Maurice Joy, 380–92. New York: Devin-Adair, 1916.

———. *Ourselves Alone*. New York: Crown, 1959.

Connolly, James. *Labour in Irish History*. Dublin: Irish Transport and General Workers' Union, 1934.

Coogan, Tim Pat. *The I.R.A.* London: Fontana/Collins, 1971.

"Courts-Martial at Richmond Barracks." In *Sinn Fein Rebellion Handbook, Easter 1916*, 84–90. Dublin: *Weekly Irish Times*, 1916.

Cousins, James H., and Margaret E. Cousins. *We Two Together*. London: Luzac, 1951.

Coxhead, Elizabeth. *Daughters of Erin*. London: Secker and Warburg, 1965.

Cronin, Sean. *The Revolutionaries*. Dublin: Republican Publications, 1971.

Curran, C. P. *James Joyce Remembered*. London: Oxford University Press, 1968.

———. *Under the Receding Wave*. Dublin: Gill and Macmillan, 1970.

Czira, Sydney Gifford. *The Years Flew By: Recollections of Sydney Gifford Czira—John Brennan*. Dublin: Gifford and Craven, 1974.

Dangerfield, George. *The Damnable Question: A Study in Anglo-Irish Relations*. Boston: Little, Brown, 1976.

———. *The Strange Death of Liberal England*. New York: Harrison Smith and Robert Haas, 1935.

Davis, Richard P. *Arthur Griffith—and Non-Violent Sinn Fein*. Dublin: Anvil Books, 1974.

Devoy, John. *Recollections of an Irish Rebel*. New York: Charles P. Young, 1929.

Duff, Charles. *Six Days to Shake an Empire*. London: J. M. Dent and Sons, 1966.

Dwyer, T. Ryle. *Eamon de Valera*. Dublin: Gill and Macmillan, 1980.

Edwards, Owen Dudley. *The Mind of an Activist: James Connolly*. Dublin: Gill and Macmillan, 1971.

Edwards, Owen Dudley, G. Evans, and H. MacDairmid. *Celtic Nationalism*. New York: Barnes and Noble, 1968.

Edwards, Owen Dudley, and Fergus Pyle, eds. *1916: The Easter Rising*. London: MacGibbon and Kee, 1968.

Edwards, Owen Dudley, and Bernard Ransom, eds. *James Connolly: Selected Political Writings*. London: Jonathan Cape, 1973.

Ellmann, Richard. *James Joyce*. New York: Oxford University Press, 1959; new and rev. ed., New York: Oxford University Press, 1982.

Fallon, Gabriel. *Sean O'Casey: The Man I Knew*. Boston: Little, Brown, 1965.

Fanning, Ronan. *Independent Ireland*. Dublin: Helicon, 1983.

Fox, R. M. *Jim Larkin: The Rise of the Underman*. London: Lawrence and Wishart, 1957.

———. *Louie Bennett: Her Life and Times*. Dublin: Talbot Press, 1958.

———. *Rebel Irishwomen*. Dublin: Progress House, 1935.

Gaughan, J. Anthony. *Thomas Johnson*. Dublin: Kingdom Books, 1980.

Gibbon, Monk. *Inglorious Soldier*. London: Hutchinson, 1968.

Glendinning, Victoria. *Elizabeth Bowen: Portrait of a Writer*. London: Weidenfeld and Nicolson, 1977.

Greaves, C. Desmond. *Sean O'Casey: Politics and Art*. London: Lawrence and Wishart, 1979.

Gwynn, Stephen. "The Dublin Play Riots." *Sean O'Casey Review* 2 (Spring 1976): 229–31. (First published in *The Observer*, 14 February 1926.)

Healy, T. M. *Letters and Leaders of My Day*. 2 vols. London: Thornton Butterworth, 1928.

Holloway, Joseph. *Joseph Holloway's Abbey Theatre*. Edited by Robert Hogan and Michael J. O'Neill. Carbondale: Southern Illinois Univeristy Press, 1967.

Hunt, Hugh. *Sean O'Casey*. Dublin: Gill and Macmillan, 1980.

Hutchins, Patricia. *James Joyce's Dublin*. London: Grey Walls Press, 1950.

———. *James Joyce's World*. London: Methuen, 1957.

Jeffares, A. Norman, and K. G. W. Cross, eds. *In Excited Reverie: A Centenary Tribute to W. B. Yeats, 1865–1939*. New York: St. Martin's Press, 1965.

Joyce, James. *Selected Letters of James Joyce*. Edited by Richard Ellmann. New York: Viking Press, 1975.

———. *Stephen Hero*. New ed. Edited by Theodore Spencer. New York: New Directions, 1963.

Joyce, Stanislaus. *My Brother's Keeper*. New York: Viking Press, 1969.

Kain, Richard M. *Dublin in the Age of William Butler Yeats and James Joyce*. Norman, Okla: University of Oklahoma Press, 1962.

Kee, Robert. *The Green Flag: The Turbulent History of the Irish National Movement*. New York: Delacorte Press, 1972.

Kettle, T. M. *The Ways of War*. Dublin: Talbot Press, 1917.

Kilroy, James. *The 'Playboy' Riots*. Dublin: Dolmen Press, 1971.

King, Clifford. *The Orange and the Green*. London: Macdonald, 1965.

Larkin, Emmet. *James Larkin: Irish Labour Leader, 1876–1947*. London: Routledge and Kegan Paul, 1965.

Lee, Joseph. *The Modernisation of Irish Society, 1848–1918*. Dublin: Gill and Macmillan, 1973.

Levenson, Leah. *With Wooden Sword: A Portrait of Francis Sheehy-Skeffington, Militant Pacifist*. Boston: Northeastern University Press, 1983.

Levenson, Samuel. *James Connolly*. London: Martin Brian and O'Keeffe, 1973.

———. *Maud Gonne*. New York: Reader's Digest Press, 1976.

Linklater, Andro. *An Unhusbanded Life: Charlotte Despard, Suffragette, Socialist and Sinn Feiner*. London: Hutchinson, 1980.

Longford, Earl of [Frank Pakenham]. *Peace by Ordeal: The Negotiation of the Anglo-Irish Treaty, 1921*. London: Sidgwick and Jackson, 1972.

Lynd, Robert. *If the Germans Conquered England and Other Essays*. Dublin: Maunsel, 1917.

Lyons, F. S. L. *Charles Stuart Parnell*. New York: Oxford University Press, 1977.

———. "Dillon, Redmond and the Irish Home Rulers." In *Leaders and Men of the Easter Rising: Dublin, 1916*, edited by F. X. Martin, 29–41. Ithaca, N. Y.: Cornell University Press, 1967.

————. Introduction to *Michael Davitt*, by Francis Sheehy-Skeffington. London: MacGibbon and Kee, 1967.

————. *Ireland Since the Famine*. London: Collins/Fontana, 1973.

————. *John Dillon: A Biography*. Chicago: University of Chicago Press, 1968.

Lyons, J. B. *The Enigma of Tom Kettle: Irish Patriot, Essayist, Poet, British Soldier, 1880–1916*. Dublin: Glendale Press, 1983.

McCann, Sean, ed. *The World of Sean O'Casey*. London: Four Square Books, 1966.

Macardle, Dorothy. *The Irish Republic*. New York: Farrar, Straus and Giroux, 1965.

MacCurtain, Margaret, and Donncha O'Corrain, eds. *Women in Irish Society: The Historical Dimension*. Dublin: Arlen House, 1978.

McDowell, R. B. *Alice Stopford Green: A Passionate Historian*. Dublin: Allen Figgis, 1967.

MacEoin, Uinseann, ed. *Survivors*. Dublin: Argenta Publications, 1980.

McHugh, Roger. "Thomas Kettle and Francis Sheehy-Skeffington." In *The Shaping of Modern Ireland*, edited by Conor Cruise O'Brien, 124–39. London: Routledge and Kegan Paul, 1960.

————, ed. *Dublin 1916*. New York: Hawthorn Books, 1966.

McInerney, Michael. *The Riddle of Erskine Childers*. Dublin: E. and T. O'Brien, 1971.

MacKenzie, Midge. *Shoulder to Shoulder: A Documentary*. New York: Alfred A. Knopf, 1975.

McKillen, Beth. "Irish Feminism and Nationalist Separatism, 1914–23." Parts 1, 2. *Eire-Ireland* 17 (Fall, Winter 1982): 52–67, 72–90.

Mannin, Ethel. *Privileged Spectator*. London: Jarrolds, 1938.

————. *Rebels' Ride: A Consideration of the Revolt of the Individual*. London: Hutchinson, 1964.

Marreco, Anne. *The Rebel Countess: The Life and Times of Constance Markievicz*. Philadelphia: Chilton Books, 1967.

Martin, F. X., ed. *Leaders and Men of the Easter Rising: Dublin 1916*. Ithaca, N. Y.: Cornell University Press, 1967.

————. "1916: Myth, Fact, and Mystery." *Studia Hibernica* no. 7 (1967): 7–126.

Martin, F. X., and F. J. Byrne, eds. *The Scholar Revolutionary: Eoin MacNeill, 1867–1945 and the Making of the New Ireland*. Shannon: Irish University Press, 1973.

Meenan, James, ed. *Centenary History of the Literary and Historical Society of University College, Dublin, 1855–1955*. Tralee, Ireland: Kerryman Press, 1957.

Milroy, Sean. *Memories of Mountjoy*. Dublin: Maunsel, 1917.

Mitchell, Arthur. "William O'Brien, 1881–1968, and the Irish Labour Movement." *Studies* 60 (Autumn-Winter 1971): 311–31.

Mitchell, David. *The Fighting Pankhursts: A Study in Tenacity*. New York: Macmillan, 1967.

――――. *Women on the Warpath: The Story of the Women of the First World War*. London: Jonathan Cape, 1966.

Murphy, John A. *Ireland in the Twentieth Century*. Dublin: Gill and Macmillan, 1975.

Nevinson, Henry W. *Changes and Chances*. London: Nisbet, 1923.

Nic Shiubhlaigh, Maire. *Story of the Irish National Theatre*. Dublin: James Duffy, 1955.

O'Brien, Conor Cruise. *States of Ireland*. Frogmore, St. Albans: Panther Books, 1974.

――――, ed. *The Shaping of Modern Ireland*. London: Routledge and Kegan Paul, 1960.

O'Brien, William. *Forth the Banners Go*. Dublin: Three Candles, 1969.

O'Brien, William, and Desmond Ryan, eds. *John Devoy's Post Bag, 1871–1928*. 2 vols. Dublin: C. J. Fallon, 1948.

O'Broin, Leon. *Dublin Castle and the 1916 Rising*. Dublin: Helicon, 1965.

――――. *Revolutionary Underground: The Story of the Irish Republican Brotherhood, 1858–1924*. Dublin: Gill and Macmillan, 1976.

O'Casey, Sean. *Inishfallen Fare Thee Well*. New York: Macmillan, 1949.

――――. *The Letters of Sean O'Casey, 1910–41*. Vol. 1. Edited by David Krause. New York: Macmillan, 1975; *The Letters of Sean O'Casey, 1942–54*. Vol. 2. Edited by David Krause. New York: Macmillan, 1980.

O Cathasaigh, P. [Sean O'Casey]. *The Story of the Irish Citizen Army*. Dublin: Maunsel, 1919.

O'Connor, Frank. *The Big Fellow: Michael Collins and the Irish Revolution*. Rev. ed. London: Burns and Oates, 1966.

O'Flynn, Grainne. "Some Aspects of the Education of Irish Women through the Years." *The Capuchin Annual*, 1977:164–79.

O'Malley, Ernie. *Army Without Banners*. London: Four Square Books, 1967.

――――. *The Singing Flame*. Dublin: Anvil Books, 1978.

O'Neill, Brian. *Easter Week*. New York: International Publishers, 1936.

Pankhurst, Christabel. *Unshackled, or How We Won the Vote*. London: Hutchinson, 1959.

Pankhurst, Emmeline. *My Own Story*. London: Eveleigh Nash, 1914.

Pankhurst, E. Sylvia. *The Suffragette*. London: Gay and Hancock, 1911.

――――. *The Suffragette Movement*. London: Longmans, Green, 1931.

Pethick-Lawrence, Emmeline. *My Part in a Changing World*. London: Victor Gollancz, 1938.

Pethick-Lawrence, Frederick W. *Women's Fight for the Vote*. London: The Woman's Press, n.d.

Reid, B. L. *The Man from New York: John Quinn and His Friends*. New York: Oxford University Press, 1968.

Roper, Esther. Introduction to *Selected Poems*, by Eva Gore-Booth. New York: Longmans, Green, 1933.

Rose, Catherine. *The Female Experience: The Story of the Woman Movement in Ireland*. Galway: Arlen House, 1976.

Rosen, Andrew. *Rise Up, Women! The Militant Campaign of the Women's Social and Political Union, 1903–1914*. London: Routledge and Kegan Paul, 1974.

Rowbotham, Sheila, Lynne Segal, and Hilary Wainwright. *Beyond the Fragments: Feminism and the Making of Socialism*. London: Merlin Press, 1979.

Ryan, Desmond. *The Rising*. 4th ed. Dublin: Golden Eagle Books, 1966.

Shaw, George Bernard. *The Matter with Ireland*. New York: Hill and Wang, 1962.

Sheehy, David. *Prison Papers*. Dublin: Weldrick Brothers, 1888.

Sheehy, Eugene. *May It Please the Court*. Dublin: C. J. Fallon, 1951.

Sheehy, Michael. *Is Ireland Dying?: Culture and the Church in Modern Ireland*. New York: Taplinger, 1969.

Sheehy-Skeffington, Francis. *A Forgotten Small Nationality*. New York: Donnelly Press, 1917.

———. *In Dark and Evil Days*. Dublin: James Duffy, 1936.

———. *Michael Davitt: Revolutionary Agitator and Labour Leader*. London: Fisher Unwin, 1908; London: MacGibbon and Kee, 1967.

———. *The Prodigal Daughter*. Dublin: n.p., 1915.

———. *Speech from the Dock*. Dublin: Liberty Hall, 1915.

———. *War and Feminism*. Dublin: n.p., 1914.

Sheehy-Skeffington, Francis, and James A. Joyce. *Two Essays*. Dublin: Gerrard Brothers, [1901].

Sheehy-Skeffington, Hanna. "Biographical Notice" in *In Dark and Evil Days*, by Francis Sheehy-Skeffington. Dublin: James Duffy, 1936.

———. *British Militarism as I Have Known It*. In *Democracy in Ireland Since 1913*, edited by Hanna Sheehy-Skeffington, 21–34. New York: Donnelly Press, [1917].

———. Impressions of Sinn Fein in America. Dublin: Davis Publishing Co., 1919.

———. *Ireland—Present and Future*. New York: Donnelly Press, n.d.

———. "Irish Militants and the War." *Irish Citizen*, 1 May 1915, 391. (First published in *Jus Suffragii*, April 1915.)

———. "An Irish Pacifist." In *We Did Not Fight*, edited by Julian Bell, 339–53. London: Cobden-Sanderson, 1935.

———. "Irish Secondary Teachers." *Irish Review*, October 1912, 393–98.

———. "A Pacifist Dies." In *Dublin 1916*, edited by Roger McHugh, 276–88. New York: Hawthorn Books, 1966.

———. "Reminiscences of an Irish Suffragette." In *Votes for Women: Irish Women's*

Struggle for the Vote, edited by Andrée Sheehy-Skeffington et al., 12–26. Dublin: Andrée D. Sheehy-Skeffington and Rosemary Owens, 1975.

———— [Hanna Sheehy]. "Women and the University Question." *New Ireland Review* 17 (May–August 1902): 148–51.

————. "Women in Politics." *The Bell* 7 (November 1943): 143–48.

————. "The Women's Movement—Ireland." *Irish Review*, July 1912, 225–27.

Sheehy-Skeffington, Owen. "Francis Sheehy-Skeffington." In *1916: The Easter Rising*, edited by Owen Dudley Edwards and Fergus Pyle, 135–48. London: MacGibbon and Kee, 1968.

Simon, John. "Report of the Royal Commission." In *Democracy in Ireland Since 1913*, edited by Hanna Sheehy-Skeffington, 36–58. New York: Donnelly Press, [1917].

Society of Jesus, Fathers of the. *A Page of Irish History: Story of University College, Dublin, 1883–1909*. Dublin: Talbot Press, 1930.

Stephens, James. *The Insurrection in Dublin*. Dublin: Maunsel, 1916.

Swift, John. "Report of Commission on Vocational Organisation (and Its Times, 1930–'40's)." *Saothar* 1 (May Day 1975): 54–62.

Tierney, Michael, ed. *Struggle with Fortune: A Miscellany for the Centenary of the Catholic University of Ireland, 1854–1954*. Dublin: Browne and Nolan, 1954.

Vane, Sir Francis Fletcher. *Agin the Governments: Memories and Adventures*. London: Sampson-Low, Marston, [1929].

Van Voris, Jacqueline. *Constance de Markievicz: In the Cause of Ireland*. Amherst: University of Massachusetts Press, 1967.

Ward, Margaret. *Unmanageable Revolutionaries: Women and Irish Nationalism*. Kerry: Brandon Book Publishers, 1983.

Young, Ella. *Flowering Dusk*. New York: Longmans, Green, 1945.

Younger, Calton. *Ireland's Civil War*. Great Britain: Fontana/Collins, 1970.

————. *A State of Disunion: Arthur Griffith, Michael Collins, James Craig, Eamon de Valera*. Great Britain: Frederick Muller, 1972.

Index

Matters, Muriel, 93
Maurice Harte, 45
Maxwell, Sir John, Commander of British Forces in Ireland, 81
Maynooth, bishops at, 17
Mellows, Liam, 106, 179
Meredith, George, 27
Metropolitan Hall, 5
"Michael Davitt: Father of the Land League, 1846–1906" (H. Sheehy-Skeffington), 153
Military Service Bill, 109
Milligan, Alice, 174
Molony, Helena, 41, 53, 118, 129
Mooney, Thomas, 107
Moore, John D., 102
Moore, W. C., 107
Moran, Gerald, 38
Moroney, William J., 104
Morris, Lieutenant, 91
Moscow, 157–158
Mountjoy Prison, 2, 5, 39, 42, 52, 61; H. Sheehy-Skeffington jailed, 38; F. Sheehy-Skeffington jailed, 59; H. Sheehy-Skeffington protesting at, 123; men on hunger strike, 134; Republicans hung at, 137
Munster Women's Franchise League, 51
Murphy, Jane, 37; jailed, 38
Murphy, Margaret, 37–38
Murray, Joseph; hunger strike and death of, 135
Murray, T. C. *Maurice Harte*, 45

National Council of Women in London, 24
National Defence Fund, 109
National Democrat, 19, 22; F. Sheehy-Skeffington co-editor, 18
National Examination Subcommittee, 20
National Gallery of Ireland, 124, 173
National Library of Ireland, 8, 11, 21, 67
National Museum of Ireland, 8, 69
National Progressive Party, 102
National Schools System, 2, 10, 156
National Student, 75
National Suffrage Bureau in New York; Ida Husted Harper editorial Chairman, 119–120

National Teachers Congress, 18
National Union of Women's Suffrage Societies, United States, 119
National University Women Graduates' Association, 174
National Women's Party, 119
Nationalist Party, 35, 40, 112
Nationist, 19; founding of, 18; Thomas Kettle as editor, 18; F. Sheehy-Skeffington as assistant editor, 18
Nazi Germany, 171
New Catholic Press of Manchester, 169
New Ireland, 15, 17, 93
New Statesman, The, 134
New York American, 142
Northcliffe, Lord, 120
Northern Committee of the Irishwomen's Suffrage Federation, 51
Northern Ireland, 148, 165; exclusion of, 139

O'Brien, Conor Cruise, 4, 5, 6, 141, 143, 164, 174; son of Kathleen Sheehy O'Brien, 10
O'Brien, Cruise, 9, 23, 28, 94, 115, 152, 175; marriage to Kathleen Sheehy, 10; joins Irish Women's Franchise League, 24; in British uniform, 75; death of, 152
O'Brien, Kate, 174
O'Brien, Kathleen Sheehy. *See* Sheehy, Kathleen
O'Brien, William, 77
O'Callaghan, Kate, 139
O'Casey, Sean, 126, 151, 162; *Juno and the Paycock*, 149, 162; *The Plough and the Stars*, 149, 150, 151
O'Connor, Frank, 132
O'Connor, T. P., 98, 136
O'Donoghue, Sighle. *See* Humphries, Sheila
O'Duffy, Eimar, 162
O'Flaherty, Liam, 162
Oldham, Miss, 11
O'Leary, Con, 162
O'Malley, Ernie, *Army Without Banners*, 121
Owens, Rosemary, 24

HANNA SHEEHY-SKEFFINGTON

was composed in 10-point Mergenthaler Linotron 202 Janson and leaded 3 points
by Eastern Graphics;
printed sheet-fed offset on 50-pound, acid-free Glatfelter B-31,
smyth sewn and bound over 80-point binder's boards in Holliston Roxite B by
Thomson-Shore, Inc.;
with dust jackets printed in 2 colors by Thomson-Shore, Inc.;
and published by

SYRACUSE UNIVERSITY PRESS
SYRACUSE, NEW YORK 13244-5160